contents

preface

Since the publication of *The Coming of the Golden Age* by Gunter Stent in 1969 there have been a number of compendiums on non growth and a world wide debate as to whether economic growth should be slowed to preserve our environment. Anxiety about pollution and natural resource scarcity, however, has tended to obscure Stent's main thesis that useful knowledge is also limited and that an eventual end to progress would have been inevitable even without an environmental revolution, unfavorable weather and a world wide energy crisis.

In this survey of the limits to growth a great deal of evidence will be presented to show that the law of diminishing returns applies to all resources, including new knowledge, and that the United States has been in the process of adjusting to a steady state economy for more than a decade.

The evidence in support of an early end to economic progress is particularly suggestive in the case of population. In the 1950s American women had an average of 3.35 children. A fertility rate of 2.11 would be required in the long run to prevent our population from increasing if there were no immigration or change in average life expectancy. In 1972 our national fertility rate dropped below this replacement level for the first time in recorded history.

The adjustment to a no-growth society is also apparent in statistics on output per manhour. When an allowance is made for fluctuations in labor productivity which are mainly cyclical, the conclusion is that output per manhour in the private domestic economy has been in a state of retarded growth since about 1963.

Smaller improvements in the productivity of men and machines have made it impossible to offset natural resource scarcity without a rise in the relative price of energy and a number of other raw materials. Both of these harbingers of a stationary economy — the decline in the growth of productivity and the differential rise in natural resource prices — have made it far more difficult to control inflation.

Efforts to achieve price stability in the wake of a worldwide food shortage and a fairly sharp decline in domestic oil and gas production have led to other problems. The restrictive monetary and fiscal policies which were followed in recent years, for example, may have helped to push the U.S. and world economies into the longest and most severe recession since the great depression of the 1930s.

Since many of our more pressing economic and social problems seem to be linked either directly or indirectly to a slowing down in the rate of economic progress, it would seem appropriate to inquire whether anything can be done to ease the adjustment to a stationary economy.

By accepting the goal of a steady state economy as being both desirable and inevitable, by stressing the need for zero population growth at home and abroad, by reducing waste and profligate consumption, and by making many of those investments in energy conservation that will be needed in the long run now, I believe that it might be possible for the U.S. and world economies to grow faster in the short run and experience far less pollution, inflation, malnutrition, unemployment and human heartache than would otherwise be the case.

This is not a doomsday book. There will be further growth. We must recognize, however, that the age of exponential growth is over, that the potential for further progress is limited, and that new attitudes, policies and institutional arrangements will be necessary to ease the adjustment to a non growth economy.

Since some of the more difficult problems of employment adjustment are likely to be borne by colleges and universities and by persons aspiring toward advanced degrees, it would seem especially appropriate that college students and their professors be better informed about some of the issues, perils, new opportunities and life styles that may have to be developed in the remainder of this century if we are to adjust gracefully to a stationary economy.

PART ONE

An Introduction to Zero Growth

chapter 1

THE END OF
PROGRESS
HYPOTHESIS

In a presidential address before the AAAS in 1970, Bentley Glass asked, "Are there finite limits to scientific understanding or are there endless horizons?" Gunther Stent, author of *Coming of the Golden Age*,[1] believes that there are limits to knowledge and that cessation of scientific advances will ultimately lead to an end to technological and social progress. Thoughtful questioning of the endless frontier concept in science comes at a time when the growth in our population has slowed down, when labor productivity has declined, and when the general public has become increasingly aware of pollution, congestion, and natural resource scarcity — particularly our irreplaceable fossil fuel reserves.

The concept of the endless frontier of economic progress must also be examined for many of the same reasons. The central hypothesis of this book is that the United States and some other industrialized economies may already be more than halfway to the end of economic progress.

From 1964 to 1974 the United States gross national product (GNP) in current dollars soared by more than 100 per cent from $685 billion to about $1.4 trillion. In a superficial sense, it would appear that this ten-year period was one of the most favorable in our history. Appearances can be deceiving, however.

When adjustments are made for price changes, the increase in real output was only about 33 per cent, compared to an increase of nearly 43 per cent from 1954 to 1964. Because the United States labor force increased by almost 24 per cent at the same time, the annual increase in real GNP per member of the labor force was actually less than 1 per cent. In the preceding decade, the annual gain in per worker output was more than 2 per cent. The last

3

decade, far from being one of strong growth, has actually been one of very slow growth in output per worker.

This sharp decline in the growth of labor productivity is one of the more important reasons for suggesting that the age of exponential growth may be over. In later sections I will examine the behavior of output per worker in greater detail and in subsequent chapters present some additional evidence and reasons for supposing that improvements in per capita income will eventually decline to zero and perhaps even become negative, on the average, in the next few decades.

Is Progress Inevitable?

In 1961 economist Sumner Slichter noted that "a large portion of technological discoveries aid in the making of an additional technological progress,"[2] and concluded that economic growth can continue indefinitely. The unlimited progress notion, which has caused futurologists like Herman Kahn and Anthony Wiener to suggest that per capita income in the United States might triple in the last half of this century, has been dampened considerably in recent years by the behavior of real spendable earnings (Figure 1.1). The average spendable weekly earnings for production workers in private nonagricultural industries in 1967 dollars increased from $66.73 in 1947 to $85.67 in 1963[3] and then rose nearly 7 per cent to $91.32 in 1965. Real spendable earnings dipped somewhat thereafter and did not recover to a new high until 1971. There was a further improvement to $96.64 in 1972. Higher food and energy prices caused real spendable earnings to decline in 1973, however, and in 1974 the purchasing power of an average production worker was less than in 1965.

The lower purchasing power does not necessarily mean that production workers are worse off today than a decade ago. The average worker can now look forward to better social security retirement benefits than were available in 1965. Improved education, a cleaner environment, and a more plentiful provision of other governmental services now provided out of higher taxes also benefit many workers and their children. Unemployment benefits have increased; public welfare benefits are generally superior and more readily available than in 1965. There is also a sense in which workers can ease the burden of inflation by substituting goods and services that have not gone up as much in price for more expensive items.

Even though the U.S. Labor Department's index of average spendable weekly earnings is not an all-inclusive measure of per capita welfare, its behavior in recent years suggests that the American worker's dream of an ever-increasing standard of living may not be realized in the future.

Although most scientists are beginning to appreciate that there are constraints to technological progress and that economic growth may eventually cease, very few have had the courage to suggest

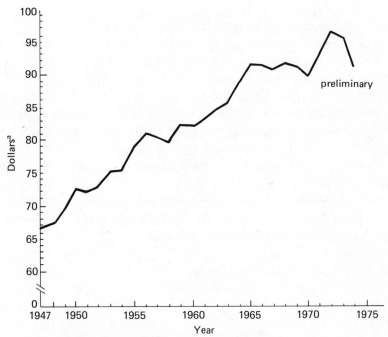

[a] Average gross weekly earnings less social security
and income taxes for a worker with three dependents.
Earnings in current dollars are divided by the consumer price index.

FIGURE 1.1

Average Spendable Weekly Earnings in 1967 Dollars for Production Workers in Private Nonagricultural Industries, 1947–
1974[a].

that this will happen in the near future. The initial reaction of most economists to the report by the Club of Rome on *The Limits to Growth*[4] was not only skeptical but highly defensive of economic growth as being both desirable and necessary to achieve such goals as the reduction of poverty and a cleaner environment.

The question of how much further growth may be possible in the future is somewhat clouded by uncertainty about the exact nature of most production functions and the degree to which these functions may have changed over time as a result of technological progress. A *production function* is simply a mathematical or statistically observed relationship between a desired output and various combinations of inputs such as land, labor, energy, and capital that might have been used to produce the output in question.

Edward Denison has made some assumptions about the nature of economic production functions.[5] He concludes that about 54 per cent of the increase in real national income from 1909 to 1957 can be attributed to increases in the quantity and quality of our employed labor force, including a dramatic increase in educational attainment, 26 per cent to increases in the amount of invested capital, and about 20 per cent to improvements in resource input productivity, which are mainly the result of technological change and economies of scale.

Although most people would probably agree that these and perhaps a million other more specific inputs to the production process have helped to increase real income, many economists disagree about how much weight should be given to the various factors that *might* have influenced economic growth.

Some economists place much more emphasis on the discovery and invention of new and improved products and production processes. Others are inclined to emphasize investments in new plant and equipment. A few, including myself, are impressed by the dramatic substitution of inanimate energy for other factors of production and would give more weight to such energy-related dimensions of progress as increased speed, scale, and improved ways of converting raw energy into useful working effects. If this view is accepted, fossil fuels become an important source of economic progress and natural resource conservation a more important concern.

Those economists with an unlimited faith in either science and technology or capital investment, on the other hand, might be inclined to dismiss natural resource scarcity as simply a minor obstacle to be overcome on the road to a golden age of general affluence in which no one will have to work for a living. Although I hope that the war on poverty will eventually be won, it does not seem likely that the average American will ever be faced with what some analysts have suggested might be a rather difficult problem of adjusting to a life of perfect leisure.

The Steady State Economy

Evidence presented in this book not only suggests that the end of economic progress is in sight but that the process of adjusting to a steady state economy is already upon us. Economic optimists and even the authors of the Club of Rome's report on *The Limits to Growth* are, I believe, essentially wrong in assuming that economic activity can continue at a very rapid rate for several more decades.

The oil embargo of 1973 and the unexpected economic recession that followed the lifting of the embargo have made it clear that the United States and most other oil-importing countries will not grow as rapidly in the future as they did from 1947 to 1973. Adjusting to a no-growth economy, it seems to me, is not something that can be postponed until we have solved all our economic problems, exhausted standing room, depleted most of our high-grade mineral resources, drowned in our own industrial wastes, or approached a world-wide heat limit which will not permit life to be sustained on earth. As I shall show in subsequent chapters, a good part of the adjustment to a steady state economy has already taken place.

The strategy that will be used in arriving at this conclusion will be to examine many important sources of economic growth and to argue that none of these sources or dimensions of economic progress is immune from a *law of diminishing returns*[6] which will eventually make further growth either unprofitable or something that is less preferred than a stationary economy, in which total population and income do not change very much over time.

Because many disagree about the weight to assign the various sources of growth, it is presumptive to suppose that there is a simple way to prove that the age of rapid economic growth is over. By examining numerous possible sources of economic growth and showing that each is subject to a law of diminished returns, however, the absence of a generally accepted theory of economic progress will probably not invalidate the end of progress hypothesis.

A detailed analysis of individual sources of growth and the evidence in support of diminishing returns for each will be deferred to later chapters. In this chapter I will examine recent changes in national income from the perspective of a simple aggregative model involving only two determinants of economic progress: the growth in the employed labor force and improvements in output per employee.

A relatively more rapid growth in the labor force has tended to obscure evidence in support of a highly significant slowdown in the growth of labor productivity. If it can be further shown that the growth rate for the employed labor force will gradually diminish to zero and that improvements in labor productivity will continue to decline to a point of zero or negative improvement, it follows that a condition which might be described as zero economic growth will have been achieved.

Most evidence supporting an end to progress is for the United States. Japan and some of the more advanced countries in Western Europe, which did not experience a significant baby boom in the post - World War II period, are probably much closer to achieving a steady state population than the United States. Many of these industrialized countries also have a dearth of high-grade mineral resources and, in some cases, appear to lack sufficient space to put all those cars, highways, appliances, and single-family dwelling units that would seem to be implied by a further doubling of real GNP. Such considerations make it reasonable to suppose that most of the richer and more industrialized nations of the world may also be at least halfway to the end of economic progress.

Growth of the Labor Force

The real gross national product of the United States has doubled five times in the last century and is now more than forty times greater than in 1873 (Figure 1.2). That it can be foolish to simply project past trends into the future without regard for inhibiting influences is suggested by population statistics. In 1950 the total American population increased by more than 2 per cent. Live births, estimated to have equaled a little over 3.6 million in 1950,

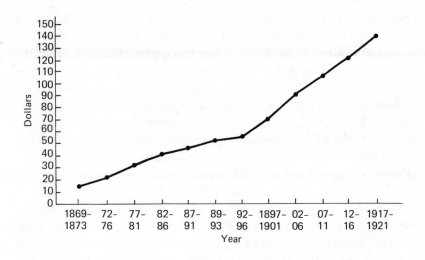

FIGURE 1.2
Gross National Product in 1958 Dollars, 1869–1973.

continued to increase to more than 4.3 million in 1957. Births remained on a high plateau until 1961 and then declined to less than 3.25 million in 1973. The even more dramatic decline in the birthrate per woman in the childbearing age range has caused the population growth rate to decline by more than 50 per cent to an average annual increase of less than 1 per cent in the years since 1967. If the fertility of American women remains at the 1973 level, young people will not quite replace themselves in the future. The total population growth could then be expected to slow to a zero growth rate in a little over 50 years.

This slowdown in population growth has not yet had a negative effect upon the growth of economic activity in the United States. The population aged 16 and over, from which the labor force is recruited, has been increasing at an average annual rate of about 1.7 per cent in recent years. This growth rate peaked in 1973, however, and can be expected to slump back to an increase of less than 1 per cent per year by 1984 as the full effects of the pill and liberalized abortion become apparent.

This decline, with other factors such as the labor force participation rate, the unemployment rate, and growth in labor productivity remaining the same, would be sufficient to lower the economic growth rate for real GNP from a remarkably constant average rate of about 3.65 per cent for the years 1953 - 1966, 1966 - 1968, and 1968 - 1973 to less than 3 per cent within about ten years.

Several developments are responsible for the rapid decline in the population growth rate. The birth control pill helped to reduce the number of unwanted babies, which some surveys suggest may have amounted to 20 per cent or more of all births in the 1960s. Liberalized abortion and a more relaxed attitude toward sex without marriage will no doubt help to reinforce the trend toward zero population growth.

Some economic factors that may have led to a reduction in fertility will be considered in Chapter 5. When fertility is viewed from the perspective of rising costs and declining benefits, it is reasonable to suppose that the American birth rate might remain at or below a replacement level and that the total population will gradually approach zero growth.

The evidence in Chapter 8 suggests that Americans are retiring at earlier ages and that the average man and woman in the twenty-first century will probably not spend more than about 30 full years in the labor force. If we assume that the number of

American-born children reaching the age of 16 plus those immigrants that might be expected to enter the labor force will
average 3.9 million persons per year in the future (see Chapter 5)
and that average employment will amount to 30 years, total
employment can be expected to increase from 86.7 million in 1973
to 117 million (3.9 × 30) in the twenty-first century, an increase of
about 35 per cent. Output per worker could then increase, on the
average, by 48 per cent and still not be enough to double real GNP.

Output Per Worker

Real GNP per person employed in our armed services and
civilian labor force increased by more than 80 per cent in the 1947 -
1973 period. To suggest that future increases in output per worker
will be substantially less than the 1947 -1973 increase is perhaps
the most unbelievable aspect to the end of progress hypothesis.
However, labor productivity clearly is no longer increasing as
rapidly as in the past. Output per manhour in the private domestic
economy, which had been increasing at a 3.5 per cent annual rate
from 1947 to 1965, slumped to an average rate of only 2 per cent
from 1965 to 1970. Of 34 industries surveyed by the Bureau of Labor
Statistics, only 6 had a higher rate of growth for labor productivity
in the 1965 - 1970 period than in the earlier period from 1953 to
1965.

This sharp decline in the growth of labor productivity raises
some perplexing questions. Was retardation a transitory
phenomenon that can be attributed to special circumstances, or
was it the result of more fundamental constraints that are likely to
persist in the future and eventually bring our economy to a state of
economic maturity?

In the 1970 *Economic Report of the President*, it was suggested
that the decline in the growth of labor productivity in the late 1960s
may have been the result of bottlenecks, labor shortages, inex-
perienced workers, absenteeism, a propensity to hoard skilled
workers, high labor turnover, other cyclical factors and adjustments accompanying an inflationary transition from war to
peace.

Rapid productivity gains from 1970 to 1973 helped to alleviate
concern about a fundamental change in the long-term growth of
productivity and have led the editors of *Fortune* to conclude that
the "1969 - 70 lag was largely due to nonrecurring factors."[7]

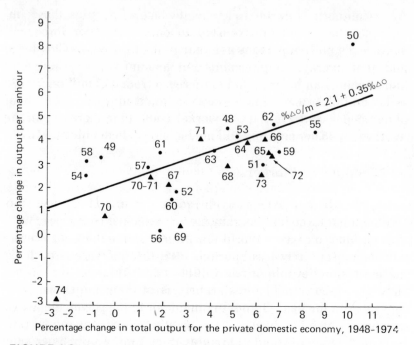

FIGURE 1.3

Percentage Changes in Output per Manhour and Gross
National Product in 1958 Dollars.

Source: Economic Report of the President, February 1974.

Evidence to support retardation in labor productivity can be
traced back to at least 1963, however, if an adjustment is made for
fluctuations in output that are related to the business cycle.[8] This
suggests that some factors responsible for retardation in labor
productivity may be more enduring.

   In Figure 1.3 the annual percentage changes in output per
manhour for the private domestic economy are plotted against the
corresponding changes in total real output for the years since 1947.
A regression line has been fitted to the original data for the period
from 1947 through 1963. Productivity has been below this line
every year since 1963 except for 1971, when output per manhour
was abnormally large in relation to the growth of total output
partly because of the General Motors strike, which caused output
per manhour in the private nonfarm sector to decline 3.1 per cent
on an annual basis in the fourth quarter of 1970 and then leap upward at an annual rate of 7.4 per cent in the first quarter of 1971.

Output per manhour was far below the long-term relation with percentage changes in real output in each of the four preceding years, which may imply a "catching up" potential in 1971 as businessmen began to take full advantage of new plant and equipment. Business investment in new equipment increased more than 80 per cent from 1960 to 1970 compared to an increase of less than 50 per cent for real GNP.

If the productivity increase in 1971 is averaged together with the increase in any of the four preceding years (as is done in Figure 1.3 for 1970 - 1971), output per manhour in the private domestic economy appears to have been in a state of retarded growth for at least a decade and perhaps even longer.

A dramatic way to illustrate the large decline in the growth of labor productivity since World War II is to divide the last 25 years of change into three subperiods that bridge years of peak prosperity. For the subperiods of 1947 - 1953, 1953 - 1966, and 1966 - 1973 the average annual growth rates were 4.1, 3.2, and 2.5 per cent respectively for output per manhour in the private domestic economy.

The downward trend in the growth of labor productivity will probably continue. Evidence suggests that the United States is now living, in part, off productivity gains which are borrowed from the past. The evidence presented in Chapter 3 is particularly strong for the oil and natural gas industries where output per manhour has been kept from declining by drawing from fuel reserves which were discovered in previous years. This cannot go on forever. As drilling activity is expanded to replace energy reserves that are now being used up, output per manhour can be expected to decline.

Improvements in labor productivity were greater, on the average, in agriculture, petroleum, natural gas, and many other natural resource industries in the years before 1968 than for the economy as a whole. The rapid improvements in labor productivity enabled producers to compensate for natural resource scarcity and, in many cases, to charge lower relative prices for these products in 1967 than in 1947.

Since 1968, when improvements in output per manhour for the private domestic economy began to lag noticeably behind the 1947 - 1968 trend, raw material prices have increased more than twice as rapidly, on the average, as other prices. The higher prices in industries that have already experienced tremendous gains in productivity as a result of mechanization, new seeds, massive doses of fertilizer, and improved production processes, reinforce a more general conclusion — that there has been a significant diminution in the power of science and technology to counteract natural resource scarcity and propel our economy forward at a steady, exponential rate of growth.

As higher prices for raw materials cause businesses and consumers to either cut back their consumption or increase their consumption at a slower rate, a negative feedback on output per manhour in other industries will follow. Once wires and pipes are in place, for example, output per manhour in the gas and electric utility industries can increase almost in proportion to the increase in total BTUs or kilowatt hours that are purchased by consumers. A slower growth rate for total energy consumption, under these circumstances, will tend to slow the growth of labor productivity in those industries responsible for energy distribution.

If higher energy prices cause people to buy smaller cars and appliances, output per manhour in manufacturing will tend to decline because some of the parts and motions that are involved in production and assembly are the same regardless of the size of the automobile or appliance.

An effective way to conserve energy is to reduce the speed of automobiles, trucks, aircraft, and ships. Reducing travel speeds, however, will tend to reduce the output per manhour of salesmen, truck drivers, and other workers in the transportation industry. Such reductions, which will be discussed more fully in Chapter 2, indicate that a cutback in the growth of energy consumption as a result of shortages or higher prices can be expected to have widespread spillover effects on the growth of labor productivity in other industries.

Natural Resource Scarcity

New inventions such as automobiles, airplanes, steel pipes, improved drilling equipment, and better compressors have been outstandingly successful in enabling us to exploit quickly low-cost oil and natural gas. From a nation that was once 100 per cent dependent upon other sources of energy such as wood, coal, and animal power, the United States is now more than 75 per cent dependent on oil and gas, both of which will be largely exhausted in the next few decades. Whether science and technology can be relied upon to quickly reverse this dependence without sacrificing some energy-intensive activities is uncertain. Our efforts to put a man on the moon have shown that it is possible to make impressive gains in applied technology with few practical spillover benefits to the civilian economy.

To postulate an end to economic progress in the near future it is not necessary to believe in an early end to improvements in scientific understanding and technological knowledge. All that is required is that an increasing share of the benefits from improved technology be devoted to such objectives as offsetting natural resource scarcity, maintaining the quality of the environment, making working conditions safer and more enjoyable, and increasing leisure time available to the average worker. In Chapter 3 we will examine the cost of achieving some of these objectives and in Chapters 2 and 4 inquire more deeply into the question of limits to technological progress.

Even more important perhaps than economic and technical limits to growth are contemporary changes in social attitudes. In the early 1970s, the U.S. Chamber of Commerce asked readers of *Nation's Business:* "Should we stop economic growth?" Two of every five said yes. Across the nation, communities and even some states are wrestling with the question of how to control, slow, and even halt economic and population growth. Tom McCall, the former governor of Oregon, called for zero growth in his state. Both seriously and jokingly, he asked visitors not to take up residence in Oregon, and put a stop to all construction along the state's Pacific Coast that might damage estuaries. A poll commissioned by the National Dividend Foundation in 1974 found that more than half the people surveyed believe that the United States has already passed its peak of economic growth.

McQuade and Aikman have suggested that ours is a taking, not a giving, society.[9] They note that industrialism works hard to project a philanthropic image by striving to satisfy people's needs "through a procession of increasingly ingenious products." The possibility that many of our economic wants may have been manufactured on Madison Avenue has also been emphasized by economist John Kenneth Galbraith in his *Affluent Society*[10] and *The New Industrial State.*[11] The general popularity of these books and the increasing respect that has been accorded to Galbraith by the economics profession suggest that relatively more workers may begin to reject an economic system which measures human success in pecuniary terms.

If this hypothesis is correct it would not be surprising if more people stop concentrating their lives around jobs, save a larger portion of their current income and begin to plan their lives around long sabbaticals, unusual projects, or early retirements for more important endeavors. This, of course, could help to bring about the kind of revolution envisioned by Charles Reich, in *The Greening of America*, in which he postulated "a renewed relationship of man to himself, to other men, to society, and to the land."[12] It could happen even if relatively more young people from affluent families begin to take their studies seriously and appreciate that a philosophy of living only for the present might simply fit them to be dishwashers, as the more industrious college students from the lower middle class prepare themselves to become a part of the new meritocracy.

Adjusting to the Steady State Economy

If the economy improves fairly rapidly in the remainder of the 1970s and better weather conditions allow a return to more normal agricultural yields, there is a danger that some of the lessons that should have been learned in the past few years will be forgotten and that similar problems will recur on even grander scales in the future.

At the World Food Conference held in Rome in 1974, for example, some experts predicted that 10 million people might die of starvation within a year, and that many millions more would suffer from malnutrition. Actual starvation was not nearly so great. Without improved weather conditions and serious efforts to limit fertility, however, a chronic condition of mass starvation could easily become a vivid reality.

In 1974 the Organization of Petroleum Exporting Countries (OPEC) quadrupled the price of imported oil. The monopolistic prices for petroleum have left economists in great uncertainty and even bewilderment about the stability and future of economic activity in the United States and the rest of the world. Oil prices are clearly suspect as one of the prime causes of the longest, most severe recession since the great depression of the 1930s.

However, the economic consequences have not been quite as bad as some economists feared. Oil prices seem to be stabilizing and may actually decline in the remainder of this decade, if not in dollars and cents, at least in real terms as more oil is discovered and as coal and other energy sources are increasingly substituted for petroleum. With economic conditions returning to a more normal state and with the OPEC nations anxious to develop their own economies, politicians around the world may tend to simply shrug off the recent energy crisis instead of planning how to adjust to an oilless world.

The fourfold rise in the price of imported oil is really rather small, however, in comparison to the additional tenfold or more price increase that can be expected as fossil fuels are used up and replaced with such substitutes as vegetable oil, wood alcohol, liquid hydrogen, and ammonia synthesized from water and air.

Natural resource scarcity is a serious problem. The longer it is ignored and the investments that might reasonably be expected to conserve exhaustible resources are delayed, the more painful it will be to adjust to a steady state economy.

Natural resources are not the only area requiring major adjustments. The rapid decline in births between 1957 and 1973 in the United States has already had a major impact on the demand for elementary and secondary school teachers. As we approach a zero-growth steady state economy there will be relatively less need for pediatricians, architects, builders, and research scientists. Recycling activities will be greatly expanded, however. There will also be a greater need for gerontologists and persons skilled in preservation and repair.

Because some of the changes in the composition of the labor force that are likely to take place as we approach a steady state population could mean needless heartache, as well as an enormous waste of resources in preparing for jobs which may not exist, young people should be better informed about zero growth.

Economists who have considered a steady state economy have differed widely in their personal regard for it. According to Adam Smith, the condition of the laboring poor and of most people seems to be happiest and most comfortable in the progressive state: "The stationary is dull: the declining melancholy."

Howard Odum and other ecologists have noted, however, that whenever an ecosystem reaches a steady state after periods of succession, the rapid net growth specialists are replaced by a new team of higher diversity, higher quality, longer living, better controlled, and more stable components: "Collectively, through division of labor and specialization, the climax team gets more energy out of the steady flow of available source energy than those specialized in fast growth."

About all one can say with confidence about the stationary economy is that some opportunities will be diminished while others will be expanded. Because mature ecosystems are generally more interesting than rapid growth successions, I am inclined to accept the view of John Stuart Mill that the stationary economy at least has the potential for being a better place in which to live. More than 100 years ago he said:

> *I cannot . . . regard the stationary state of capital and wealth with the unaffected aversion so generally manifested towards it by political economists of the old school. I am inclined to believe that it would be, on the whole, a very considerable improvement on our present condition. I confess I am not charmed with the ideal of life held out to those who think that the normal state of human beings is that of struggling to get on; that the trampling, crushing, elbowing, and treading on each other's heels which forms the existing type of social life, are the most desirable lot of human kind.*
>
> *I know not why it should be a matter of congratulation, that persons who are already richer than anyone needs to be, should have doubled their means of consuming things which give little or no pleasure except as representative of wealth. . . . It is only in the backward countries of the world that increased production is still an important object: in those most advanced, what is economically needed is a better distribution, of which one indispensable means is a stricter restraint on population. . . .*
>
> *It is scarcely necessary to remark that a stationary condition of capital and population implies no stationary state of human improvement.* There would be as much scope as ever for all kinds of mental culture, and moral and social progress; as much and much more likelihood of it being improved, when minds cease to be engrossed by the art of getting on. *Even the industrial arts might be as earnestly and as successfully cultivated, with this sole difference, that in serving no purpose but the increase of wealth, industrial improvements would produce their legitimate effect, that of abridging labor.*[13]

William Bowen, president of Princeton University, has expressed similar thoughts:

> *An end to growth in material output would not necessarily be incompatible with economic growth of kinds not well measured by our*

present stock of indicators, notably growth in the quality of goods and services. With a renaissance of craftsmanship, of pride in work, of willingness to serve, a society poorer than ours by some statistical measures could enjoy goods of greater durability and higher aesthetic quality, and services performed with more courtesy, cheerfulness, and competence. And stability in material growth, finally, would not necessarily be incompatible with individual excellence, with devotion to one's craft, with love for one's children, with high achievement in the arts, with eloquence, and with precise thought or careful expression, with enhanced sense of community, with deepened religious faith, or with care for the scarred yet still nurturing earth itself.[14]

Notes

1. Gunther S. Stent, *The Coming of the Golden Age: A View of the End of Progress* (New York: Natural History Press, 1969), p. 112.

2. Sumner Slichter, *Economic Growth in the United States* (Baton Rouge, La.: State University Press, 1961), pp. 101 - 106.

3. In 1963 I examined various sources of economic growth, noted that none of these sources are open-ended, and suggested that real wages, which had doubled, redoubled, and then doubled for a third time in about 100 years might "never double again." This conclusion was so out of tune with contemporary economic thinking, which assumed that there would be another doubling before the end of this century, that is was virtually ignored at the time. See "The Substitution of Inanimate Energy for Animal Power," *The Journal of Political Economy* (June 1973), pp. 284 - 292.

4. Donella H. Meadows et al., *The Limits to Growth* (New York: Universe Books, 1972).

5. Edward Denison, *Sources of Economic Growth in the United States* (Committee for Economic Development, 1962).

6. The *law of diminishing returns* states that as the quantity of any variable input that is combined with a fixed quantity of other inputs increases, the incremental increase in total output per additional unit of the variable input will eventually decline. In the 1963 - 1973 decade, GNP increased less rapidly than total capital investment, total energy consumption, and expenditure for civilian research and development. This suggests that the law of diminishing returns is already operative and that the growth in output per manhour will probably continue to decline.

7. *Fortune* (June 1973), p. 30.

8. This point was first publicized by me in "Why Economic Uptrend May be Short Lived," *Commercial and Financial Chronicle* (December 3, 1970), p. 1.

9. Walter McQuade and Ann Aikman, *Stress* (New York: Dutton, 1974), p. 10.

10. John Kenneth Galbraith, *Affluent Society* (Boston: Houghton Mifflin, 1958).

11. John Kenneth Galbraith, *The New Industrial State* (Boston: Houghton Mifflin, 1967).

12. Charles A. Reich, *The Greening of America* (New York: Bantam, 1971), p. 2.

13. John Stuart Mill, "The Stationary State," in *Principles of Political Economy*, book 4. Italics supplied.

14. William Bowen, "A Choice of Futures — Black or Gray," *Fortune* (September 1971), p. 132.

PART TWO

*The Advent of the
Steady State Economy*

chapter 2

SOME LIMITS TO GROWTH

The idea of growth has become as deeply entrenched in contemporary economic thinking as rain dancing has in some other societies, according to Alan Wagar. He suggests that too little thought has been given to the results of headlong expansion, particularly those which affect the environment: "Although we still seem confident that technology will solve all problems as they arise, the problems are already far ahead of us, and many are growing faster than their solutions."[1]

Rising concern about the impact of economic growth on the environment has not only led to a revival of interest in the stationary state but also to suggestions that laws should be passed to hasten what John Stuart Mill envisioned in 1857 as inevitable:

> It must have been seen, more or less distinctly by political economists, that the increase in wealth is not boundless; that at the end of what they term the progressive state lies the stationary state, that all progress in wealth is but a postponement of this, and that each step in advance is an approach to it.

Speaking before the Institute on Man and Science in 1970, Dr. Rene Dubos gave voice to a growing number of scientists and humanists who feel that the times have caught up with John Stuart Mill:

> The ecological constraints upon population and technological growth will inevitably lead to social and economic systems different from the ones in which we live today. . . . Whether we want it or not, the phase or quantitative growth which has prevailed throughout technical civilization during the 19th and 20th centuries will soon come to an end.

In this chapter I will first examine economic progress from the point of view of some economic and environmental constraints, and then consider mechanization from the perspective of employed horsepower. The speed, scale, and efficiency of mechanical horses provide an understandable basis for expecting real GNP to grow more rapidly than the employed labor force. None of these energy-related dimensions of progress can be considered open-ended or exempt from the law of diminishing returns, however. Analyzing the substitution of inanimate energy for animal power shows that the United States and other industrialized nations are probably much closer to an end of strictly economic progress than most persons engaged in research and development would care to admit.

Environmental Constraints

Since the publication of the *General Theory of Employment, Interest and Money* by John Maynard Keynes in 1936, most economists have considered a decline in profitable investment opportunities to be a key cause of economic stagnation. In his presidential address before the American Economic Association in 1938, Alvin Hansen suggested that investment activity could usefully be related to three main factors: population growth, opening of new territory and discovery of new resources, and technological innovations.[2] Hansen dismissed the opening of new territory and the discovery of new resources as no longer important in the development of the American economy. He then rationalized the cause of the great depression of the 1930s as a decline in the population growth and a lack of new industries comparable to the invention of the railroad and the automobile.

The surge of economic and investment activity that occurred during and after World War II has tended to discredit Hansen's theory of stagnation. Many Western European countries have achieved very impressive rates of economic growth despite comparatively low population growth. Larger houses and fancier automobiles also can be effective substitutes for new industries. Natural resource scarcity and the closing of old frontiers are now regarded by some economists, such as Kenneth Boulding, as a more important reason for expecting an eventual end to economic growth.

Boulding has a vision of a global equilibrium built around the principle of a spaceship economy.[3] However, it does not provide a very clear picture of when such an equilibrium might be achieved. The spaceship that carried men to the moon was, after all, a resounding technological success. Such optimists as economist Frank W. Notestein have responded with the suggestion that there are no substantial limits in sight either in raw materials or in energy that alterations in the price structure, product substitution, anticipated gains in technology, and pollution control cannot be expected to solve. Lord Zuckerman has suggested that pollution is not an irreversible menace: "that devastation of the landscape can be corrected, that rivers can be cleaned, and that the skies can be cleared." He points out that the Thames River in England is now clean enough to support the growth of more than fifty species of fish, and that the once-notorious pea-soup fogs of London are now a thing of the past.[4]

New York City has strikingly reduced sulfur dioxide emissions since 1966. The President's Council on Environmental Quality recently reported that many other large cities have also reduced sulfur dioxide, carbon monoxide, and total suspended particles. If pollution were the only constraint on economic activity, economic growth, by itself, might bring on an environmental revolution against pollution.[5]

In the early stages of industrialization, the amount of pollution is likely to be quite small in comparison to the absorptive capacity of the environment. Private benefit from increased output is probably higher than the social cost of the residuals that must be disposed of in production and consumption. The tendency to do little or nothing about increased pollution is likely to be reinforced by the large unit costs of recycling or treating small quantities of waste products.

As output increases and market demands become more saturated, however, pollution becomes more noticeable. The social costs or external damages produced by an increase in waste products, moreover, can be expected to increase not in direct proportion to the increase in output but in proportion to the increase in output times the number of people who are forced to observe it, or might be adversely affected by it.

As costs increase more rapidly than the benefits from additional pollution, public outrage and increased recycling and waste treatment efforts are to be expected, with a consequent redirection of inventive effort toward product and input substitution, improved clean-up methods, and the conversion of waste products into productive assets. Reducing noxious pollutants will be further accelerated if the demand for an improved environment increases with higher incomes and if the per unit cost of treating or recycling large amounts of waste products is less than for small amounts of waste products.

The costs of a cleaner environment have generally been rather modest. The catalytic converters required on new automobiles, for example, only cost between $100 and $150, but in comparison to 1967 models, they are expected to reduce unburnt hydrocarbons more than 90 per cent, carbon monoxide 83 per cent, and nitrogen oxides 48 per cent. By permitting automobile manufacturers to retune their engines for better fuel economy, these devices are also expected to increase average fuel efficiency about 14 per cent over 1974 models.

A 1974 study by the President's Council on Environmental Quality suggests that environmental programs in the United States had accounted at most for roughly 0.5 per cent of inflation, 1 per cent of GNP, 2 to 3 per cent of all investment expenditures, and 5 to 6 per cent of total expenditures on industrial plants and equipment.

Pollution would probably not be a serious constraint on economic growth in a world with an abundant supply of natural gas and low-sulfur oil and coal. It is likely to become a more serious constraint in a world of increasing natural resource scarcity, however.

In a pioneering analysis of coal's environmental debt, Gerald Garvey has examined some economic costs associated with land sinking into mined-out tunnels, uncontrolled fires in abandoned mines, acid mine drainage, and the need for greater earth waste reclamation and soil conservation in Appalachia. He concludes that at least $4 billion would have been required in 1970 to correct cumulative damages and achieve something approaching a full environmental restoration of abandoned coal mines in the United States and their unsightly waste heaps.[6] This debt estimate, interestingly enough, was slightly greater than the economic value of the coal mined in 1970.

Because coal supplied less than 20 per cent of the energy used in the United States in 1970, the cost of rectifying environmental damage can be expected to rise rapidly as oil and gas, which currently supply more than three-quarters of our energy, are replaced with synthetic fuels derived from coal and shale. Garvey notes that mine acid discharges in Appalachia already exceed the ecosystem's natural absorptive ability by at least 10 per cent and that spoil banks multiply erosion by a factor of ten, worsening both land degradation and stream siltation. As energy production shifts to the more fragile ecologies of Alaska and the arid West the environmental damage will be more severe.

The problem of maintaining a reasonably clean environment will be exacerbated not only by the use of relatively more coal, which is inconvenient and rather dirty, but also by the fact that relatively more energy will be used up in mining, processing, upgrading, and transporting such energy to consumers. If it is true, as some studies have suggested, that almost as much energy will be needed to extract shale oil as the shale produces, the environmental burden of maintaining a liquid fuels economy could turn out to be enormous. As high-grade fossil fuel reserves and other mineral resources are used up the problem of waste disposal might turn out to be even more severe.

In a rebuttal to the Club of Rome and other ecodoomsters Wilfred Beckerman, an economist at the University of London, has noted that there is about one million times the known reserves of every industrial element within a mile of the surface of the earth.[7] He suggests that with substitution and higher prices we might be able to postpone the problem of physical bankruptcy for 100 million years or more. All the oxygen in the earth's atmosphere would soon be used up, however, if only a small proportion of the ferrous iron in the earth's crust were oxidized to ferric iron.

Geologist Thomas Lovering has pointed out, moreover, that the enormous quantities of usual waste produced for each unit of metal in ordinary granite (in a ratio of at least 2,000 to 1) are more easily disposed of on a blueprint than in the field. "To recover minerals sought, the rock must be shattered by explosives, drilled for input and recovery wells, and flooded with solutions containing special extractive chemicals. Provisions must then be made to avoid the loss of solutions and the consequent contamination of groundwater and surface water."[8]

Though such problems do support the theory of an eventual

end to economic progress, I feel that other factors will tend to be more limiting in the near future. Of the factors that help to restore one's faith in the law of diminishing returns, none has been more neglected by economists than the substitution of inanimate energy for animal power. Mechanical horses provide an understandable basis for expecting real GNP to grow more rapidly than the employed labor force as well as a basis for suggesting that we may be very close to the end of strictly economic progress.

The Mechanical Horse

In 1928 C. R. Daugherty noted that it is impracticable to make a census of machines: "They change and become obsolete too rapidly, and they cannot be reduced to any satisfactory common unit."[9] An index of installed machinery can be compiled, however, by ascertaining the total horsepower of the engines that drive the different kinds of machinery. The horsepower of electric motors and other installed prime movers and the work performed by prime movers are among the few inputs of economic consequence that have increased more rapidly than total output.[10]

Total horsepower used in the United States, including automotive horsepower, increased more than twice as rapidly as real GNP between 1940 and 1972. The increase in nonautomotive horsepower was only slightly greater than the percentage increase in GNP; this is impressive, however, considering the extent to which buses, trucks, and private automobiles have replaced non-automotive horsepower in factories, railroads, and public transit.

If one accepts the idea that economic progress is largely the result of mechanization, growth in labor productivity can be considered a process which is partly self-generating or induced by a spillover of wage benefits to a comparatively scarce supply of labor. The higher wage rates then provide an economic incentive for innovations and adjustments leading to a further substitution of mechanical horses for human labor.

Improvements in labor productivity are also partly the result of discoveries and inventions that cheapen inanimate energy by improving the efficiency of converting heat into work. A man or a horse can convert carbohydrate food energy into useful work with efficiencies ranging up to 35 per cent. Without the development of internal combustion engines with efficiencies ranging between 20 and 30 per cent, horses might still be used for work as well as for pleasure. A 1956 study of horse and tractor costs indicates that the horse was still more economical than a tractor in some agricultural situations, even in technically advanced countries like Great Britain.[11]

Changes in conversion efficiency are probably even more important than such comparisons indicate, because they help to offset natural resource scarcity. Without improving the efficiency of converting energy into useful working effects, improvements in labor productivity become analogous to a free-wheeling vehicle propelled by its own momentum — a vehicle that will gradually lose momentum and inevitably coast to a stop as a result of friction and a natural scarcity of good roadbed.

The limits to technological efficiency are well understood in the case of large-scale power plants and are rapidly being approached. Higher fuel prices probably will stimulate much research in ways to improve the combustion and work efficiencies of small-scale energy converters. It does not seem likely, however, that these efforts will be successful enough to fully offset natural resource scarcity without a relative sacrifice of such energy-intensive activities as operating motorboats or large automobiles at high speeds.

To obtain greater efficiencies from internal combustion engines, it is necessary to utilize scarce materials that can withstand higher temperatures. Alloy steel for construction that does not have to withstand high temperatures typically contains from between 0.1 and 2 per cent of such alloying elements as nickel, chromium, molybdenum, and silicon. Steels that will stand temperatures up to 500° F. contain from 4 to 6 per cent chromium. Alloys designed to withstand temperatures above 1,000 degrees contain practically no iron but are based mainly on cobalt, nickel, and chromium with smaller additions of columbium, tungsten, molybdenum, and tantalum — materials which are not nearly as abundant in nature as iron.

Analogous to, but somewhat distinct from the notion of technical efficiency, are a host of road-type investments that contribute to the same overall objective. The Erie Canal, which is alleged to have reduced the cost of shipping a ton of wheat from

Buffalo to New York from $100 to $10 is a classic example of road-type efficiency. The Panama and Suez canals are even more spectacular examples.

Somewhat more subtle, but nevertheless in the road-type category, are clothing and shelter — two of the most important ways of maintaining and increasing the efficiency of animal power in the face of a sometimes hostile environment. Half or more of what is usually regarded as wealth consists of buildings and shelter to keep human beings, domesticated animals, and various artifacts intact. Because many mechanical horses can be compacted into a smaller space than is required to house one live animal, phenomenal economies can sometimes be obtained by switching to mechanical horsepower which also has the advantage of not consuming energy when the inanimate horses are not working.

The assembly-line principle is another device for straightening out the productive process and making it more efficient. Savings are accrued not only in labor but in floor space, inventories, storage, machinery, and auxiliary equipment and maintenance, and by eliminating waste, reducing spoilage, and shortening the time in process.

The main difficulty with the road-straightening analogy applied to assembly lines is that the gains from reorganizing and concentrating production in a few metropolitan centers are not entirely net. Large-scale assembly-line production is, in an important sense, at cross-purposes with the minimization of travel costs and possibly worker preferences as well. The road-straightening analogy does help one to perceive that the assembly-line principle is not an open-ended source of improved efficiency, however.

To understand better how inanimate energy can be a marvelous yet imperfect substitute for human beings and other resources it is helpful to consider two of the more important ways in which mechanical horses can be substituted for human effort. These ways are basically related to the economically important dimensions of speed and the scale of productive operations.

Speed

Today information can be transmitted at 2,400 words per minute via teletype. It is estimated that computer to computer transmission will soon be at 86,000 words per minute. Add to this the barrage of infor-

*mation beamed via TV and radio and consider that human beings
can process only about 250 to 1,000 words per minute. In an attempt
to understand ever more by generating more information we
overload our capacity to integrate or assimilate what we are doing.
The barrage of information has led society to a condition where it is
"data rich but perceptually poor." We have all the numbers but can't
seem to make sense of them.*

*The quest for information appears to lead to a condition which
could be described as "information neurosis." We can't get enough
primarily because we don't know what we are looking for or why we
want it. We just have a vague feeling that more information is better
than less information.*[12]

A large gap in our knowledge of labor productivity is
systematic information on travel, working, and processing speeds
for different industries at various times. Using changes in the
transportation industry, however, it is reasonable to suppose that
between a third and a half of all improvements in labor productivity in this century may have been either directly or indirectly
the result of faster travel times and speedier production processes.
Speed is one area where evidence in support of retardation and
diminishing returns is easy to obtain and where economic limits
have already retarded the growth of labor productivity.

An electronic computer can do in minutes what would take a
lifetime of human calculation. In 1945, at a labor cost of $1 per
hour, at a rate of 16 operations per minute, it cost about $1,000 to do
a million operations on a keyboard and took at least a month.
Modern computers can now do a million operations in a second or
less for about one penny. Although further improvements can be
expected, the data suggest that the percentage growth in computer
speeds has been slowing down for more than a decade.

A man or a horse cannot move heavy loads long distances at
speeds of more than about 2.5 miles per hour. A modern diesel
engine, on the other hand, is capable of moving much heavier
loads faster than 50 miles per hour — a twentyfold increase. The
advantage of higher operating speed is twofold. Savings occur not
only in labor and travel-time inputs but also in interest and amor-
tization of fixed capital. Within fairly wide ranges, horsepower is
the only input of consequence that must be increased in proportion
to total output.

Intercity freight trains in the United States had an average
speed of only 16.8 miles per hour in 1950. Their speed increased at

a rate of 2.1 per cent per year from 1950 to 1955. Improvements in freight train speed declined to a 1 per cent growth rate from 1955 to 1960 and then slipped to an annual increase of 0.6 per cent per year from 1960 to 1965. In 1973 the average speed of freight trains was only 19.8 miles per hour or slightly less than the 1965 level of 20.1 miles per hour. The low average speed and retarded rates of improvement help to explain why trucks have captured a larger share of the intercity freight business (Table 2.1).

The average speed of trucks on straight sections of main rural highways during off-peak hours increased from 39.8 miles per hour in 1945 to 56.2 miles per hour in 1972, an average annual increase of about 1.2 per cent. Between 1950 and 1969 the speed of intercity air passenger service in the United States more than doubled from 180 miles per hour to 394 miles per hour, an average annual increase of 4.2 per cent per year. Air as well as ground speeds are now being cut back in some instances, however, to conserve energy.

Better roads and faster travel times have greatly helped to increase labor productivity in other industries. Health is a classic example. The comfort and convenience of the private automobile has made it possible to move most patients to doctors or hospitals, greatly improving the productivity of the medical profession in comparison to a system in which doctors spent most of their time traveling to see their patients.

Better roads and faster travel times have also helped traveling salesmen and persons in the repair industry to cover larger territories and become more specialized. The direct savings from a

TABLE 2.1
Average Speed of Trucks and Freight Trains, 1950–1973.

	Trucks	Freight trains
1950	43.0	16.8
1955	45.6	18.6
1960	48.2	19.5
1965	51.8	20.1
1970	54.7	20.1
1971	56.1	20.4
1972	56.2	20.0
1973	55.0	19.8

Source: *Statistical Abstract.*

reduction in on-the-job travel time may be small, however, compared to the indirect savings in manhours that result from being able to locate new facilities in uncongested areas that would not be accessible without the speed and convenience of motor vehicles.

Single-story manufacturing and distribution facilities are more efficient than multilevel ones and businesses can often obtain additional economies by moving to the suburbs where land is cheaper and parking less expensive. The possibility that large increases in the scale of manufacturing and commercial establishments may be dependent upon the larger markets that can be quickly reached with faster transport raises an interesting question. Will changes in labor productivity from other kinds of adjustments, such as increases in the size of an operation, continue to be of significance now that the economic limits to motor vehicles speed have generally been reached and in some instances surpassed?

One drawback to higher operating speeds is that the work performed usually requires an expenditure of relatively more energy. A modern destroyer can cruise at speeds up to 35 knots for short periods. A further increase in speed to 38 knots without sacrificing any other military characteristics would require an increase in displacement of 33.5 per cent and an increase in fuel consumption at cruising speed of 21 per cent — all for an increase in speed of less than 10 per cent. Significantly higher operating speeds for surface ships are impossible without resorting to hydrofoils or hovercraft, both of which are costlier in terms of capital outlay and have low propulsion efficiencies.

Richard Rice, a professor at the Carnegie-Mellon University Transportation Research Institute, has estimated that a heavy 30,000-ton freight train with 200 cars that travels at a speed of 25 miles per hour can move 420 tons of cargo per gallon of fuel over fairly level terrain.[13] A 3,000-ton freight train with 100 cars traveling at 40 miles per hour would have a lower propulsion efficiency of 250 ton miles per gallon. A faster 3,000-ton, 40-car freight train traveling at 90 miles per hour would have a propulsion efficiency of only 97 ton miles per gallon. Most American railroads do not have track that is straight enough and adequately maintained to permit safe travel at speeds over about 50 miles per hour.

Buses and passenger trains are from three to four times as efficient in moving passengers as the private automobile. Because of the many stops and starts involved in loading and unloading passengers, however, it usually takes at least twice as long to get to one's destination using public transportation. Moses and Williamson suggest that because of the extra time loss, negative prices are necessary on practically all modes of public transportation in metropolitan areas to divert at least 50 per cent of those individuals now using private automobiles.[14] Transit companies, in other words, would probably have to pay many automobile owners to use their service.

Former President Nixon suggested in a 1973 energy message that a car traveling 50 miles per hour uses 20 to 25 per cent less gasoline per mile than the same car traveling at 70 miles per hour. Airplanes require almost two and one-half times as much galoline and jet fuel per passenger mile, on the average, as private automobiles.[15] A supersonic aircraft (SST) is estimated to consume almost twice as much fuel as a subsonic jet of comparable size.

The propulsion efficiency of the SST is so low as to put it in a class with oceangoing superliners, helicopters, and Pullman night trains — innovations that have either ceased to be economic or have never been very successful economically. Long-distance travel at very high speeds can be so upsetting to sleeping, eating, and working habits, moreover, as to be counterproductive in many instances.

Whether faster travel times should be considered more instead of less productive depends on how society chooses to value fossil fuels. As liquid hydrocarbons become increasingly scarce there will be an economic incentive to shift from air to ground and water transport, to reduce the size and speed of private automobiles, and to make better use of public transport even if it means more waiting and greater travel time. All these economizing measures will tend to lower labor productivity either directly or indirectly. Because some costs of building and servicing an automobile are fixed and independent of its size, there is bound to be an indirect loss of labor productivity per pound of automobile produced or gallon of gasoline sold as a result of smaller automobiles, even if their owners are not seriously inconvenienced.

Whether measures to conserve energy can also be expected to reduce economic well-being is more conjectural. Henry David Thoreau long ago noted:

Most of the luxuries, and many of the so-called comforts of life, are not only not indispensable, but positive hindrances to the elevation of mankind. . . .

Our inventions are wont to be pretty toys, which distract our attention from serious things. They are but improved means to an unimproved end, an end which it was already but too easy to arrive at; as railroads lead to Boston or New York. . . . To make a railroad round the world available to all mankind is equivalent to grading the whole surface of the planet. Men have an indistinct notion that if they keep up this activity of joint stocks and spades long enough all will at length ride somewhere, in next to no time, and for nothing; but though a crowd rushes to the depot, and the conductor shouts, "All aboard." when the smoke is blown away and the vapor condensed, it will be perceived that a few are riding, but the rest are run over.[16]

Although speed, as much as any factor, probably accounts for many revolutionary changes that have occurred in the last century, it is not an unmixed blessing. The capability of the average automobile is already so great that ground speeds must be reduced and controlled for safety and accident prevention.

The problem of unsafe speed is not unique to the transportation sector. Damage occurring to goods in process and delays resulting from equipment breakdown are two reasons why the average worker in manufacturing industries employed less than six horses in 1972 compared to the hundred or more horses under the hood of the automobile that may have been used to bring him or her to work. The speed characteristics of the average farm tractor, interestingly enough, are not very different from those that can be supplied by a live horse.

Though many improvements may increase working speeds in a minor way, the age of spectacular advances in practical working speeds is rapidly drawing to a close. As the limits to practicable working speeds are reached in most industries — probably before the end of this century — the growth in output per manhour can also be expected to stop unless workers can operate larger machines or control more and more machines operating at the same rate of speed.

Scale

A major difference between inanimate prime movers and animals is the possibility of teaming together hundreds of mechanical horses in a smaller space than is required to house and harness one live animal. The compactness of the mechanical horse has had a profound effect upon the scale of many productive operations and has led to economies in the housing and use of additional horsepower.

Some increases in plant size since World War II have been truly phenomenal. Fifteen years ago an ammonia plant, driven by the old reciprocating compressors, might produce only 150 tons a day. Using modern, compact, and more powerful centrifugal compressors, some plants now produce over 1,500 tons a day and designers are working to double that size. A pump motor of a few hundred horsepower used to be big; today some motors have reached 9,000 hp. and are headed even higher. *Supertankers*, a word coined when such ships reached 28,000 deadweight tons in the 1940s, are now sailing at 477,000 dwt. and up.

The economics of big machines start to cut two ways, however, as the market for them narrows and development costs must be spread over fewer units. Shipments of huge pieces of equipment can butt up against the hard realities of rail and highway underpasses. In some areas, equipment designers have nearly reached the limits of the available materials and components. Reliability standards intensify as the user tries to ensure the success of an enormous financial commitment. Big Allis, Consolidated Edison's largest generating unit in New York, is an interesting example. It could supply 10 per cent of Con Ed's power demand but because of the difficulty of replacing that much electricity on short notice if the unit were unexpectedly forced out of service it has generally been operated below full capacity.

Statistics presented in the 1970 National Power Survey also show that large-scale generating units have been forced out of operations more often than smaller units. This unreliability raises serious doubts as to whether the process of scaling up electric power plants will go on indefinitely.

In 1970 the editors of *Business Week* noted that older industries are more likely to reach plateaus in size than newer industries.[17] The new sheet mills then being built by the steel industry were a foot narrower than the biggest existing one. Similarly, no one was rushing to duplicate U.S. Steel's 260-in plate mill at Gary, Indiana, which serves the shipbuilding industry. They observed that Caterpillar Tractor, which has a standard scraper capable of pushing 54 cu.yd. of dirt, was not sure whether it could build a 72-cu.yd. scraper that would deliver dirt at the same cost per yard, let alone a lower cost.

As plants get larger and production becomes more concentrated in fewer and fewer plants it is often necessary to move materials and finished products longer distances. The higher costs for transportation will tend to offset economies of scale at the plant. Public policy, in the form of concern over excessive pollution, noise, or safety, may also intrude and prevent such plants from being either built or sited at optimal locations.

The larger the ship, other things equal, the smaller the fleet, and the fewer trips required to deliver a given quantity of output. To save time in port, the horsepower of the unloading facilities must be increased in proportion to the size of the ship; but because of fewer trips this horsepower will tend to be idle a larger fraction of the time. Greater inventory will be required between ships; and, because some ports are not equipped to handle large ships, additional losses are likely to exist as a result of greater "roundaboutness" in the transport of people and commodities. As less frequent and more marginal activities of the human operator are mechanized, one automatically increases both the average idleness of total horsepower and the number of gadgets that might fail and possibly idle the entire complex.

Because many time losses tend to be proportional to area, an increase in width or speed of a machine cannot be expected to result in a proportional increase in effective field capacity. Increasing the width of a planter 50 per cent, from four to six rows, for example, raises effective capacity only 35 per cent. Popular articles emphasizing technology and economies of scale now place more emphasis on barriers to progress and statements such as that of K. W. Anderson of John Deere, "In farm equipment, a 24 ft. harvester is about as wide as you can go."[18] As farms have become larger and the distance between homes and the field of operation greater, farmers have also discovered that theft of unattended, expensive equipment is increasing.

Though it might be argued that there is a problem of unwieldy equipment that will soon catch up, if it has not already done so, with road transportation, agriculture, and people in the earthmoving business, the most important size limits probably have to do with human preferences and flexibility.

Most people, for some reason, do not prefer to live in barracks, consume the same meals, move about in busses at prearranged schedules, and in other ways avoid duplication of effort. The taste of the consumer for variety, for individuality, for goods in small packages, for freedom in travel and consumption, and for a bit of ground he can call his own, greatly limits the size and efficiency of the equipment that can be employed in fabrication, packaging, and distribution.

The flexibility of the human operator also allows him to jump from task to task and from special situation to special situation, and in so doing remain more or less fully employed, at a time when larger and more specialized equipment would remain idle, be in the way, or consume valuable storage space.

Given human flexibility and preferences for variety and for goods in small quantities, it does not seem probable that the scale factor, which has been of tremendous importance in freeing labor from primary production, can possibly have a comparable impact at the distribution stage of production.

In 1963 I predicted that, when the agricultural, mining, industrial, utility, and transportation sectors of the economy begin to run into a problem of unwieldy equipment — a development that is already occuring — the preferred pattern of consumption might be inconsistent with opportunities for marked improvement in labor productivity in other sectors of our economy.[19]

Since 1963 the growth of labor productivity in most industries that employ a substantial amount of horsepower has declined markedly. Electric and gas utilities, for example, increased output per manhour at an average rate of about 7 per cent annually between 1947 and 1965. From 1965 to 1972 the increase averaged only 5.1 per cent. Declining sales of natural gas and the higher prices now being charged for electricity make it reasonable to suppose that the future growth in gas and electric utility sales may be less than half the 1965 - 1972 rate of 7 per cent, and that improvements in output per manhour will also fall to less than half the 1965 - 1972 rate of 5.1 per cent.

In 1969 output per manhour in the bituminous coal industry rose to a new all-time peak and then slumped precipitously in 1970 and 1971. By the middle 1970s it had not recovered to a new high. Between 1947 and 1973 output per manhour in the farm economy increased at an average annual rate of 5.9 per cent compared to an average rate of only 2.6 per cent for the nonfarm sector. The overall average, however, obscures a pattern of accelerated growth followed by marked evidence in support of retardation. For the 6 five-year intervals from 1940 to 1970 the average annual sub-period growth rates for labor productivity in the farm economy were 5.2, 5.3, 6.1, 7.4, 6.3, and 4.4 per cent respectively.

For years it has been fashionable to talk of "excess capacity" in agriculture. Our farm population is now stabilizing. Most acreage restrictions have been lifted. With large amounts of rather marginal land now being brought back into cultivation, it is hard to believe that a 4 per cent growth rate for farm labor productivity can be sustained in the rest of the 70s.

Automation

With machine size determined by unwieldiness or the package size that consumers prefer, the hope for further substitution of inanimate energy for muscle power rests on better integration of complementary machinery and the elimination of machine tenders. Although computers and other electronic devices could possibly take over routine control functions, automation seems more likely to give the average worker less to do than to eliminate him completely, because repairs must be made and normal stoppage corrected. In agriculture the introduction of bigger and better machines employing more and more horsepower has, until recently, created a condition of almost chronic underemployment.

The operation of farm tractors by means of radio control devices has been studied since the 1920s. However, the extreme variability of farm operating conditions are not conducive to efficient programming and remote control. Even if it were economically feasible to collect and transmit enough information about differences in agricultural terrain to make remote control as technically efficient as control by a human operator, accidents and normal downtime still would require the services of an attendant. With thousands of dollars invested in complicated harvesting equipment and reaping time limited, farmers are unlikely to be willing to run the risk of either not having pertinent information at their fingertips or finding it impossible to respond creatively and constructively to unexpected information.

Greater opportunities exist for adapting electronic controls to complex industrial processes, but with half a million dollars worth of digital and analog computers replacing perhaps one supervisor in a refinery or power station, it is rather difficult to imagine far-reaching repercussions. In most cases the main justification will be improved operating efficiency, which tends to be inherently limited by natural laws. If an allowance is made for fabricating and maintaining the control equipment, it would not be at all surprising if elaborate controls created more jobs than are directly eliminated.

Energy and Capital

Though it would be an oversimplification to attribute all improvements in productivity to a mere substitution of inanimate energy for human beings and other resources, there is a sense in which it is more enlightening to speak in terms of factors affecting the speed, scale, and technical efficiency of converting heat into work than to simply measure that portion of total output which cannot be explained by an increase in labor and capital and, for want of a more rational understanding, call it all "technical progress."

Economists, in any event, are beginning to realize that the horsepower of prime mover deserves to be considered a separate and distinct factor of production that ought not to be omitted from empirical production functions. G. S. Maddala has shown that employed horsepower can explain almost all the growth in labor productivity in the coal industry without resort to technological change.[20]

In 1963 Murray Foss of the Department of Commerce analyzed the consumption of energy in manufacturing and various other industries, compared this consumption to the horsepower of electric motors and installed prime movers, and concluded that the utilization rate for capital equipment may have increased more than one-third between 1929 and the mid-1950s.[21]

After making other adjustments for changes in the quality of capital and labor, Griliches and Jorgenson have computed new indices of capital and labor inputs. Their effective stock of capital has increased more rapidly than total output, and they conclude that, "If real product and real factor input are accurately accounted for, the observed growth in total factor productivity is negligible."[22]

The pioneering work of Chenery[23] and Smith[24] has shown that production functions can be derived from engineering data and then analyzed to determine the substitutability of energy for capital. Their work supports the hypothesis that capital can be used to help conserve energy. The trade-off between capital and energy is far from perfect, however, and not immune to the law of diminishing returns.

Dewhurst has estimated that work animals contributed 52.4 per cent of total work output in the United States in 1850; human workers, 12.6 per cent; wind, water, and fuel wood, 27.8 per cent; and fossil fuels, 6.8 per cent. In 1950, work animals are estimated to have contributed only 0.7 per cent of total work output; human workers, 0.9 per cent; wind, water, and fuel wood, 7.8 per cent; and fossil fuels, 90.8 per cent.[25]

As the economics profession begins to appreciate better the importance of inanimate energy as a substitute for other inputs, and also considers the difficulties of converting from an economy run mainly on oil and natural gas to one that is entirely dependent upon other sources of energy, it is almost certain to develop and test new theories of economic growth. Those economists who are not afraid to meet the disciplines of science and engineering halfway will probably not make the mistake of assuming that technological progress is open-ended and exponential, and that capital investment is likely to continue to be an almost perfect substitute for other resources such as land, labor, capital, and energy. When these two assumptions are relaxed, the conclusion is almost sure to be that economic growth in the United States and the more advanced countries of the world will soon come to an end whether we want it to or not.

Notes

1. Alan Wagar, "Growth Versus the Quality of Life," *Science* (June 1970), 1180.

2. Alvin Hansen, "Economic Progress and Declining Population Growth," *American Economic Review* (March 1939), 1 - 15.

3. Kenneth E. Boulding, "The Economics of the Coming Spaceship Earth," *Environmental Quality: In a Growing Economy*, ed. H. Jarret. (Baltimore: Johns Hopkins, 1966): reprinted in *The Environmental Handbook*, ed. Garrett de Bell (New York: Ballantine, 1970), 96 - 97.

4. Lord Zuckerman, "Science, Technology, and Environmental Management," *Who Speaks For Earth*, ed. Maurice F. Strong (New York: Norton, 1973), 137.

5. The theoretical argument in behalf of an environmental revolution brought on by a process of population growth is developed in a more rigorous way in my "Note on Private Goods and Public Bads," *The Journal of Environmental Education*, Summer, 1975, pp. 45 - 49.

6. Gerald Garvey, *Energy, Ecology, Economy*, (New York: Norton, 1972), p. 88.

7. Wilfred Beckerman, *In Defense of Economic Growth* (London: Cape, 1974).

8. Thomas S. Lovering, "Mineral Resources from the Land," in *Resources and Man* (San Francisco: Freeman, 1969), pp. 122 - 123.

9. C. R. Daughterty, A. H. Horton, R. W. Horton, and R. W. Davenport, *Power Capacity and Production in the United States* (U.S. Geological Survey Water Supply Paper No. 579, 1928), p. 13.

10. In addition to my own article on this subject see Murray F. Foss, "The Utilization of Capital Equipment," *Survey of Current Business* (June 1963), 8 - 16; and G. S. Maddala, "Productivity and Technological Change in the Bituminous Coal Industry, 1919 - 54," *The Journal of Political Economy* (August 1965), 352 - 65. Maddala's index of output per employee in bituminous coal mining increased from 100 in 1919 to 228.5 in 1954; horsepower per employee rose from 100 to 772 during the same time. Index changes in gross farm output per person employed in agriculture and a combined index of animate and inanimate horsepower per person imply a marginal rate of substitution in agriculture from 1910 to 1955 that is about the same as that observed for the bituminous coal industry. Output per manhour in manufacturing increased 381 per cent between 1899 and 1962. The horsepower of installed prime mover per manhour increased 556 per cent during the same time. Murray Foss's finding that electric motors and other installed prime movers were utilized from one-third to one-half more hours per day in the mid-1950s than in 1929 suggests that the trade-off between human energy and inanimate energy — adjusted for changes in conversion efficiency — may have been quite a bit worse than implied by the increase in inanimate prime mover.

11. Keith Dexter, "A Study of Economic Costs of Production: An Analysis of Horse and Tractor Costs," *Journal of Agricultural Economics* (June 1956), pp. 73 - 81.

12. Arthur J. Cordell, "The Socio-Economics of Technological Progress," a paper prepared for the Faculty of Science Lecture Series on Human Environment — Problems and Prospects, Carleton University (February 23, 1972), pp. 18 - 19.

13. Richard A. Rice, "System Energy as a Factor in Considering Future Transportation," a paper presented at the ASME annual meeting, November 29, 1970.

14. N. Moses and H. F. Williamson, "Value of Time, Choice of Mode and Subsidy Issue in Urban Transportation," *The Journal of Political Economy* (1963), p. 262.

15. Council on Environmental Quality, *Energy, Environment, and the Electric Power* (August 1972), p. 4. Larger planes loaded to capacity and those flying longer distances between stops consume less energy per passenger mile.

16. Henry David Thoreau, *Walden:* reprinted in *Economic Growth vs. The Environment*, ed. Warren Johnson and John Hardesty (Belmont, Calif.: Wadsworth, 1971), pp. 186 - 187.

17. "In Industry, Sheer Size Really Pays," *Business Week* (October 17, 1970), pp. 172 - 174.

18. Ibid.

19. Edward F. Renshaw, "The Substitution of Inanimate Energy for Animal Power," *Journal of Political Economy* (June 1963), p. 288.

20. "Productivity and Technological Change in the Bituminous Coal Industry, 1919 - 54," *Journal of Political Economy* (August 1965), pp. 352 - 365.

21. Murray F. Foss, "The Utilization of Capital Equipment," *Survey of Current Business* (June 1963), pp. 8 - 16.

22. Z. Griliches and D. W. Jorgenson, "The Explanation of Productivity Change," *Review of Economic Studies* (July 1967): reprinted in *Survey of Current Business* (May 1969), part 2, p. 31. This conclusion has since been modified somewhat. See, "The Measurement of Productivity," *Survey of Current Business*, May 1972, Part II.

23. Hollis B. Chenery, "Process and Production Functions from Engineering Data," in *Studies in the Structure of the American Economy*, ed. V. Leontief et al. (New York: Oxford University Press, 1955), pp. 297 - 325.

24. Vernon L. Smith, *Investment and Production* (Cambridge: Harvard University Press, 1961), pp. 17 - 62.

25. J. Frederick Dewhurst, *America's Needs and Resources* (New York: Twentieth Century Fund, 1955), p. 1116.

chapter 3

THE ENERGY
SHORTAGE

The importance of energy as a source of economic progress is vividly illustrated by the fairly strong correlation between per capita consumption of energy in different countries and per capita GNP (Figure 3.1). United States energy production increased at an average annual rate of 2.5 per cent from 1947 to 1970, while energy consumption increased by 3 per cent. Consumption increased even faster from 1970 to 1973. Domestic energy production during the same time actually declined. Coal, natural gas, and petroleum production were all lower in 1973 than in 1970.

In 1970 oil imports amounted to only about a quarter of American consumption. After the oil embargo was lifted in 1974, petroleum imports increased to nearly 40 per cent of domestic consumption. This growing dependence on imported oil was one factor that made it possible for the Organization of Petroleum Exporting Countries (OPEC) to more than quadruple the price of imported oil.

In this chapter I will first consider how difficult it will be for the United States to become self-sufficient in basic energy. Fossil fuel consumption will then be examined from the perspective of its effect upon total long-run wealth.

The High Cost of
Energy Self-Sufficiency

The wholesale price index for fuels, related products, and power more than doubled in the 18-month period from the beginning of 1973 to the middle of 1974. In commenting on "Project Independence" and the feasibility of becoming self-sufficient in

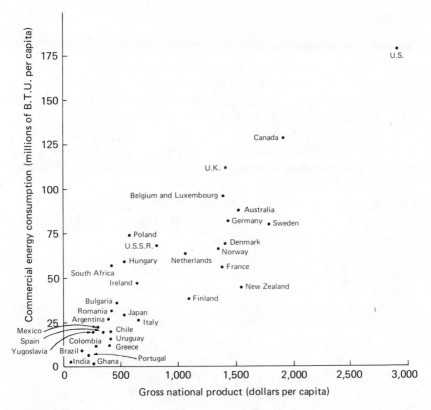

FIGURE 3.1

The Correlation Between Energy Consumption and Gross
National Product.

Source: United Nations Statistical Yearbook.

energy by 1980, a group of economists and energy experts at the
Massachusetts Institute of Technology have suggested that there
would probably have to be another round of price increases for
consumers as great as that experienced in 1973 - 1974 to overcome
economic bottlenecks and technological and environmental constraints.

Part of the difficulty in quickly becoming self-sufficient in
basic energy can be illustrated by examining the domestic
petroleum industry. Diminishing returns have been obscured to a
considerable extent by a regulatory system that has kept many
productive oil wells operating at less than full capacity throughout
most of the post - World War II period. The National Petroleum

Council estimates that surplus crude oil capacity in the United States equaled about 3.75 million barrels of oil per day in the 1965 - 1967 period, or about 45 per cent of total domestic production.

The large increase in surplus capacity was mainly caused by large new oil fields that were discovered in the late 1940s and early 1950s, extensions of undeveloped oil fields, and improvements in the percentage of oil recovered from older fields. Discoveries of new onshore oil fields in the original forty-eight states have sharply declined for more than twenty years. About three-quarters of the gross additions of American oil reserves were from newly discovered oil fields in the 1946 - 1949 period. By 1965 - 1967 the fraction of added reserves from new oil fields declined to about 26 per cent. The percentage was even lower in later years, but data on recent discoveries are incomplete.

The sharp decline in the discovery of new oil fields in the late 1950s and early 1960s was more than offset by a host of new techniques used to increase the percentage of oil recovered from existing reservoirs. By 1969 about 90 per cent of the 548,000 working oil wells in the United States were receiving some form of ar-tificial stimulation. As the less costly techniques of increasing oil production from known oil fields were adopted, the growth of domestic oil production slowed appreciably. In eight of the thir-teen years before 1974, annual reserve finds for crude oil were less than annual production. In 1970 total oil production in the United States reached an all-time peak (Figure 3.2) and has since been declining. It was not until April 1972, however, that the Texas Railroad Commission increased the allowable oil production from wells in the largest oil-producing state to 100 per cent of their so-called maximum efficient rate. Now that excess capacity is no longer available to help offset the natural decline in production from existing wells, the oil industry will have to increase its drill-ing activity substantially to merely keep domestic production from declining.

The natural rate of decline, without advanced recovery technology[1] and regulatory arrangements that limit production below the efficient rate, appears to be about 10 per cent or more per year for existing onshore wells outside Alaska. New oil wells in 1973 and 1974 apparently were only able to offset about 65 per cent of this decline. This implies a required increase in drilling ac-tivity of more than 50 per cent simply to halt the downward trend in domestic oil production in the United States until the Alaska pipeline is completed, if drilling efficiency is to remain the same as in 1973 - 1974.

Some analysts, including M. King Hubbert of the U.S. Geological Survey, believe that we have already discovered and produced more than half the oil that can be economically recovered from known and undiscovered oil fields in the United States. Hubbert's careful analysis of historical production and new discoveries as a function of cumulative exploratory drilling has led a committee of the National Academy of Sciences to conclude that most of the remaining supplies of oil and gas could be used up before the end of this century.[2]

In 1974 petroleum (including imported oil) supplied about 46 per cent of our gross energy consumption; natural gas, 30.1 per cent; coal, 18.3 per cent; hydroelectric power, 4.2 per cent; and nuclear energy, 1.4 per cent. Natural gas reserves were very large in relation to total consumption in the early post - World War II period and continued to increase each year until 1967. From 1968 to 1972, however, net additions to reserves were less than half as large, on the average, as net withdrawals of natural gas for con-

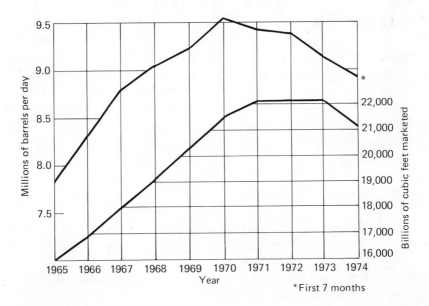

FIGURE 3.2
U.S. Production of Crude Oil and Natural Gas.

sumption. Total production of natural gas continued to increase somewhat from 1968 to 1972 but has since trended downward (Figure 3.2).

Natural Gas

Most additions to natural gas reserves from 1947 to 1967 were the result of extensions to known gas fields and revisions in the estimated amount of recoverable, existing gas. Reserve additions from extensions and revisions of known gas fields fell from 15.7 trillion cubic feet in 1967 to only 4.8 trillion cubic feet in 1972. New discoveries also declined but only from 5.4 to 4.6 trillion cubic feet during the same period. The dramatic decline in reserve additions due to extensions and revisions of known fields strongly suggests that it has become far more difficult to find new gas fields with large amounts of reserves which require a great deal of time to develop.

Total reserve additions per new gas well fell from 4.8 billion cubic feet in 1967 to only 1.6 billion cubic feet in 1972. If reserve additions per well were to remain the same, almost three times as many new gas wells would have to be brought into production each year, in the future, to restore and maintain natural gas production at the 1972 level.[3]

Large deposits of natural gas may be found in either Alaska or mostly unexplored offshore areas. It does not seem likely, however, that onshore natural gas production in the continental states will ever be restored to former levels. Because it will take time to develop offshore deposits and to build a pipeline to transport natural gas from Alaska, natural gas production will probably continue to decline throughout the remainder of the 1970s.

Coal and Shale Oil

The United States has large reserves of coal and rock from which shale oil can be extracted. Efforts are now underway to develop large-scale facilities for converting some of these reserves into synthetic gas and liquid hydrocarbons, it is hoped, at prices equal to or less than the price of imported oil. However, much of the technology that energy companies plan to use for manufacturing synthetic fuels has not been developed beyond a pilot plant state. Actual costs are uncertain. Environmental constraints, technological delays, and the need for water, roads, and utilities in the arid West where large supplies of shale and low-sulphur coal are readily available could easily delay the advent of a significant synthetic fuels industry for more than a decade. In the meantime we must either become more dependent on energy imports, and possible supply disruptions, or curb our growing appetite for oil and gas.

Negative Social Wealth

In the United States — with its heretofore abundant supplies of iron ore needing only to be lifted into the blast furnace, large deposits of unexploited coal and shale, and the postwar vision of nuclear fission opening up an almost unlimited supply of new energy — it has been easy to minimize and even neglect the social cost of natural resource scarcity.

Though electric railroads, large ships powered by atomic reactors, small cars with speeds up to 35 miles an hour and ranges up to 40 miles powered by electric batteries, and even atomic-powered space ships are feasible, no one has seriously proposed that atomic reactors be designed for small boats, large automobiles, mobile trucks capable of delivering heavy loads long distances, farm tractors, or commercial aircraft. The danger of accidents and contamination from radioactivity is simply too great.

The seriousness of natural resource scarcity, in the long run, can perhaps best be illustrated by comparing the caloric price ratios for petroleum and vegetable oil. Crude oil at $12 per barrel is only about a tenth as costly per calorie as vegetable oil at 40 cents per pound. Petroleum is scarce, however, and will eventually be used up. Oil production in such historically important states as Pennsylvania, California, Illinois, Indiana, Colorado, Kansas, Nebraska, and Utah has already peaked and is now in absolute decline. As existing and as yet undiscovered supplies of liquid hydrocarbons are used up, caloric prices will rise to equal and perhaps even exceed the price of vegetable oil, which is more perishable and not as good a source of materials for some essential chemicals.

Suppose petroleum consumption were valued not in terms of

its historical production cost, but in terms of its probable replacement cost, using the price of vegetable oil, which has averaged more than ten times as much per calorie as petroleum.

Figures provided in the Resources for the Future compendium, *Energy in the American Economy, 1950 - 1975*, indicate that the United States produced at least 304,982 trillion BTU equivalent of crude oil before 1956. The price of oil relative to the wholesale price index, though quite volatile, was rather trendless from 1900 to 1955.[4] Starting with an average price per barrel of $2.77 in 1955 and assuming an eventual tenfold increase in the relative price of crude petroleum, the cumulative negative wealth value for petroleum produced in the United States through 1955 is equal to $1.5 trillion. This can be compared to Raymond Goldsmith's estimate of $1.3 trillion for reproducible tangible wealth in 1957 and Schultz's estimate of $848 billion for educational capital invested in the U.S. population.[5]

Although educational capital has increased more rapidly than petroleum consumption since 1957, largely because of the postwar baby boom and the trend toward relatively more higher education, it is rather doubtful whether reproducible tangible wealth has grown as rapidly as the negative social wealth associated with petroleum consumption. Crude oil has supplied considerably less than half our energy requirements. If an allowance were made for the probable future price increases for coal, natural gas, and other scarce mineral resources, the implication is that the United States has been growing poorer instead of richer. Monetary incomes are, of course, much higher than formerly, but only at the expense of a rapid deterioration in our stock of mineral wealth.

Most tangible wealth that has been assigned a monetary value, moreover, may be of a fleeting character. It is doubtful, for example, whether the huge investment in large automobiles, superhighways, sprawling suburban housing, jet aircraft, oil refineries, gas stations, and energy pipelines can be fully maintained as fossil fuel reserves run out. In 1915, Wilford King, a pioneer in national income accounting, noted: "Each year, our social wealth, as represented by minerals, grows less and less and the more flourishing the condition of our mining industry, the more rapid the disappearance of our mineral estate."[6]

The idea that we may be growing poorer instead of richer has recently been given a modern twist by Nicholas Georgescu-Roegen.[7] He notes that, thermodynamically, energy enters the economic process in a state of low entropy and comes out of it in a valueless state of high entropy. Fossil fuels are an ideal source of low-entropy energy, but once they have been burnt, their value as a source of useful energy is gone forever.

Roegen points out that every time we produce a Cadillac, we irrevocably destroy an amount of low entropy that could otherwise be used for producing a plow or a spade: "Economic development through industrial abundance may be a blessing for us now and for those who will be able to enjoy it in the near future, but it is definitely against the interest of the human species as a whole, if its interest is to have a lifespan as long as is compatible with its dowry of low entropy."

Concepts of Wealth

Such concepts as power and wealth have been subject to evolutionary changes throughout the history of economic thought. During the Middle Ages, when the church was a dominant power and owned much of the land in Europe, wealth was considered to be any good or instrument that could lead a person to a virtuous life. With the rise of nation-states and the development of mercantilism, the concept of wealth became increasingly associated with gold and silver, which could be used to maintain military and political power.

In France during the late 1600s, the concept of wealth changed and became more closely identified among the Physiocrats with agricultural land. After the industrial revolution, the emphasis shifted to investment in capital goods. In the late 1950s and early 1960s, when real GNP in the United States was still increasing more rapidly than investment in new plants and equipment, the capital concept applied to man was revived, with education being considered an important source of economic wealth.

The oil embargo of 1973 has shown that large stocks of conventional wealth are of little value without abundant supplies of relatively cheap energy. Notions as to which countries are rich and which are poor are changing rapidly. In the next decade or two it seems likely that the concepts of power and wealth will increasingly be reckoned in terms of a country's command over fossil fuels and other stocks of "low-entropy" energy.

The dramatic rise in the price of imported oil has already transferred a great deal of financial wealth and purchasing power from the more industrialized nations to less developed countries with exportable petroleum. The 600 billion barrels of proven oil reserves in the world are quite limited, however. They could be exhausted in less than seventeen years if consumption were to continue to increase at the 7 per cent annual rate that prevailed before the Arab oil embargo. If per capita consumption in other countries were increased to United States levels, it would be theoretically possible to exhaust all the world's proven oil reserves in less than five years.

The amount of oil remaining to be discovered is highly conjectural. Some energy experts believe that half or more of the world's recoverable oil reserves may have already been discovered, which would seem plausible if the international oil companies have been reasonably successful in identifying the best areas in which to search for new oil.

Others have noted, however, that large portions of the earth's surface and outer continental shelves have never been test-drilled. They suggest that total recoverable reserves may turn out to be several times as great as existing proven reserves. Even if the optimists are correct, by American standards of consumption, little oil is left to be consumed on a per capita basis.

Most oil discovered to date is located in Africa and the Middle East. Though countries like Saudi Arabia are extremely rich in petroleum, most petroleum-exporting nations are rather poor in coal reserves. Only about 1.4 per cent of the world's coal reserves, which are estimated to be at least ten or more times as great as the world's petroleum reserves, are located in Africa and the Middle East. The dearth of coal and other mineral resources suggests that most petroleum-exporting countries will have to carefully husband their oil reserves, make wise investments, and eventually export petrochemicals, nitrogen fertilizer, aluminum, and light manufactured products if they are to achieve a condition of sustained prosperity.

OPEC Conservation

Though it might be possible for the United States to rely more heavily on imported energy for a few more years, those countries with either large existing or undiscovered oil reserves will probably be increasingly reluctant to export large quantities of liquid petroleum. Such OPEC countries as Venezuela, Kuwait, and

Libya have already cut back production in an effort to maintain high prices for their oil and lengthen the useful life of their reserves.

As OPEC members become more industrialized they are likely to be even more reluctant to maintain high exports. Because Japan, many Western European industrialized nations, and developing countries without oil reserves will probably need imported oil more than the United States, it would not be surprising if the United States was largely rationed out of the international market for oil and gas before the end of this century. In the early part of the twenty-first century, as most natural gas and liquid petroleum reserves are used up, the United States will almost certainly be forced to become more self-sufficient in basic energy.

Conserving Low-Entropy Energy

In 1915 crude petroleum supplied less than 10 per cent of total energy requirements in the United States. Consumption, including imports, has since risen to more than 45 per cent of total gross energy inputs. Although new technology may help us to preserve an affluent way of life, its overall impact to date seems to have made our society even more dependent on exhaustible resources. Reverting back to an economy that utilizes only small amounts of liquid hydrocarbons will not be easy and may indeed be rather dangerous.

Nuclear Energy Safety

The scientific community has long held deep but, until recently, suppressed doubts about the adequacy of nuclear reactor safety research and the wisdom of quickly converting to a nuclear economy. Allen Kneese has noted that if so unforgiving a technology as large-scale nuclear fission energy production is adopted, "it will impose a burden of continuous monitoring and sophisticated management of a dangerous material essentially forever." The penalty of not bearing this burden might be unparalleled disaster:

> When one factors in the possibility of sabotage and warfare, where
> power plants are prime targets not just in the United States but also
> in less developed countries now striving to establish a nuclear in-
> dustry, then there is almost no limit to the size of the catastrophe one
> can envisage.[8]

It has been estimated that a cubic mile of ocean water would
be required to properly dilute and safely dispose of all the
radioactive wastes created by generating enough electricity to con-
tinuously light only 640 100-watt bulbs. A 500-megawatt power station, operated for three years, contains as much strontium 90 as
was left in the atmosphere by thermonuclear weapons testing.
Inhaling one-millionth of a gram of plutonium — about the size of a
grain of pollen — appears to be sufficient to cause lung cancer. If
breeder reactors containing hundreds of pounds of plutonium turn
out to be an economic success, one serious accident might be sufficient to render a large land mass almost totally uninhabitable for
thousands of years.

Whether we should strike a Faustian bargain with atomic
scientists by quickly substituting nuclear fission power plants for
electricity from fossil fuels is an unresolved issue. There does
seem to be a growing realization, however, that we must begin to
conserve natural resources. A slower growth rate for total energy
consumption might be a way to buy the time needed to reduce the
hazards associated with a nuclear economy. Because the United
States does have large coal reserves that can be burned to produce
electricity, the economic costs of delaying the transition to a
nuclear economy would not appear to be unduly great if electric
power consumption were slowed.

Energy Efficiency

Government studies made before the Arab oil embargo
suggest that only about 40 per cent of the energy consumed in this
country is used for productive purposes, and that the remaining 60
per cent is wasted.[9] After examining energy consumption for
different countries and the conservation measures that could be
taken in the future, Makhijani and Litchtenberg conclude that a 37
per cent reduction in per capita energy consumption is possible in
this country by the year 2000 without reducing the standard of
living.[10] A zero energy growth scenario developed by the Ford
Foundation's Energy Policy Project also supports the hypothesis

that it might be possible to achieve further improvements in economic and material well-being in the United States without increasing per capita energy consumption.[11]

A 1974 study by scientists and engineers at MIT indicates that electric power constituted 58 per cent of the total life cycle costs for refrigerators; by spending 20 per cent more to improve insulation and increase motor efficiency, manufacturers and consumers could halve the consumption of electrical power over the life of a refrigerator.

Consumers began to revolt against large gas-guzzling automobiles even before the Arab oil embargo. Auto men have since learned to think small and by March 1974, articles in *The New York Times* had such titles as "The Great American Auto Conversion." Though large car sales have picked up since the oil embargo was lifted the demand for such automobiles will probably never again be the same.

A rapid shift to smaller, more efficient automobiles is particularly good for the economy, because it could mean a return to full employment in the automobile industry without a recurrent prospect of gasoline shortages and a deteriorating balance of payments. If conservation of energy in both the home and the business sector were emphasized and inefficient appliances and equipment rapidly replaced the domestic economy could be stimulated without greatly increasing oil imports or making huge investments in the development of new energy resources. This in turn could perhaps free enough scarce capital resources to revive the residential construction industry.

As thoughtful citizens begin to appreciate the difficulties and high costs of quickly becoming self-sufficient in basic energy I hope that there will be increasing interest in policies that might help to promote zero energy growth in the United States. (The problem of too much energy consumption will again be considered in Chapter 7.) A much slower growth rate for energy consumption would give the United States more time to develop new technologies and explore alternative energy choices. Massive new commitments to offshore drilling, nuclear power development, and the production of synthetic gas and oil from coal and shale in arid sections of the West could be delayed. A slower growth rate would make us less dependent upon energy imports, less vulnerable to supply disruptions, and allow us to pursue a more neutral and independent foreign policy in the Middle East. In view of the high costs, risks, and uncertainties associated with rapid growth in energy consumption, it seems only prudent to conserve more of our limited stocks of low-entropy wealth.

Notes

1. *Advanced recovery technologies* include the use of water, heat, or special solvents to extract a greater fraction of the oil in existing fields.

2. M. King Hubbert, "Methods of Estimating Oil and Gas Resources," *The Energy Crisis and Proposed Solutions* (Washington, D.C.: U.S. Government Printing Office, 1975), part 3, pp. 1110 - 1138.

3. This calculation ignores natural gas produced in conjunction with oil wells. Most natural gas is produced from gas wells, however. In 1972, only a little over 20 per cent of gas reserves was associated with oil wells.

4. Sam Schurr and Bruce C. Netschert, *Energy in the American Economy: 1850 - 1975* (Baltimore: Johns Hopkins, 1960).

5. Theodore W. Schultz, *The Economic Value of Education* (New York: Columbia University Press, 1963), p. 51.

6. Wilford I. King, *The Wealth and Income of the People of the United States* (New York: Macmillan, 1922), pp. 33 - 34.

7. N. Georgescu-Roegen, *The Entropy Law and the Economic Process* (Cambridge: Harvard University Press, 1971).

8. Allen Kneese, "The Faustian Bargain," *Resources* (Resources for the Future, September 1973), pp. 1 - 5.

9. "Conservation of Energy," Report of the Committee on Interior and Insular Affairs, U.S. Senate, Serial No. 92 - 18 (1972); "The Potential for Energy Conservation, A Staff Study," Office of Emergency Preparedness (October 1972); "Conservation of Energy: The Potential for More Efficient Use," *Science* (December 8, 1972); and "Initiatives in Energy Conservation," Staff Report of the Committee on Commerce, U.S. Senate (1973).

10. A. B. Makhijani and A. J. Lichtenberg, "Energy and Well-Being," *Environment* (June 1972).

11. *Exploring Energy Choices*, a preliminary report by the Energy Policy Project of the Ford Foundation (1974), pp. 51 - 53; and *A Time to Choose* (New York: Ballinger, 1974).

chapter 4

TECHNOLOGY
AND NATURAL
RESOURCE
SCARCITY

Our creative resources are not only inexhaustible, they grow every day. As far as we can tell, the frontier of creative scientific knowledge is limitless. So who can doubt that we have the capacity to make the scientific and technological advances required to build our new dream world of fresh air, pure water and an undefiled countryside — while at the same time continuing an orderly economic expansion, including more employment opportunities.[1]

Federal expenditure for research and development, as a percentage of GNP and the federal budget, has drifted downward since 1965. Total expenditure, adjusted for inflation, is now substantially lower than a decade ago, which has caused many scientists and some economists to forecast a slower growth rate for our gross national product.

If budgetary priorities are rational, however, the implication is that congressmen now consider the socioeconomic and political payoff from additional research and development to be lower than the return from other kinds of government expenditure.

For example, enthusiasm for space research has noticeably declined as people realize that there isn't much of economic value on the moon or any great urgency for human beings to make a trip to Mars. Attitudes about national defense also have undergone revolutionary change as more congressmen appreciate that a never-ending stream of newer and fancier weapon systems may be a rather poor substitute for the hard negotiations necessary to limit arms and secure peace.

If expenditures for new weapons systems and space exploration are removed from the budget, however, an opposite impression is obtained. Both federal and private expenditures for civilian research and development have been increasing at least as rapidly, on the average, as the gross national product since 1965 and in some recent years even faster.

This is not the only factor which should have helped to create a condition favorable to an accelerated growth in economic activity in the last decade. In the 1965 - 1973 period almost twice as many persons joined the employed civilian labor force as from 1957 to 1965; the share of GNP devoted to gross private domestic investment increased slightly after having accelerated dramatically from the stagnant levels experienced between 1957 and 1961; and the educational attainment of the employed labor force also continued to increase impressively. With all these conditions favoring an accelerated increase in the GNP growth rate, surprisingly it actually declined slightly from 1965 to 1973 compared to the 1957 - 1965 period. Growth in output per manhour in the private domestic economy plunged by more than 25 per cent.

This implies, it seems to me, that persons engaged in research and development may be finding it more difficult to discover and invent new products and productive processes that are unambiguously superior to older commodities and ways of producing goods and services.

In this chapter I will examine the problem of natural resource scarcity from several technological perspectives, ranging from computers and new products to conversion efficiency and various other dimensions of economic progress. All these dimensions tend to support the hypothesis that we may be nearing an end to beneficial progress and that new technology may not be sufficient to compensate for natural resource scarcity and preserve the energy-intensive way of life in contemporary America.

Computers

In the thirteen-year period from 1955 to 1967 there were only three years when the percentage change in undeflated GNP in the current year divided by the money supply at the beginning of the year (what economists have termed the "velocity of money income") increased less than 3 per cent. In the 1967 - 1973 period in only one year has the velocity of money increased by as much as 3 per cent.

The slower growth in what might be termed "monetary productivity" is particularly puzzling considering the rapid rises in prices and interest rates since 1967. They should have caused businessmen and consumers either to spend their incomes more quickly or to shift idle cash balances into time deposits and other earning assets. It is also puzzling because of the large increase in credit cards, computer-based cash management systems, and such financial innovations as no-minimum-balance bank accounts.

Though a decline in the growth of monetary productivity is not serious from an economic point of view — because the stock of money can be increased almost without limit by simply "printing" or crediting the commercial banking system with quantities of new money — the decline does suggest that money is not likely to go out of fashion in the near future. It also suggests that high-speed computers, telecommunications, and modern data-processing equipment may never have as dramatic an impact on our economic system of exchanging goods and services as some enthusiasts have supposed.

The development of language translators and computers which play a better than average game of chess has, in a sense, shattered the illusion of sectors and operations that cannot be mechanized. It remains to be seen, however, whether computers will ever be given an opportunity to "learn" anything of value that could not be learned more economically with conventional programs.

If a computer did discover something of value that was not already known, it is questionable whether scientists and engineers would have either the time or the inclination to appreciate its true merit. Dr. Simon Ramo has suggested that the computer can optimize the control of electric power distribution better and faster than humans, therefore cutting down power shortages. At the same time, however, "it is being used just as often to produce stacks of reports automatically that executives don't have the time to read."

The amazing changes and developments in data processing and high-speed computers have not had a comparable economic effect to that wrought by the mechanization of agriculture and the coal industry. Clerical workers, as a proportion of the nonfarm civilian labor force, have continued to increase throughout the last two decades. Even before the recent slowdown in the growth of labor productivity *Fortune* magazine featured articles with such catchy titles as "The Real News about Automation," which implied that computers were not having the revolutionary effect on the economy that many futurists predicted.

A fundamental factor narrowing the use of computers in manufacturing is that most industrial processes can be broken down into a set of simple feedback or thermostatic control operations. British engineers interviewed by *The Economist* in 1961 were inclined to argue, "that by the time they have studied a process closely enough to know how best to apply a computer to it, they often know enough to be able to do without the computer."[2]

Though electronic devices for controlling motor vehicles on major highways have been studied, computer monitors are unlikely to be anything more revolutionary than more complicated traffic signals. Controlling an automobile is, from an economic point of view, not only a "free" resource — because to propel an empty vehicle down a freeway would generally defeat its function — but also a prestige occupation that the public would be reluctant to relinquish.

The Dearth of New Products

In 1938, Alvin Hansen, noted, "When a revolutionary new industry like the railroad or automobile, after having initiated in its youth a powerful upward surge of investment activity, reaches maturity and ceases to grow, as all industries must, the whole economy must experience a profound stagnation, unless indeed new developments take its place."[3]

Almost all the great new technological innovations in the last decade seem to be in materials and capital goods. But even this progress can be quite limited. In 1957 Douglas Hague noted that the concerted efforts of the hundreds of scientists who have examined thousands of possible products during the last twenty-five years have led to only five classes of synthetic fibers. Creating a structurally different fiber, it seems, is rather rare.[4]

The mid-third of this century is now considered by some scientists as the golden age of medicine because of such important developments as the discovery of antibiotics, surgical invasion of the heart, kidney transplants, and the unmasking of viruses. But the pace has slowed considerably in the last decade, with relatively fewer new, chemically distinct drugs being marketed. This appears to support a 1970 warning by Dr. Ernst Chain, the co-discoverer of penicillin, that there may be few rabbits left in the hat.

The consumption goods market also seems to be suffering from a profound technological depression. A recent ad by Amoco Chemicals Corporation says: "The next great appliance is waiting for an inventor ... not the materials." Except possibly for permanent-press pants, it is hard to think of any new and exciting consumption good that was introduced in the last decade with a market potential close to 100 per cent.

A 1971 Conference Board survey found that even the largest companies find it increasingly difficult to introduce new products that are automatically successful. Ben Gaynes, vice president of Clark Dodge, lamented at the same time that no single new industry is ready or even on the drawing board to carry the economy forward in the remainder of the 1970s.

According to Amoco Chemicals Corporation, "The inventor of the decade may well be the person who designs an appliance to wash windows ... that last great bastion of drudgery in the American home."

The most impressive evidence in support of an eventual end to technological progress is provided by science itself, however, and is related to the efficiency of converting various forms of energy into comfort heat and useful working effects.

Conversion Efficiency

When wood or coal is burned in an open fireplace, less than 20 per cent of the energy is radiated into a room. A well-designed home furnace, on the other hand, can convert up to 75 per cent of the energy in the fuel for space heating. The average efficiency of the conversion of fossil fuels for space heating is now nearly triple what it was at the turn of the century.

In 1900 less than 5 per cent of the energy in fuel was converted into electricity. Today the average efficiency is around 33 per cent. The modern incandescent lamp is about five times as efficient as lamps used in 1900. By shifting to fluorescent lamps modern consumers can obtain another fourfold increase in lighting efficiency.

Old steam locomotives had a maximum thermal efficiency of 10 per cent and usually operated much below this limit; diesel-electric locomotives, on the other hand, have a thermal efficiency of about 35 per cent. In 1920 railroads accounted for about 16 per cent of the nation's total energy demand. With the shift to trucks, buses, and more efficient energy converters the railroads' share of the nation's total fuel budget has fallen to about 1 per cent.

Claude Summers has estimated that the efficiency with which fuels were consumed for all purposes increased by a factor of about four between 1900 and 1970: "Without this increase the U.S. economy of 1971 would already be consuming energy at the rate projected for the year 2025 or thereabouts."[5] The economy would not be consuming fuels at this rate without such improvements; however, that does not alter the profound importance of improved conversion efficiency as a mechanism for saving other inputs in the productive process and for promoting rapid economic growth.

Increased conversion efficiency not only saves fuel but also saves corresponding amounts of labor and capital that would otherwise be employed in mining, transporting, and utilizing our energy resources. A major reason supporting a fundamental change or reduction in the long-term growth of labor productivity is that it has now become much more difficult to improve the efficiency of devices which convert fossil fuels and electricity into comfort heat, cooler temperatures, and useful working effects. The limits to conversion efficiency are well understood in the case of heat engines and electrical generators and are rapidly being approached.

Even more disturbing, in some respects, is mounting evidence which suggests that it may be possible to achieve some important ends too efficiently. DDT, phosphate detergents, and leaded gasoline are perhaps classic examples of important developments that are economically and technically efficient but that produce undesirable side effects. About 5.5 per cent more crude oil must be processed to obtain a lead-free gasoline with the same performance characteristics as leaded gasoline; the loss is largely caused by the extra energy consumed in the additional refining process.

Improvements in the efficiency of converting raw energy into comfort heat and useful working effects allowed the gross national product in constant dollars to grow more rapidly than the consumption of mineral fuels between 1920 and 1965 (see Figure 4.1). The

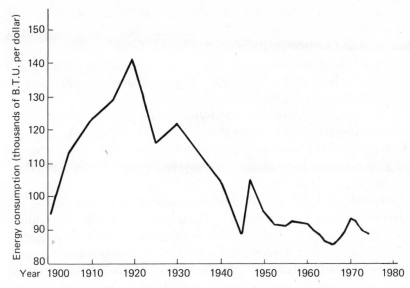

FIGURE 4.1
Variations in the Ratio of U.S. Energy Consumption to Gross
National Product. *Source:* Adapted from "The Flow of Energy
in an Industrial Society," by Earl Cook. Copyright © 1971
by *Scientific American,* Inc. All rights reserved.

slowing down of improvements in conversion efficiency caused
energy consumption per dollar of GNP to spurt upward from 1965
to 1970. Sharp increases in the relative price of fuels and related
products have led Americans to conserve more energy since 1970.
Overall conversion efficiency was still less in 1974, however, than
in 1965.

Francis H. Schott, vice president and economist of the
Equitable Life Assurance Society of the United States, has said:

> Assuming the United States decides to become independent of Arab
> oil, the economic life style of this country will undergo its biggest
> change since World War II. Suburban sprawl, the three-car family,
> the production of heavy cars and of power options, highway con-
> struction, the distant vacation home, the sharp rise in air con-
> ditioning, even the businessman's transcontinental commute — all
> of these will be significantly dampened.[6]

Even the editors of *Business Week* have begun to appreciate
that the United States is becoming a "have-not nation" and that to
avert further crises in the future, we need a national energy policy,
something we have never had.

In 1960 Resources for the Future published *Energy in the American Economy: 1850 - 1975*, which concluded that the United States could satisfy its demand for energy from domestic sources of supply by about 1975 at no significant increases in costs, except for those which might be brought about by a rise in the general price level.[7]

The price of fuels, related products, and power expressed as a ratio to the wholesale price index for all raw materials and industrial commodities remained remarkably stable from 1960 to 1972. It has since shot upward at an alarming rate to now more than double the 1960 average.

Harold Barnett and Chandler Morse note a tendency to regard technological advance as a chancy phenomenon or "a bit of luck that is sure to run out sooner or later."[8] They remark that Alfred Marshall conceived the law of diminishing returns to be a historical law that was only temporarily set aside by the industrial revolution and the opening up of new lands:

> The world is really a very small place . . . and there is not room in it for the opening up of rich new resources during many decades at as rapid a rate as has prevailed during the last three or four. When new countries begin to need most of their own food and other raw produce, improvements in transport will count for little. From that time onward the pressure of the Law of Diminishing Returns can be opposed only by further improvements in production; and improvements in production must themselves gradually show a diminishing return.[9]

Barnett and Morse are inclined to reject Marshall's view and accept the premise that technological progress is self-generating:

> A strong case can be made for the view that the cumulation of knowledge and technological progress is automatic and self-reproductive in modern economies, and obeys a law of increasing returns. Every cost-reducing innovation opens up possibilities of application in so many new directions that the stock of knowledge, far from being depleted by new developments, may even expand geometrically. Technological progress, instead of being the adventitious consequence of lucky and highly improbable discoveries, appears to obey what Myrdal has called the "principle of circular and cumulative causation," namely, that change tends to induce further change in the same direction.

William Nordhaus, an economist at Yale University, has developed an econometric model that gets the United States through at least the next two centuries without any significant slowing of the long-term growth rate caused by energy shortages.[10] His basic model assumes that society will be able to leapfrog from technology to technology in the decades ahead as lower-cost energy sources are exhausted and give way to higher-cost sources. Beyond the next two centuries he counts on breeder nuclear reactors and other new energy technologies to carry the economy into the indefinite future.

Nordhaus's theory is that "we should not be haunted by the specter of the affluent society grinding to a halt for lack of energy resources." As Leonard Silk of *The New York Times* has commented, "In these gloomy days, every bit of cheer is gratefully received — at least until the opposition knocks it down."

The Nordhaus model, like most other growth models examined by mathematical economists in the last three decades, assumes that the growth rate of technical change is of the nature of a compound rate. If one starts with this assumption and also assumes that capital investment is a very good substitute for other resources such as labor, land, energy, pure water, and clean air, economic growth will go on forever. Using the assumptions built into the Nordhaus model, there is simply no way that it can ever grind to a halt.

The only possible justification for seriously considering such models is the fact that labor productivity and other measures of technological progress have increased at a compound rate until fairly recently. The historical data could just as easily be consistent with many other types of technical change, however. Many of the S-shaped growth models used in biology, for example, have a compound growth phase. Assuming that the S-shaped curve is symmetric, it would generally not be easy to distinguish between it and the Nordhaus model until after the golden age of technological change was more than halfway over. Georgescu-Roegen has noted that:

> The unprecedented achievements of the Industrial Revolution so amazed everyone with what man might do with the aid of machines that the general attention became confined to the factory. The landslide of spectacular scientific discoveries triggered by the new

technical facilities strengthened this general awe for the power of technology. It also induced the literati to overestimate and, ultimately, to oversell to their audiences the powers of science. Naturally, from such a pedestal one could not even conceive that there is any real obstacle inherent in the human condition.

The sober truth is different. Even the lifespan of the human species represents just a blink when compared with that of a galaxy. So, even with progress in space travel, mankind will remain confined to a speck of space. Man's biological nature sets other limitations as to what he can do. Too high or too low a temperature is incompatible with his existence. And so are many radiations. It is not only that he cannot reach up to the stars, but he cannot even reach down to an individual elementary particle, to an individual atom.[11]

Kenneth Boulding has gone beyond Georgescu-Roegen to suggest that the second law of thermodynamics, the principle of increasing entropy, is a special instance of a more general principle that he describes as the second law of practically everything. The entropy principle covers the exhaustion of potential: once a potential has been realized it has been used up and cannot be used again. In thermodynamics the potential for work arises because of temperature differences. Once the work has been performed the temperature difference disappears and the work cannot be done a second time.

There is a similar principle of increasing material entropy. Man has inherited a united endowment of concentrated deposits of ore and fossil fuels. He is now spending this endowment by diffusing the concentrated materials and burning up the stored energy.

Boulding also postulates a second law of cultural dynamics, that creative acts are essentially nonrepeatable and that once they have been done, they cannot be done again: "Once Beethoven has written the Ninth Symphony, no one else can write it." Toward the end of an old cultural or artistic period, the frenetic search for the new often produces things that are worse than the old.

In the past, according to Boulding, we have always been able to escape the steady state by developing new cultural potential: a new vision of the world or a new religion. When the potential for creating new cultural potential is exhausted, however, creativity can only go off in corrupt forms, making things worse instead of better. Because the normal rate of evolutionary development seems to be much slower than what we have experienced in the last two centuries, he asks: "Do we not, therefore, have a great slowdown ahead of us? Should we not expect the restoration of a pace of change that seems more normal in light of evolutionary history?"[12]

Gunther Stent suggests that "There is imminent in the evolution of a bounded scientific discipline a point of diminishing returns; after the great insights have been made and brought the discipline close to its goal, further efforts are necessarily of ever-decreasing significance."[13] Stent believes that progress — a "better" world in which man has a greater power over external events, is economically more secure, and has gained a greater dominion over nature — is rapidly nearing an end.

This vision of an end to economic and scientific progress does not deter him, however, from postulating a golden age or Utopian world in which most people are extraordinarily healthy, happy, and do not have to work very hard. "As a result of eugenics and euphenics, mortal men will soon be free from the miseries of old age, their legs and arms will never fail, and when they die, it will be as though they were overcome with sleep."

Those who predict the future by simply examining past trends and employing models which assume that rapid rates of growth will continue for several more decades are advised to contemplate Mark Twain's observation:

> In the space of one hundred and seventy-six years the Lower Mississippi has shortened itself two hundred and forty-two miles. That is an average of a trifle over one mile and a third per year. Therefore, any calm person, who is not blind or idiotic, can see that in the old Oolitic Silurian Period, just a million years ago next November, the Lower Mississippi River was upward of one million three hundred thousand miles long. . . . By the same token any person can see that seven hundred and forty-two years from now the Lower Mississippi will be only a mile and three-quarters long. . . . There is something fascinating about science. One gets such wholesale returns of conjecture out of such a trifling investment of fact.[14]

In *The Limits to Growth* Meadows and others discuss a world growth model that is basically exponential but does not include technology as a specific variable.[15] Though their model is useful in suggesting that natural resource scarcity and waste disposal problems might bring growth to a halt, it doesn't directly consider whether technological progress is open-ended and will continue

forever and whether capital investment will continue to be a very
good substitute for other resources. If technological improvements
are nearing an end and if capital investment ceases to be a good
substitute for labor and energy, the world growth rate could slow
to a creep in the next few decades, instead of coming to a
screeching halt in the twenty-first century after several more
doublings of GNP.

Some Dimensions of Progress

To argue that economic optimists and even the authors of The
Limits to Growth are essentially wrong in assuming that economic
activity can continue to increase rapidly for several more decades
one must show that the law of diminishing returns can also be
applied to technological progress. Although technological changes
have been extremely diverse, some important dimensions of
progress, such as speed, size, and conversion efficiency, suggest
that the economic benefits of a particular progress dimension will
first increase at an increasing rate, reach a maximum, and then increase at a rapidly diminishing rate.

Conversion efficiency is an important method of saving
energy. In the early 1900s almost 10 pounds of coal were required
to generate 1 kilowatt hour of electricity. By 1965 less than 0.86
pounds were needed, but the amount has since been trending upward. The efficiency of new fossil-fired generating units apparently reached a peak around 1967 and has since been reduced
somewhat to lessen the need for costly alloy materials, to obtain
greater reliability in plant operation, and to reduce the cost of
boiler equipment and maintenance.

Conventional generating units only convert about 40 per cent
of the energy in fossil fuels into electricity. Higher efficiencies can
be reached but they have not yet proven to be very economical for
most purposes. The fuel cells used by astronauts, for example, can
convert hydrogen into electricity with an efficiency of more than
50 per cent, but are so costly as to be of limited value except in outer space and other remote locations.

Jet aircraft, with their higher speeds and easier maintenance,
have made large propeller-driven aircraft obsolete. The next
logical step, in terms of speed, is the supersonic passenger plane.
The Concorde, which was developed by the French and British

governments, must be considered a technological success. It now seems destined to become a museum piece, however, because of its extremely high capital costs, environmental side effects, and very poor economy in the use of energy per passenger mile.

As fossil fuels are used up new sources of energy must be developed. Nuclear fission power plants, after several billion dollars of research effort and more than thirty years of fairly intensive development, are still a fairly minor source of electric power and cannot easily compete on a favorable cost basis with coal in many parts of the United States. Technical, environmental, personnel, and other factors have intervened to such an extent that actual nuclear power capacity in 1985 is now expected to fall far short of previously projected capacity.

The next big step in nuclear fission is the development of a breeder reactor that would greatly increase the amount of electricity to be obtained from a given quantity of uranium. But there are many disquieting aspects to the liquid metal fast-breeder program, such as the very large amount of plutonium required for each reactor and the possibility that some of this material might be accidently dispersed to the atmosphere or used to produce an unauthorized atomic explosion. The technological difficulties in perfecting a breeder reactor have been enormous. Many scientists are no longer very confident that these problems can be solved, and even if they can, breeder reactors appear to be sufficiently uneconomical that their use will probably be deferred until well into the twenty-first century when the price of fossil fuels and high-grade uranium will have risen to much higher levels.

Suppose that scientists and engineers are fairly successful at first making those discoveries and undertaking those improvements which are the best, easiest, and most profitable to implement. The outlook for sustained economic growth would then be murky, even if the pace of scientific achievements seemed to be accelerating and there was no end in sight to the number of achievements that might be possible from a scientific and technical point of view.

The proposition that scientists have been reasonably successful in first exploiting the easiest and most profitable technology has been strengthened to some extent recently by efforts to revive the steam-powered automobile. The steam car emits fewer pollutants to the atmosphere. William Lear, who has spent about $12.5 million on steam-powered experiments, has admitted, however, that the steam engine is twice as heavy and twice as expensive as a gasoline engine of similar power output.

Other power plants involving substantially different technologies have also turned out to be economic disappointments. Chrysler's turbine-powered automobiles have been taken off the road and relegated to the scrap heap. Efforts to revive the electric automobile have been something less than spectacularly successful. In 1974, General Motors indefinitely suspended testing its new rotary engine because of its inability both to obtain high fuel economy and to satisfy California's pollution control standards.

The end of progress hypothesis is further supported, I believe, by the space program and by the resounding flop of many new technologies with futuristic possibilities. To go to the moon it was necessary to develop several new materials and technologies that are still far too expensive to yield many practical benefits on earth. The solar cell is a particularly good example of space-age technology with futuristic possibilities. Its capital costs are still so great and its electrical power density so low, however, as to make it of limited value except in outer space.

Shortly after World War II many experts predicted a private flying boom. Peter F. Drucker has noted that some fairly elementary mathematics could have disproved this particular technological assessment but "no one then realized how finite air space is."

Arthur Clarke's interesting and provocative book *Profiles of the Future*, which was first published in 1958 and labeled a daring look at tomorrow's fantastic world, includes chapters on the quest for speed and the future of transport. Clarke recognized that the helicopter, for all its importance in more specialized fields, has had little effect on public transportation but believed that this would not be true of winged aircraft with vertical take-off and landing (VTOL) capabilities.[16] However, VTOL and the helicopter, because of their enormous consumption of energy per passenger mile and the finiteness of air space, will never solve the problem of automobile congestion.

Clarke also wondered if cargo submarines would ever be economical because of heavy initial costs and problems of underwater operation. He proposed an interesting compromise "which almost certainly is economical" — the flexible towed container then being developed in the United Kingdom for liquid cargos:

> These giant plastic sausages (which can be rolled up when they are
> not in use) have now been built in lengths of up to three hundred
> feet, and there is no obvious limit to size. Since they can be towed
> completely submerged, they have the efficiency of the submarine
> without its mechanical and navigation complications. And they can
> be built very lightly and cheaply, since their structural strength is
> extremely low.[17]

Because of the low structural strength and the serious problem
of oil spills, we can be glad that these sausages are not being towed
into New York harbor at the present time.

Clarke also extolled the virtues of ground-effect or hovercraft
machines and suggested that "it is obvious that industry and heavy
engineering will find many uses for these floating saucers." The
hovercraft and the supersonic aircraft suffer from the same basic
weaknesses. Both are extremely capital-intensive and require a
great deal more energy per passenger mile than other conveyances.

In reading *Profiles of the Future* after almost twenty years of
impressive achievements in outer space it seems likely that Clarke's
analysis may ultimately be more valuable for its illumination of
what is not likely to happen than for its vision of an utterly fantastic future. He noted, for example, that the energy of sunlight at
sea level is about one horsepower per square yard:

> So far we have been able to convert about one-tenth of this energy
> into electricity (at a cost of roughly $100,000 per horsepower for
> present-day solar cells!) so a hundred horsepower automobile
> would require about a thousand square yards of collecting surface
> — even on a bright sunny day. This is hardly a practicable
> proposition.[18]

A major problem with solar cells, aside from high capital cost,
is that they may not be much more efficient at converting sunlight
into convenient forms of stored energy than conventional
agriculture. Howard Odum has said that many advocates of solar
energy do not understand that the concentration of sunlight is very
low and that much of the available energy has to be used to upgrade the remaining energy to carbohydrates, cellulose, and other
harvestable forms.[19]

Many scientists and even federal energy officials, however,
now think that solar electric power production should rank equally

with the breeder reactor and nuclear fusion as one of the three unproven but potentially inexhaustible sources of energy for the twenty-first century. The Energy Research and Development Administration has suggested, however, that basic energy costs are likely to double by the year 2000 no matter which technology is developed.

Nuclear fusion is sometimes considered to be the ultimate solution to our energy problems. The technical difficulties of containing and controlling a hydrogen explosion are so great, however, that most scientists are not confident that it can ever be accomplished. And if the technical problems are surmounted and a device is built that produces more power than it consumes, it does not necessarily follow that such a device would be economical. Present design estimates are that fusion reactors, which become highly radioactive, would have to be replaced every year or two. The average investment and waste disposal costs in that event are likely to be much higher than for the present generation of nuclear reactors.

The last three decades of rather intensive effort to develop new energy conversion devices and exploit other sources of energy besides fossil fuels generates at least as much pessimism as optimism. Improving the efficiency of converting energy into useful working effects is becoming more difficult. Without further improvements, the energy cost of extracting additional energy and materials from the crust of the earth can be expected to increase.

As the percentage of organic material removed from waste water increases, the cost of waste treatment increases not in proportion to the percentage removed but at a rapidly increasing rate. The same phenomenon has been observed in connection with petroleum reservoirs and must surely hold in the case of most other mineral resources. The energy required to concentrate iron ore from taconite for the blast furnace is about thirty-five times greater than the energy required to prepare Mesabi ores, which were concentrated and softened by nature over a very long time.

More than 85 per cent of the total usable energy — including that supplied by water, wood, food, and nuclear energy — is presently derived from fossil fuels, compared to less than 20 per cent in 1850. Technological progress has, until recently, made us even more dependent on fossil fuels and raw materials from other parts of the world.

From a nation that was once a large exporter of raw materials the United States is now the world's largest importer. We are now more than 90 per cent dependent upon imports of manganese, platinum, cobalt, graphite, chromium, and bauxite. More than 50 per cent of the tin, nickel, antimony, bismuth, mercury, and zinc comes from other countries, and more than 25 per cent of the silver, tungsten, gypsum, petroleum, and iron ore is currently imported.

The United States has about 6 per cent of the world's population but it has been consuming about a third of the world's mineral wealth. As other countries become more developed and as the suppliers of other basic materials attempt to emulate the international oil cartel, the United States will probably be forced to become more self-sufficient in basic energy and mineral production.

In a thought-provoking analysis of natural resource scarcity, Preston Cloud has noted that optimism and imagination are happy human traits: "They often make bad situations appear tolerable or even good." He points out, however, that man's ability to imagine solutions to important problems often outruns his ability to find them.[20]

One solution to the problem of dwindling reserves of natural petroleum is shale oil. The Department of the Interior has estimated that the United States has enough rock containing at least 15 gallons of oil per ton to yield 1.8 trillion barrels of shale oil. This would provide enough energy to satisfy future petroleum needs, at present rates of consumption, for about 300 years.

A study prepared for the Federal Energy Administration by Resources Planning Associates suggests, however, that it may take almost as much energy to extract oil from shale as the shale oil will produce. If this assessment is correct, the United States would have to be considered much poorer in readily available net energy than has commonly been supposed. Unless atomic energy can be safely used to shatter the rock and generate some of the heat necessary to extract shale oil, the huge reserves of oil-bearing rock may never be of much practical benefit to American motorists.

The U.S. Geological Survey has estimated that coal resources at the beginning of 1967 totaled over 3,000 billion tons. Half this amount was based directly on mapping and exploration. The other half was "probable." Economically recoverable resources are estimated to equal about 600 billion tons, or about a thousand times the current annual production. Coal is a rather dirty and inconvenient fuel, however. It currently supplies less than 20 per cent of our energy. If this share increases and if substantially more than half the energy in our coal reserves is either lost in mining and transit or wasted by converting the coal into cleaner and more convenient forms of energy such as electricity, high-BTU gas, or synthetic oil, the net energy to be obtained from these huge coal reserves really is not as great as is sometimes supposed.

As fossil fuels reserves are used up, prices and costs can be expected to rise. The amount of the cost increase, in some instances, will be truly mind-boggling. In some parts of Saudi Arabia, for example, oil can be pumped out of the ground and loaded aboard ocean-going tankers for about ten cents per barrel. In 1974 it would have paid American oil producers to keep marginal wells in operation until the cost of producing oil had risen to over $10 a barrel — a hundredfold difference in costs. Since the price of vegetable oil was about ten times as expensive as crude oil in 1974 it is not illogical to suppose that the price and cost of producing crude oil will eventually increase to within the vicinity of $100 per barrel in 1974 dollars.

The Tennessee Valley Authority was able to buy coal at a price of less than $3 per ton in 1964. It has recently paid as much as $30 for new coal supplies. For some purposes coal is worth as much per calorie as crude oil. For those purposes coal would be worth $452 per ton if crude oil is assumed to sell for $100 per barrel.

Ores are now being mined with uranium concentrations between 1,000 and 3,000 parts per million. The mean abundance of uranium in the earth's crust, however, is only 4 parts per million. If uranium were to become the principle source of energy, its price would eventually rise a thousand times or more.

The future prices of other mineral resources are less certain. It is reasonable to suppose, however, that the energy and real effort necessary to extract precious metals and scarce alloy materials from the earth will also increase by factors ranging upward from ten to perhaps a thousand times current costs.

As fossil fuels and other high-grade mineral resources are consumed, the nature and direction of technological progress will have to change if mankind is to become self-sufficient in basic energy and eventually be able to extract all the minerals and materials we need from harvested crops, common rock, the oceans, and the air. Whether technological progress will be sufficient to offset natural resource scarcity and allow the United

States and other advanced industrialized nations to maintain a reasonably high standard of living for hundreds of years, without sacrificing an energy-intensive way of life, is still uncertain. It will no doubt be one of the most important questions to be debated during the rest of this century.

Notes

1. Address by Gerald R. Ford at Expo 74, Spokane, Washington, August 15, 1974.

2. "Instruments in Evolution," *The Economist* (March 25, 1961), p. 1220.

3. Alvin Hansen, "Economic Progress and Declining Population Growth," *American Economic Review* (March 1939), pp. 1 - 15.

4. Douglas C. Hague, *The Economics of Man-Made Fibres* (London: Duckworth, 1957), p. 118.

5. Claude Summers, "The Conversion of Energy," *Scientific American* (September 1971), pp. 148 - 164.

6. Francis H. Schott, "Costs High to Rid U.S. of Dependency on Oil from Arabs," *The Money Manager* (December 24, 1973), p. 7.

7. Sam H. Schurr and Bruce C. Netschert, *Energy in the American Economy, 1950 - 1975* (Baltimore: Johns Hopkins, 1960).

8. Harold J. Barnett and Chandler Morse, *Scarcity and Growth* (Baltimore: Johns Hopkins, 1963), p. 235.

9. Ibid., p. 236.

10. William Nordhaus, "The Allocation of Energy Resources," *Brookings Papers on Economic Activity* (March 1973), pp. 515 - 528.

11. Nicholas Georgescu-Roegen, "The Entropy Law and the Economic Problem," in *Toward A Steady-State Economy*, ed. Herman E. Daly (San Francisco: Freeman, 1973), p. 43.

12. Kenneth E. Boulding, "The Shadow of the Stationary State," in *The No-Growth Society*, ed. Mancur Olson and Hans H. Landsberg (New York: Norton, 1973), p. 98.

13. Gunther S. Stent, *The Coming of the Golden Age: A View of the End of Progress* (New York: Natural History Press, 1969), p. 112.

14. Mark Twain, *Life on the Mississippi* (New York: Sagamore Press, 1957), p. 102.

15. Donella H. Meadows et al., *The Limits to Growth* (New York: Universe, 1972).

16.   Arthur Clarke, *Profiles of the Future* (New York: Harper and Row, 1958), pp. 35, 144 - 145.

17.   Ibid.

18.   Ibid.

19.   Howard T. Odum, *Environment, Power, and Society* (New York: Wiley, 1971).

20.   Preston Cloud, "Mineral Resources in Fact and Fancy," in *Toward a Steady-State Economy*, ed. Herman Daly (San Francisco: Freeman, 1973), pp. 2 - 75.

chapter 5

ZERO POPULATION GROWTH

The United States population is estimated to have increased about 0.75 per cent in 1973. If this growth rate continues, and if output per member of the labor force remains the same, real GNP will double in less than a century. Growth projections such as this suggest that zero population growth (ZPG) is a basic element in any theory of a steady state economy.

The prospects for attaining zero population growth in the near future are related to three variables: the number of live births, net immigration, and longer life expectancy. In this chapter I will briefly examine each of these variables and also consider some problems of economic adjustment that may tend to reinforce the trend toward ZPG.

The Downward Trend
in the Birth Rate

In the 1950s American women had an average of 3.35 children. By the early 1960s, this figure had dropped to 2.78. In 1970 it was 2.45. A long-run fertility rate of 2.11 is required to prevent the total population from declining if there is no immigration or change in average life expectancy.

In 1972 the national fertility rate dropped below this replacement level for the first time in history; in 1973 it was only 1.9 children per family (Figure 5.1). If fertility remains at this level the population of the United States will probably reach a peak and begin to decline sometime in the first half of the twenty-first century.

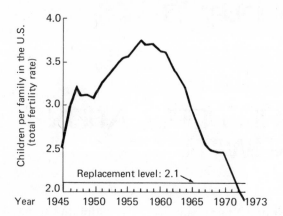

FIGURE 5.1
Children per Family in the United States (Total Fertility Rate).
Source: U.S. Census Bureau.

Though the recent dip in fertility may have been partly the result of trends toward later marriage and childrearing, considerable evidence suggests that the desired number of children has been trending downward. A 1967 survey by the Census Bureau showed that wives aged 18 to 24 expected to have an average of 2.9 children. By 1971 this figure had dropped to 2.4, and by 1974 the expected number of children was only 2.2.

A Social Research Incorporated study suggested that most wives of blue-collar working-class men still believed that the ideal family should have four children in 1965. By 1973 over 70 per cent of those blue-collar wives in their early twenties said they planned to have only one or two children.

Though demographers are somewhat at a loss to explain the downward trend in the desired number of births, part of the explanation is economic. In a largely urbanized society, children's work — in either the home or the market place — has ceased to be a valuable asset. Nor can children be relied upon to provide economic and financial security for their parents' old age.

Producing children, moreover, is extremely labor-intensive and not subject to rapid improvements in labor productivity. Low productivity in housing, education, health, and the child care industries has tended to raise the price of children relative to other consumer goods and encourage young people to invest in fewer offspring.[1] Rising concern about a population explosion, higher levels of expected educational attainment, social pressures that encourage young people to borrow for the purpose of immediately acquiring all the consumer durables and amenities that their parents acquired over a much longer time, increasing acceptance of women in the labor force at less discriminatory rates of pay, and new lifestyles for both men and women may have also helped to reduce the number of desired children.

Attitudes about women's careers, marriage, and childbearing have changed radically since the early 1950s, when to remain single for any extended period often condemned persons 20 and over to the status of a social outcast. Rising affluence and modern birth control technology, however, have helped to create a singles culture in which the pressures not to marry and have children may be almost as great as the earlier social pressures in the opposite direction.

A recent poll has suggested, however, that about 96 per cent of all women still see marriage as the best way of life. If they wait until their late twenties and early thirties, though, a disproportionate number may discover that they have waited too long to have children, acquired pregnancy fears, or developed a taste for lifestyles that would be seriously disrupted by even one or two children.

In 1971 the Commission on Population Growth and the American Future issued a report suggesting that it will cost a typical family $147,154 in direct expenditures and foregone income to raise two children and put them through college. These figures assume that the typical mother is a high school graduate who would lose income equal to $58,437 while staying home to raise her family. A woman with a college degree would lose more foregone income. The cost of sending two children to college would be higher if they were sent to private schools rather than public institutions. Many childcare cost elements — such as doctor's visits and babysitting — moreover, contain a high proportion of labor inputs subject to a relatively more rapid rate of inflation than the economy in general.

If adjustments are made for inflation and if the mother has either gone to college or acquired some professional training, the cost of raising two children and sending them through college is probably more than a quarter of a million dollars. These high costs are likely to reduce further the number of families that feel they can afford to educate more than one or two children.

Some Problems of Adjustment

The revolution of birth control technology that began in the early 1960s has already created some adjustment problems which are likely to reinforce the trend toward ZPG. The number of live births fell to about 2.2 million in the 1930s, recovered to about 3 million by the end of World War II, and subsequently climbed to an all-time peak of 4.3 million in 1957. The number of live births remained on a high plateau until 1961 and then fell from an average of about 4.25 million per year to less than 3.2 million in 1973. If fertility remains at a replacement level during the rest of this century, there will not be a secondary baby boom because American women are tending to marry later and waiting longer before having their first child.

New capital expenditures in education will decline because most schools are relatively new and can be expected to last for many years. New teaching positions also will drop sharply. However, colleges and universities are geared to producing more qualified educators at every degree level, because most teachers hired to help educate the baby boom are still alive and are not yet ready to retire.

Projections by the U.S. Office of Education show a drop of over 50 per cent in the number of new teaching jobs in higher education during the 1970s compared to the 1960s. At the elementary and secondary education levels an absolute decline in the total number of teachers can be predicted during the remainder of the 1970s. In the past, about a third of all college graduates trained to be teachers. Less than 10 per cent of all college graduates in the future will replace retiring teachers.

A large surplus of qualified teachers is not the only problem that is likely to be encountered in adjusting to a replacement level of fertility. The 25 per cent fewer babies that were born in 1973 than in 1957 has already brought about a closing of many maternity and pediatric hospital wards and will continue to reduce the demand for pediatric services in many neighborhoods. No doubt other industries that provide goods and services for a youth-oriented market will be negatively affected.

A discouraging aspect to the emerging surplus of highly educated young people is that the number of challenging job opportunities outside of the educational sector does not seem to show a compensating rise. From the end of World War II until 1957, when the growth in the United States population reached a post-war peak, unemployment equaled or exceeded 4.5 per cent of the civilian labor force in only three years. Since 1957 there have been only four years — during the Vietnam build-up — in which the unemployment rate was *below* 4.5 per cent.

The Housing Sector

It has sometimes been assumed that the baby boom might be able to trigger its own employment boom. The housing sector is perhaps the classic example of an industry that should expect to benefit from a rapid increase in the number of persons reaching the age of household formation. The future demand for new housing starts was so exaggerated in the early 1970s, however, that the number of conventional housing starts may never exceed the record 2.4 million new units of 1972.[2]

Housing starts were much higher in the postwar period than were necessary to accommodate ordinary replacement demand plus growth in the adult population. In the last thirty years the number of adults per household has dropped from about four to less than two mature persons per family. This undoubling process may actually reverse itself by the end of the 1970s as a disproportionate number of the older members of the emerging singles culture get married.

The population age 20 and over is only projected to increase 2.42 million per year on the average between 1975 and 1980. Dividing this figure by two (assuming that most young people will either remain at home, get married, or live with friends and relatives before they demand a new house or apartment) implies a basic growth demand for nearly 1.2 million new dwelling units per year. When this figure is added to a replacement demand, which has been averaging about 700,000 units per year, the basic new housing needs are about 1.9 million units per year. It seems clear that residential construction could remain in the doldrums for the rest of this decade.

A suspicion that the postwar boom in conventional housing may be over is reinforced by several other factors. Low productivity and differential inflation in the building industry, combined with high interest and mortgage rates, make it more difficult for young families to afford new homes. In some congested and highly unionized metropolitan areas with strict zoning ordinances it is estimated that less than 15 per cent of all families now can afford new homes.

The high cost of home building has led to a dramatic rise in the purchase of mobile homes, from less than 100,000 units in the 1950s to over half a million in 1973. In more rural and less densely settled areas, mobile homes have become an important substitute for conventional housing. In some parts of the country they are about the only kind of housing that families with moderate incomes can afford.

Federal subsidies to public housing projects and nonprofit organizations that sponsor newly constructed housing for families with moderate incomes account for much of the increase in new housing starts in the early 1970s. However, many of these projects were poorly planned and of low quality. Poor administration, insufficient maintenance, and security problems have led to abandonment and widespread vandalism that has left thousands of these units uninhabitable.

Such problems are not limited to federally assisted construction. Abandonment of structurally sound older buildings in many central cities has accelerated. The chronic shortage of decent units for persons with low and moderate incomes in cities has caused many housing experts to suggest that the production of new housing units has been overemphasized, and that more effort and resources ought to go into preserving the present housing through better services and maintenance.

One way of achieving this goal might be through the creation of a housing allowance for all persons with low and moderate income. It would allow them to live in either new or used housing, whichever was cheaper, provided it satisfied minimum standards.[3] More emphasis on the upgrading and preservation of older housing would, of course, reduce the need for new housing starts.

As of April 1967, there were only 1,547,000 second homes in the United States for about 58,845,000 households. In a 1970 HUD report on national housing goals, it was assumed that the number of second homes would increase by 1,245,000 units between 1969 and 1978, an increase of about 80 per cent over such homes in 1967, but still a rather small increase of only about 125,000 per year.

However, higher taxes, inflationary increases in gasoline

prices and new homes, and uncertain availability of motor fuel are causing some affluent families to question the value of a second home.

The dramatic rise in conventional housing starts from less than 1.5 million units in 1969 and 1970 to almost 2.1 million in 1971, 2.4 million in 1972, and over 2 million in 1973 was clearly one of the more important forces behind the somewhat belated yet vigorous recovery from the economic recession of 1970. The possibility that there will not be a sustained recovery in housing construction comparable to the average amount of new housing constructed from 1971 to 1973 raises an interesting question: Is it plausible to expect a prompt return to a condition of reasonably full employment from the more recent recession, which began in the first quarter of 1974?

A relatively stagnant housing industry combined with such factors as a tapering off of the growth of state and local government employment, an end to the era of cheap energy, and relatively more stringent monetary and fiscal policies designed to curb price inflation at a cost of somewhat greater unemployment, could slow the growth of full-time employment in the United States. This, in turn, could make it far more difficult for young men to find jobs that are suitable for maintaining an accustomed or expected lifestyle while supporting a nonworking wife and more than one or two children.

Between 1947 and 1973 nearly 1.5 times as many women were added to the employed labor force in the United States as men. With high-paying jobs for young men rather scarce, and with the real spendable earnings of most production workers now less than in 1965 (see Chapter 1), most young married women will probably feel that they should obtain either part- or full-time jobs to help their husbands provide the family with decent incomes. This in turn might make the prospect of having more than one or two children seem like an excess burden.

The 1930s and other recessionary periods have shown that economic stagnation and adversity can increase infant mortality and also have a rather depressing impact on the birth rate.[4] If my forecast is correct, such factors as a trend toward mobile homes, apartments, and smaller housing units as well as a lack of full-time jobs for young men and women at all educational levels should help to keep fertility low and reinforce the trend toward ZPG.

Immigration

To remain on a path to ZPG, however, it may still be necessary for the United States to re-examine its present immigration policy. Some evidence suggests that immigration will be adversely affected by high unemployment even with no change in the existing statutes.

In 1974, the U.S. Immigration and Naturalization Service ruled that foreign students would not be permitted to accept jobs during the summer vacation because such employment would deprive young Americans, particularly minority group members and Vietnam veterans, of job opportunities. Work experience during the summer is probably one factor that has encouraged many foreign students either to remain in this country or to return to the United States after their studies have been completed.

Population growth after World War II indicates that net immigration reached a high of over 450,000 persons in 1969, the last year in which the national unemployment rate was below 4 per cent, and has since been trending downward. My own guess would be that concern about unemployment will become so great in the remainder of the 1970s that net immigration will be slowed to a trickle either through tighter administration or changes in the law.

In 1973 there was an average of slightly less than 3.8 million persons in each age year below 25. A policy of limiting immigration and the total number of live babies born in a particular year to a predetermined sum such as 3.8 million would help considerably to promote population stability.

A population policy of this sort would affirm the desirability of ZPG without denying American youth the right to replace themselves. It would also put future immigration on a "space-available" basis and notify other countries that they cannot expect to solve their own population problems by exporting surplus residents to the United States.

Life Expectancy

If the number of births and immigrants remains about the same each year, total population will eventually be equal to this sum times average life expectancy. It follows that to achieve a condition of ZPG, a point must eventually be reached at which there will be no further improvements in life expectancy.

From 1920 to 1950 the life expectancy of American residents increased on the average by about 4.7 years per decade. In the 1950s the improvement in life expectancy dropped to 1.5 years and in the 1960s the improvement was only 1.1 years. The sharp reduction in improved life expectancy is particularly surprising considering the explosive advances in medical science. Expenditures for research and development by the U.S. Department of Health, Education and Welfare — which are mainly in the health area — increased almost twentyfold between fiscal years 1954 and 1969, from $63 million to an estimated $1,310 million.

The rapid increase in expenditures has enabled molecular biologists and geneticists to make great strides in unraveling the code of life, which was broken by James Watson and Francis Crick in 1953 when they found that the DNA molecule is a double helix, composed of two intertwined polynucleotide chains. Although much remains to be learned about life and death, it now seems clear that the determinants of old age and some degenerative diseases are woven into the genetic structure of the human species and that there may not be much that can be done to alter the aging process significantly and safely.

Dr. Robert R. Kohn of Case Western Reserve Medical School has noted that until about age 18 the body continues to synthesize new collagen, the connective tissue that supports the cells of the body in the same way that mortar supports bricks. There is a plateau period until about age 25 or 30, after which the collagen begins to stiffen. In later years, the collagen fibers become increasingly brittle just as rubber, paint, and paper become fragile with age.

Because collagen is distributed throughout the body and presumably ages at the same rate, people can die of "old age" like the wonderful one-horse shay with everything collapsing together if accidents, disease, and genetic defects do not trigger a premature death of some vital organ of the body.

Recently, Massachusetts Institute of Technology studies have reported progress in deciphering most of the "on" signal for a gene, as well as a significant portion of the corresponding "off" signal. Although the signal to stop synthesizing new collagen may be found, it is not clear that this would be sufficient to provide the secret to eternal life on earth.

Juvenile hormones with the power to lengthen the life of some insect larvae have already been synthesized. Such hormones have been so disruptive to the insects' other life stages, however, as to have laid the foundation for a new pest control industry. They also raise doubts about the safety of analogous experiments on human beings, even if all the genes and other factors responsible for body repair and aging are ever identified.

To reduce such risks and obtain the benefit of a more controlled environment, scientists would probably find it desirable or necessary to transfer human genetic material to bacteria and other simpler organisms. A committee of the National Academy of Sciences has expressed fears that such experiments might increase the incidence of cancer and create drug-resistant strains of mutant germs that would cause new diseases. The committee has asked scientists to postpone or abandon research in this field — even though it could benefit mankind — because of its "potential hazards."

A major hazard is that genetically hybrid molecules are typically grown in the bacterium *Escherichia coli* which is commonly found in the human digestive tract. In some experiments new types of plasmids have been created in these bacteria as a result of transferring genetic material from animals to the bacteria. The plasmids can multiply by themselves and are able to carry and impart a resistance to antibiotics.

Although I expect more progress in the prevention and treatment of disease as well as in the repair and replacement of damaged body parts, it doesn't seem likely that a great deal of research priority will be given to the difficult and possibly very hazardous problem of unraveling the aging process.[5] My own guess, in any event, is that there will be some improvement in life expectancy in the next hundred years, but not a great deal. If the number of live births plus net immigration averages 3.8 million or less per year, and if life expectancy in the United States eventually increases from 71.1 years in 1971 to 75 years, the total population will level off at a steady state number of less than 285 million people in the next half century or so. This would be an increase of about 35 per cent from the estimated 210 million Americans as of 1973.

A total population in the 250 - 300 million range is, I believe, both a reasonable and a desirable goal. To reach ZPG without any further increase in the present population would require an immediate end to net immigration and a further reduction in the number of new babies from about 3.2 million in 1973 to slightly less than 2 million babies per year. The annual birth rate would then correspond to the annual death rate.

To achieve such a large reduction in the birth rate, young people would have to be denied the right to fully replace themselves. The average number of children per family would have to be reduced to a figure that is not much greater than one child per couple. This, I suspect, is too big an adjustment to be accepted socio-economically — and politically — at least in the United States, where food shortages are not serious.

If new births were reduced to less than 2 million for a sustained period about half the schools could be closed, and no new teachers trained for a decade or two. Such a drastic decline in the number of children being born and raised would make it very difficult for the economy to support the post - World War II baby boom when they are old enough to retire, because the ratio of retired people to working adults could be expected to rise dramatically in the first half of the twenty-first century.[6]

Another reason for moving fairly rapidly toward ZPG is that a relatively small population may be necessary in the long run to preserve such basic human rights as the freedom to choose where to work and live. John Holdren has suggested that the optimum population must be kept well below the physical maximum levels to provide sufficient social, cultural, and environmental diversity for personal satisfaction: "Diversity in the social and physical environments is related to personal options — access to a variety of employment possibilities, degrees of privacy, and so forth. The optimum population size is that beyond which further growth closes more options than it opens."[7]

Holdren is unable to think of many options that would be opened by further population growth in the United States. The scores of communities across the country now erecting such barriers to newcomers as restrictive zoning ordinances, building permit moratoria, and prohibitive development fees strongly suggest that many Americans are inclined to agree.

Though a case can be made for an eventual end to population growth and a gradual reduction in the number of people in the United States, halting population growth should not be the responsibility of individual communities. As the courts have noted in invalidating some local barriers to city growth, if all communities erected such mechanisms, where could young people settle who are now leaving home to establish their own, first households?

I hope that a steady state population can be achieved in the United States gradually, without coercive intervention by the federal government, but population forecasting is at best a hazardous art. If the fertility of American women does not remain at or below a replacement level, the United States will eventually be forced to adopt a national fertility policy.

Population and Consumption

Paul and Anne Ehrlich have estimated that raising the annual output of the rest of the world to American levels would require 75 times as much iron, 100 times as much copper, 200 times as much lead, 75 times as much zinc, and 250 times as much tin as was being consumed throughout the world in the late 1960s.[8] The same basic disparity in the distribution of population and consumption can be expressed in another way by noting that the United States, with a little over 5 per cent of the world's population, now consumes about a third of the world's energy and mineral resources — a large part of which is imported.

Because we are so affluent and because we consume energy and other raw materials at a rate far in excess of our own capacity to produce such materials, the United States appears to have more of a social responsibility than less developed countries to keep fertility low and move quickly toward ZPG. It can also be argued that the United States has more to lose than other countries in not endorsing the ZPG goal.

In India and other less developed countries commonly considered to be overpopulated there cannot be a very large decline in per capita income without an equilibrating condition of mass starvation, which would tend to restore the ecological balance between population and resources and make it possible for the surviving population to enjoy a higher standard of living.

The United States could easily support a much larger population without much danger of mass starvation. The oil embargo of 1973 and the unexpected recession that followed, however, have shown how dependent our own economic prosperity is on energy and raw materials from abroad. Not to move fairly quickly toward zero population growth would make this prosperity even more vulnerable to political events outside our borders, as well as to unfavorable trade changes that could depress the accustomed standard of living. To enjoy a high standard of living, it is clearly in the best interests of the United States to accept the idea of only one or two children per family and strive for a total population that is far short of the maximum number of people that could be fed, sheltered, and clothed.

Notes

1. This thesis has been further developed in "Marriage, Family, Human Capital and Fertility," edited by T. W. Schultz and published as a supplement to the March 1974, issue of the *Journal of Political Economy.*

2. Edward F. Renshaw, "The Demand for Housing in the Mid 1970's," *Land Economics* (August 1971), pp. 249 - 255.

3. The housing allowance alternative was seriously considered in an excellent set of papers submitted to the Subcommittee on Housing Panels of the House Committee on Banking and Currency, 92nd Congress (June 1971), and in *Setting National Priorities: The 1972 Budget,* by Charles Schultze and other analysts at the Brookings Institution (Washington, D.C.: 1973).

4. See Hudson Hoagland, "Mechanisms of Population Control," *Daedalus* (Summer 1964), pp. 812 - 829.

5. In a recent discussion of the outlook for medical science in the year 2024, Dr. Michael DeBakey, a pioneer in open-heart surgery, has suggested that "considerable emphasis will be directed toward gerontological research; ways will be explored, and found, of making the elderly healthier, happier and more productive." There was no mention at all of trying to halt the aging process. See "The Medical Prognosis: Favorable, Treatable, Curable," *Saturday Review World, Part 2 — The Next 50 Years* (August 24, 1974), p. 46.

6. *Daedalus* (Fall 1973); reprinted in Mancur Olson and Hans H. Landsberg, eds., *The No-Growth Society* (New York: Norton, 1973).

7. John P. Holdren, "Population and the American Predicament: The Case Against Complacency," in *The No-Growth Society,* ed. Mancur Olson and Hans H. Landsberg (New York: Norton, 1973), p. 40.

8. Paul and Anne Ehrlich, *Population, Resources, Environment: Issues in Human Ecology* (San Francisco: Freeman, 1970), pp. 61, 62.

PART THREE

*Adjusting to a
Steady State Economy*

chapter 6

EMPLOYMENT

The prospects for employment growth in a number of industries where future patterns might be different from the trends that emerged from 1947 to 1970 will be examined in this chapter, particularly employment opportunities in agriculture, mining, manufacturing, government, and the service sector of the economy. The rapid growth of government employment appears to have been of unrecognized importance in ensuring reasonably full employment for the economy since World War II.

Some evidence in this chapter suggests that government employment will not need to grow as rapidly in the future as in the past. With young people now entering the labor force in peak numbers it is difficult to imagine how the private sector can be relied upon to provide most of the new jobs that will be desired in the rest of this decade.

Rising unemployment has already renewed the debate about whether state and local governments, with financial assistance from the federal government, should accept the responsibility of being the employer of last resort. This might turn out to be a major issue of public policy to be considered by Congress in the transition to a steady state economy.

Agriculture

A salient characteristic of economic progress is its unevenness. Data compiled by Nobel laureate Simon Kuznets for the 1869 - 1948 period suggest that about 40 per cent of the rise in net national product per worker can be accounted for by interindustry shifts, the most important being the shift from farm to nonfarm employment.[1]

In 1890, work animals, mostly horses and mules, contributed over 90 per cent of the horsepower employed on farms; farm labor contributed another 5 per cent; windmills and steam engines, the remainder. Improvements in the internal combustion engine and the commercial development of electricity set the stage for a rapid transition. By 1955, horses and mules contributed less than 2 per cent of the total horsepower; labor, less than 1 per cent; and in-animate movers, like the tractor, 97 per cent of the nonautomotive horsepower used to produce agricultural products (Figures 6.1, 6.2).

The impact of this transition on farm labor has been dramatic. Between 1929 and 1972 farm employment declined by more than 65 per cent. Most job opportunities were lost in subsistence agriculture or on small farms with very little output. The loss of such farmers helped to boost the growth rate for agricultural labor productivity after World War II to a level that was more than twice the growth rate for the rest of the economy. The aggregate growth rate for the entire economy was also increased because most peo-ple leaving agriculture were able to obtain jobs in industry and the commercial sector that were more productive, on the average, than the jobs they left.

Much of the decrease in farm labor, however, has been ob-tained at the expense of increased purchases from other sectors. The U.S. Department of Agriculture's index of farm output per unit of total input — which includes machinery, fertilizer, and other industrial inputs — was very flat from 1963 to 1970. These figures imply that the United States is nearing a point where a further reduction in farm labor will be largely, if not entirely, offset by an increase in nonfarm labor used to produce

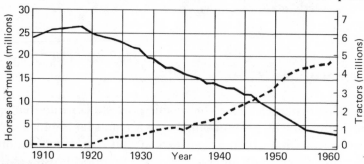

FIGURE 6.1

Replacement of Animals by Machines on U.S. Farms. *Source:* "Energy and Power," by Chauncey Starr. Copyright © 1971 by *Scientific American,* Inc. All rights reserved.

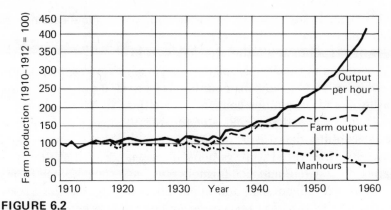

FIGURE 6.2
The Increase in Farm Output per Manhour. *Source:* "Energy
and Power," by Chauncey Starr. Copyright © 1971 by
Scientific American, Inc. All rights reserved.

agricultural inputs. This has not yet occurred because nonfarm
labor tends to be more expensive than farm labor, giving it a
higher weight in the Agriculture Department's productivity index
for all farm inputs.

If the farm population continues to decline at the same absolute rate as it did from 1950 to 1970, there will be no farmers left
in another twenty years. In 1969, when unemployment was very
low and jobs outside of agriculture easy to obtain, however, the
decline in the farm population was less than a fifth of the decline
in any other postwar year with a peak in business activity. Since
1971 farm population, farm employment, and the number of
manhours used to produce farm output have only slightly declined.
Though the small decline may have been partly caused by a fairly
large increase in the acreage of crop land harvested since 1972, it
does not seem likely that the reduction in farm employment will
ever again be as dramatic as in the 1950 - 1970 period. What
agricultural economists are now beginning to call a "stabilization"
of the farm population may, indeed, be a good thing, even if it
means a much slower growth rate for the gross national product.

In 1920, before trucks and tractors began to rapidly replace
horses and mules, almost 30 per cent of the American population
lived on farms. The substitution of mechanical horses for animal
power has now reduced the farm population to less than 5 per cent
of the total population. Though trucks and tractors have greatly increased labor productivity, they may also be creating social dis-
economies. Fewer people can now observe natural rhythms and
continually experience the joys of nature. That these losses can be

real is strongly suggested by the time and money some commuters pay to move their families to the suburbs.

A 1969 Gallup poll found that 30 per cent of American families prefer to live in rural areas, 25 per cent in small towns, 18 per cent in suburbs, 15 per cent in mountainous areas, 9 per cent by the seashore, and only 6 per cent in large cities.

One of the sadder aspects of the rural-to-urban migration is the possibility that disproportionate numbers may have been drawn by differential welfare benefits or been forced off the land against their will. Some rich farmers may have consolidated farms to obtain tax advantages and some affluent city dwellers have bought small farms for recreation or speculation, which in turn forced some farmers to move to the city.

Mason Gaffney has said that property is a paramount tax shelter which allows many persons with large amounts of earned income to escape much of the personal income tax. Many investments that enhance the value of agricultural land can be written off as current operating expenses. No taxes need to be paid on the resulting capital gains until the property is sold; when it is sold, the capital gains tax is less than for ordinary income. Though a strong case can be made for allowing mechanization to minimize or replace most disagreeable jobs, it would be folly to force people off the farm for the benefit of land speculators and wealthy tax evaders.

The income tax shelter provided by agricultural land near major cities has also helped to generate a sizable speculative component in the price of suburban agricultural land. In many cases this speculative component is being taxed at nonagricultural rates to support, for example, suburban schools. Such arbitrary taxation can create an income squeeze that may force many farmers to sell their properties to suburban developers and land speculators before the land is needed for housing, commercial, or industrial developments. To avoid paying capital gains taxes many uprooted suburban farmers move even farther from the city. By bidding up the price of agricultural land in remote locations they impart a speculative component to almost all agricultural land, regardless of its location.

With land values everywhere inflated beyond their worth as sources of agricultural products, only rich farmers, wealthy businessmen, doctors, lawyers, real estate speculators, and housing developers can afford to buy farm land. Many poor farmers and their children, as a consequence, have been prematurely forced off the land into towns and city ghettos. Agricultural production, in turn, has declined fairly dramatically in some parts of the United States. Although improvements in crop yields have been sufficient to offset such losses, the number of cattle on farms has declined since 1964 in such heavily populated areas as New England, the Mid-Atlantic, and East North Central states.

Cattle production, at least in northern states, is a labor-intensive business. Suitcase farmers, who may only visit their property on weekends, land speculators, and even wealthy farmers are often too busy to be bothered with managing a few cows and calves.

When the price of beef, which rose to record levels in 1973 and 1975, is viewed from this perspective, it becomes even more questionable whether land speculation, absentee ownership, and large-scale farming should be allowed to continue. Because much of the capital deterioration in our central cities can also be linked to tax evasion, speculation, and absentee ownership, the United States should seriously consider agrarian reforms that limit the size of agricultural enterprises and impose a special tax on all property owned by absentee landlords.

Mining

Agriculture is not the only industry in which large productivity advances caused an absolute decline in the number of job opportunities. Between 1920 and 1971 the number of persons employed in mining declined by more than 50 per cent. In 1920 coal supplied over 70 per cent of American energy needs. Its share of gross energy consumption had fallen to less than 18 per cent by 1971.

Since 1971 the total employment in mining has increased. During 1974, for the first time in more than a decade, the rate of employment increase in mining was more rapid than for total employment. This trend will probably continue for several more decades as efforts are made to replace oil and natural gas with electricity and synthetic fuels derived from coal and shale.

Historically, coal mining has been a dirty, rather hazardous occupation. Working conditions have been improved somewhat, however, as a result of the Health and Safety Act of 1969. The cost has been rather high, with output per manhour in coal mining in 1974 still less than in 1968. The estimated average daily wage, including fringe benefits, of organized coal miners was $65 in 1973. In a 200-work-day year, this wage would be equivalent to an annual income of $13,120. Wages increased rather substantially in 1974. Coal mining is one of the few industries in which it is reasonable to suppose that real wages might double in the next several decades.

Manufacturing

Employment in manufacturing increased to 10.7 million workers in 1929, fell to 7.4 million in 1933, recovered to 10.3 million in 1939, and subsequently rose to 17.6 million in 1943. Employment declined to less than 15 million in 1949. It almost equaled the 1943 level in 1953, at the height of the Korean War, but did not exceed the World War II level until 1965, when the United States became significantly involved in the Vietnam War. During 1969, at the end of direct involvement in Vietnam, employment in manufacturing had risen to almost 20.2 million workers. This record, despite the vigorous economic recovery in 1972 and 1973, has not yet been broken. Although I feel that employment in American manufacturing will eventually rise to a new high, this might not occur during the remainder of this decade unless a major effort is made to properly insulate old buildings and make numerous investments which conserve energy.

The electrical equipment industry is almost certain to experience a significant decline in employment opportunities. Electric power consumption grew at an average annual rate of about 7 per cent from 1925 to 1970. At the beginning of the 1970s consumption was projected to increase at 7.3 per cent annually during the 1970s. Even after the Arab oil embargo in 1974, however, some sectors of the economy and parts of the United States still consumed less electricity than in 1973.

The slowdown in the growth of electricity consumption has caused many utilities to sharply curtail their expansion plans. Because most manufacturing capacity in the electrical equipment industry has been for growth, rather than replacement, it seems clear that excess manufacturing capacity is substantial.

Other industries, like electrical appliance and automobile manufacturing, have also been adversely affected by higher energy prices. To avoid prolonged periods of chronic unemployment, American consumers should be encouraged to replace large automobiles and inefficient electrical appliances with new and more energy-efficient consumer durables.

The Service Economy

Total employment within the service sector of the economy, which includes transportation, public utilities, wholesale and retail trade, government, medical services, finance, insurance, and real estate, has grown from approximately 40 per cent in 1929 to over 60 per cent in 1973. What is the reason for the shift of employment toward services? Victor Fuchs has postulated three hypotheses: a more rapid growth in the demand for services by consumers; a relative increase in the demand for services by businesses; and a relatively slow increase in output per man in the service industry.[2]

The first hypothesis accounts for very little of the change. Total output in the service sector in constant dollars was about the same proportion in 1965 as in 1929. In current dollars the service sector increased its share of GNP from 47 per cent to about 50 per cent. Fuchs has found that the second hypothesis explains less than 10 per cent of the total change. The major explanation was that output per man grew much more slowly in the service sector than in other sectors, which implies that most service industries are inherently less subject to technological change than the rest of the economy.

In an interesting article on the anatomy of urban crisis, William Baumol has argued that many urban problems are basically the result of differential productivity.[3] Baumol suggests that such differences could lead to an end of economic growth. Suppose that increases in output per manhour are not the same in different industries and that consumers prefer to increase their consumption of all goods by about the same proportion. The percentage of total hours worked in service and other industries with slowly rising output per manhour will then have to increase, which will cause the overall average growth rate for total output per manhour to decline, because a larger share of the total labor force will be employed in industries with low productivity.

In 1971 Leon Greenberg, staff director of the National Commission on Productivity, pointed out that the increasing importance of low-productivity industries will lower the productivity growth rate in the United States by 0.2 per cent during the 1970s. In the preceding 20 years interindustry shifts raised the growth rate by 0.2 per cent. The overall result is a 0.4 per cent swing, "which translates into a lot of GNP dollars."

The service sector of the economy is not homogeneous. In addition to miscellaneous services, it includes employment in transportation, public utilities, wholesale and retail trade, finance, insurance, real estate, and federal, state, and local government employment. The government sector, including the armed services, provided less than 7 per cent of all employment in 1929. Its share has since increased to over 18 per cent in 1973.

There is a strong possibility, however, that the growth of government employment in such traditional areas as health, education, public safety, and welfare might not be nearly as rapid in the future as in the past two decades. This, I believe, could pose a rather serious problem of employment adjustment in the remainder of this decade when the number of young people seeking jobs will be at an all-time maximum.

The Military

In 1945 more than 11 million men and women were serving in the American armed forces. This figure dropped to a little less than 1.5 million in 1948, rose to almost 3.6 million in 1952, slumped to almost 2.5 million in 1960, rose to over 3.5 million in 1968 and then declined to 2.2 million in 1974 — the lowest figure in more than two decades. I believe that the size of the armed forces will continue to decline somewhat.

Two reasons that support this view are inflation and the voluntary army, which have helped to erode the real purchasing power of the Defense Department. With the economy caught in the midst of stagnation and inflation, and with military expenditures a bit more controllable than expenditures for social welfare programs, it seems likely that the armed forces will be required to make further cuts in men and material. Deficits in the United States balance of payments could also add to sentiment within Congress to bring more servicemen home from overseas.

Other factors, however, can be expected to keep the armed services from shrinking to very low levels. The army has always been something of a sump for juvenile delinquents and other unemployables. The assertion that the new volunteer army has been recruited, to some extent, by criminal court judges who have offered young lawbreakers the choice between jail and enlistment probably contains some truth. Such a recruitment policy is not necessarily undesirable from a social point of view. A well-run army is probably much cheaper and more cost-effective than the average jail, with less danger that an offender upon release will revert to a life of crime. There is also less stigma to having been released from the armed services. The discipline and training received in the service often help one-time delinquents to obtain and hold civilian jobs.

Although the Vietnam War did lower the prestige of the armed services in the eyes of many young people, attitudes are beginning to change. Reserve officer training (ROTC) is apparently making a cautious comeback at many colleges. The Air Force probably will continue to train a significant fraction of the pilots employed by commercial airlines; the military will no doubt remain an important source of financing for medical students. Valuable mechanical and electronic education and training is also provided by the military establishment. Turnover in these areas as well as in the junior officer corps is likely to remain relatively high, and provide more opportunities for training and leadership experience than the general shrinkage in the size of the armed services implies.

Government Employment

Federal employment of civilian workers reached an all-time peak of a little over 2.9 million workers in 1944, drifted downward to less than 1.9 million in 1947 - 1948, rose to a little over 2.75 million workers in 1969, and declined to almost 2.6 million employees by 1973. I expect federal employment to drift slowly upward in the years ahead.

One of the most dynamic parts of the service sector has been employment by state and local governments. Their share of the civilian labor force was only a little over 5 per cent in 1929 but has since risen to almost 13 per cent in 1974. During the 1960s more than a quarter of all new civilian jobs were provided by state and local governments. From 1960 to 1972 about 65 per cent of all the net new jobs in the state of New York were in government.

Of the new jobs that were created by state and local governments in the 1960s, about 60 per cent were in education. As school enrollments at the elementary and secondary levels decline, and as college enrollments peak in the next few years, the growth of state and local government employment will not have to be as rapid in the last half of the 1970s as during the preceding twenty-five years.

The possibility that the increase in state and local government employment will soon sag to less than half the average annual increase of 391,000 workers between 1960 and 1974 is disturbing because the growth of total employment seems to be influenced to some extent by the growth of public employment.

When the increase in employment at all government levels, including the armed services, is averaged over a two-year period and related to the current year's increase in nongovernment employment, a fairly striking relationship can be observed for the twenty-two years from 1948 to 1970. During those eleven years when the average increase in public employment amounted to 300,000 or more, private employment increased at a rapid rate of about 935,000 per year.

When the average increase in government employment was less than 300,000 employees, changes in private employment were quite erratic and amounted to an average annual increase of only 276,000 workers. Most large increases in private employment during these eleven years were simply a recovery of employment opportunities following business recessions, with little growth in long-term employment.[4]

School attendance until age 16 is compulsory in most states. As the postwar baby boom reached school age, government officials and local taxpayers had little choice but to build new schools and hire increasing numbers of teachers. Local purchasing power increased, which probably bolstered the confidence of local businessmen in the prospects for continuing growth for the local economies.

Declining enrollments and the rising costs of maintaining the existing teaching force have already made it much more difficult to get school budgets and bond issues passed in many communities. In education as well as in other discretionary service areas, the tendency may even be to reduce government employment because of rising costs resulting from relatively small improvements in labor productivity.

Mental health is an interesting example of a service industry that has been strongly affected by rising costs. The New York State Department of Mental Hygiene has reduced the number of patients in state mental hospitals from 84,000 in 1964 to 38,000 in 1974. Though new drugs and community treatment programs are often used as a rationale for justifying what some detractors have called a "revolving-door" treatment policy at state hospitals, part of the reason for the new approach to mentally ill persons is the enormous cost of maintaining mental hospitals. When adequate services are provided, annual costs can average between $10,000 and $20,000 per patient. If patient problems can be satisfactorily dealt with at nursing homes, halfway houses, outpatient clinics, or other appropriate home-based facilities, the savings to state and local taxpayers can be significant.

Our system of criminal justice is another area in which reform-minded officials, reinforced by rising costs, may be able to reduce the number of people locked up full-time at public expense. In 1974 the Citizens' Inquiry on Parole and Criminal Justice, headed by former United States Attorney General Ramsey Clark, labeled the New York State parole system as "oppressive and arbitrary," "a tragic failure," and "beyond reform." The citizens' group called for the eventual abolition of parole, the establishment of a "short and definite" sentencing system, and a restructuring of the entire postconviction criminal justice system. It noted that offenders released on parole return to prison at almost the same rate as prisoners that serve out their sentence.

In 1972 a Wisconsin task force on criminal justice planning recommended that the state phase out its prisons over a five-year period. The task force became convinced that "no amount of resources, however great, can enhance a convicted citizen's chances for productive re-entry to a democratic society when that citizen has been confined in an institution too large to provide individual services, too geographically remote to provide vital life contacts, and too regimented to foster self-esteem."

The Wisconsin statement could describe almost any state or federal prison and succinctly explains why prisons, according to the National Council on Crime and Delinquency, "have proved to be (1) ineffectual, (2) probably incapable of being operated constitutionally, (3) themselves productive of crime, and (4) destructive of the keepers as well as the kept." The council then recommended that the imprisonment of "nondangerous" offenders should be virtually abandoned, with the courts turning instead to greater use of pretrial diversion, probation, suspended sentences, deferred conviction, fines, restitution and other "community-based programs." The Council estimated that no more than 100 prisoners in any one state are sufficiently dangerous or so deeply involved in organized crime as to require tight-security confinement.

In 1971 the New York State Department of Corrections began an experimental program of halfway houses at eight different locations in New York, Buffalo, and Rochester. In 1973, a departmental statement indicated that 95 per cent of the parolees in the project were making community adjustment without incident. Initial studies indicate a financial saving of at least $250,000 for the first group of 85 inmates.

Leslie Wilkins concludes that humanitarian systems of treatment are no less effective at reducing the probability of a return to crime than severe forms of punishment and also notes that they are normally cheaper than the methods that stress supervision or security.[5] The road to prison reform may be set back to some extent, however, by broader based economic studies which suggest that longer prison terms and more severe forms of punishment do tend to reduce crime rates, perhaps by deterring others from engaging in crime.[6]

In 1971 the nation's public police forces cost the taxpayers $6.2 billion. Though the United States has as many uniformed policemen as steelworkers, annual expenditures to improve law enforcement productivity have only averaged from 1 to 5 per cent of the amount spent annually to improve productivity in the steel industry. The National Commission on Productivity has noted that per capita law enforcement expenditures for communities with equal crime rates vary by a factor of four or more and has concluded that "There is little question that the average American could get more police services for his tax dollar."[7] To help local officials and police managers deal with the rapid rise in police costs, in 1973 the commission set up an Advisory Group on Productivity in Law Enforcement.

Young men and women are more likely to engage in crime and

delinquency than older persons. As the postwar baby boom grows up, the proportion of the population engaged in criminal investigation and law enforcement activity should begin to decline even without significant reforms in police efficiency, court procedures, and criminal justice systems.

Between 1957 and 1972 the number of persons receiving public welfare benefits in the state of New York increased fourfold. Most of this increase was in Aid to Families with Dependent Children (AFDC). Tighter administration and a declining birth rate helped to reduce AFDC caseloads in 1973 and 1974. Because the eligible population is declining, fewer caseworkers and persons will be needed to administer this program once the economy recovers from the severe recession of 1975.

Roadbuilding and maintenance is another area where future public employment may not have to increase as rapidly as total employment. Construction and reconstruction completed on our federally aided highway system amounted to 20,000 miles in 1960, declined to 17,000 miles in 1965, and fell to 11,000 miles in 1969. As the interstate highway system nears completion, and with almost half of all new housing units being constructed for two or more families, compared to less than a quarter in the 1950s, roadbuilding, street, and highway maintenance employment growth will not have to be as rapid in the future as in the the last two decades.

A 1974 study for the federal government by the Real Estate Research Corporation of Chicago shows that planned urban fringe and suburban development can save communities up to 50 per cent in land costs, construction costs, energy consumption, air and water pollution, and municipal operating costs, as compared with haphazard growth. The Environmental Protection Agency has announced that it will pay more attention to land use patterns in the future when awarding federal grants for sewers to reduce urban sprawl and ensure more efficient use of public resources.

The future growth of public employment will also be more moderate in ordinary hospitals than in the past two decades. In the *Special Analyses* of the 1973 U.S. budget, it was noted that Hill-Burton assistance grants have virtually eliminated a national shortage of hospital beds. Hospital beds increased from 1,436,000 in 1946 to 1,616,000 in 1970: "one out of every five of these hospital beds is unoccupied. . . . The critical area of need for construction today is outpatient and other ambulatory health care facilities which provide alternatives to costly hospital care."

The peak year for growth in government employment was 1966, when 531,000 people were added to state and local government payrolls. If my analysis is correct, the growth rate could drop from an average of about 400,000 additional employees for 1971 - 1974 to less than half that rate of increase. Some nongovernment sectors, such as mining, can be expected to grow rapidly. Mining is a very capital-intensive industry, however, and the total employment base of 672,000 miners in 1974 was really quite small in comparison to the more than 11.5 million persons employed in state and local government. A large percentage increase could occur in the mining industry, in other words, without an appreciable impact on the overall employment picture.

The postwar baby boom is now entering the labor force in peak numbers. With less need for a rapid expansion of government services, I find it rather difficult to visualize how the private sector can be relied upon to provide a larger share of the new jobs that young people will desire in the late 1970s. If this view is correct the unemployment rate for the civilian labor force could remain at very high levels for an extended period.

Unemployment

The national unemployment rate rose above 6 per cent in only four years between the end of World War II and 1973. After the 1970 recession Congress passed the Emergency Employment Act of 1971 to provide 178,000 new public service jobs in fiscal year 1972. Within nine months the Public Employment Program had created 152,000 jobs. The success of PEP soon led to suggestions that the Public Employment Program be expanded substantially and redirected to provide additional training, work experience, and permanent employment for disadvantaged people who might otherwise be unemployable or remain on public welfare.

The debate over public jobs for the jobless waned considerably during 1973 as the national unemployment rate was reduced to less than 5 per cent. In late 1974, however, when the unemployment rate rose to 7.2 per cent, Congress enacted an expanded program to provide more than $4 billion of financial support for additional public service jobs and extended unemployment compensation benefits.

Robert H. Haveman, director of the Institute for Research on Poverty at the University of Wisconsin, has criticized large-scale public employment because it would probably be "wasteful and inequitable." It would generate "arbitrary choice among applicants," "make-work jobs," and also threaten present government employees. Haveman has urged a permanent income-support system that would automatically trigger cash-assistance payments to cushion earnings losses from whatever source.

Another criticism of public employment programs for the unemployed is that a large part of the federal funds may be used to displace state and local funds with only a small net impact on total government employment, especially in the long run.[8] My own guess, however, is that unemployment will remain at uncomfortable levels during the rest of this decade and that Congress will not only be forced to adopt major reforms in the present welfare system but will also move further toward becoming an employer of last resort.

Notes

1. Simon Kuznets, *Income and Wealth of the United States, Trends and Structures* (Cambridge, England: Bowes and Bowes, 1952).

2. Victor Fuchs, *The Service Economy* (New York: Columbia University Press, 1958).

3. William J. Baumol, "Macroeconomics of Unbalanced Growth: The Anatomy of Urban Crisis," *American Economic Review* (June 1967), pp. 419 - 420.

4. Edward F. Renshaw, "The Steady State Economy: Some Immediate Problems of Employment Adjustment," *Governmental Finance* (May 1972), pp. 5 - 9.

5. Leslie T. Wilkins, *Evaluation of Penal Measures* (New York: Random House, 1969), p. 110.

6. For a brief review of the economic versus the sociological views of crime see Richard B. McKenzie and Gordon Tullock, *The New World of Economics* (Homewood, Ill.: Irwin, 1975), chapter 12. More detailed economic studies can be found in Gary S. Becker and William M. Landes, eds., *Essays in the Economics of Crime and Punishment* (New York: Columbia University Press, 1974).

7. National Commission on Productivity, *Third Annual Report* (March 1974), pp. 18 - 19.

8. Alan Fechter, *Public Employment Programs* (Washington: American Enterprise Institute for Public Policy Research, 1975).

chapter 7

CONSUMPTION

A rather useful principle for predicting human behavior is the assumption that more consumption is preferable to less. It does not necessarily follow, however, that a person who consumes twice as much as another is twice as well off. In our preoccupation with adding up the monetary value of goods and services that are bought and sold in the marketplace, economists may have lost sight of other values that might possibly lead to a revolution in which relatively less time and effort is devoted to the kinds of production and consumption included in the gross national product.

In this chapter I will first consider a potpourri of views about consumption and the relation between economic growth and basic human welfare, and will then enumerate some of the quantities that are consumed on a per capita basis in the United States. In the last part of this chapter I will consider the excess consumption arising from the underpricing of domestic energy. If energy consumption is not priced or taxed enough to cover the full social cost to society, an economic case can be made for the adoption of energy-labeling and efficiency standards that will tend to encourage conservation.

By accepting the goal of a steady state economy and by making many of the investments in energy conservation that will be needed in the long run, the United States may be able to grow faster in the remainder of this decade and experience less unemployment than would otherwise be the case.

Staffan Linder has noted:

> Most people seem to think that wants are inexhaustible. . . . The idea
> that there may be some point at which not only the stomach, but the
> whole body, including head and heart is fed, if not fed up, is usually
> denied. John Stuart Mill's views on the bliss of the stagnant state
> have a queer ring in modern ears. Talk of a consumption maximum

is contemptuously referred to as "idealism" or "Utopianism" — concepts which have nowadays acquired pejorative overtones as being impractical. These commentators are, of course, honest in their disbelief in a saturation of wants. They are also hostile to the very idea. This is perhaps surprising. We have come to dislike ultimate success. The means have become the end. Dissatisfaction with one's material conditions is regarded as the stimulus of life. Our hopes and ambitions are tied to material "progress." Our enterprising spirit requires it as an outlet. Efforts to achieve economic growth have created their own values and vested interests. Saturation appears as a threat of greater dimensions than a mere problem of economic policy. . . . Economists and non-economists alike take comfort in the fact that people are conspicuously interested in material advancement, even after centuries of what, in fact, has been an accelerating growth of consumption. As new consumption heights are reached, people dare — thank God — to raise their aspiration levels. Whether through advertising or not, the appetite of the mass consumer can always be relied upon to be whetted. Decreasing marginal utility might affect individual commodities but not aggregate consumption. What George Katona has reverently referred to as "the miracle of consumption" will, it is believed, be an even greater miracle a hundred years hence.[1]

Since Linder's commentary on a growth-minded society was written in the mid-1960s, a significant minority of the American population, particularly the young, are becoming dissatisfied with an economic philosophy based upon selfishness, greed, and conspicuous consumption. Charles Silberman, an editor of *Fortune* magazine, noted that basic economic assumptions are now being challenged and has suggested that: "the new values could profoundly alter consumer demand, on the one hand, and the growth of productivity and the labor force, hence of the economy's capacity to produce, on the other."[2]

Silberman singles out a rising involvement by executives and professionals in social problems and issues outside their office lives, as increased professional enlistments in the Peace Corps attest. More young lawyers are working on *pro bono publico* cases with the approval of their often prestigious law firms. And, Silberman notes, "corporate presidents and chairmen increasingly seem to feel the need to justify business operations not in traditional profit terms but by referring to their corporate contribution to solving urban, racial, or environmental problems."

Younger economists are increasingly disposed to wonder

whether John Stuart Mill and even John Maynard Keynes were not correct in believing that growth in per capita income may be subject to a law of diminishing marginal utility once such basic necessities as food, clothing, and shelter are acquired. J. A. Livingston recently noted that to reread Keynes's essay, "Economic Possibilities for Our Grandchildren," written in 1930, is to say: "Yesterday he explained today." Keynes believed that in the long run mankind would solve its economic problem:

> I see us free to return to some of the most sure and certain principles of religion and traditional virtue — that avarice is a vice, that the exaction of usury is a misdemeanor, and the love of money detestable, that those walk most truly in the paths of virtue and wisdom who take least thought for tomorrow.
>
> We shall once more value ends above means and prefer the good to the useful. We shall honor those who can teach us how to pluck the hour and the day virtuously and well, the delightful people who are capable of taking direct enjoyment in things, the elites of the field who toil not, neither do they spin.[3]

Keynes recognized that economic growth had become an obsession in some parts of the world, and was even inclined to speculate that the transition to a steady state economy might be difficult:

> If the economic problem is solved, mankind will be deprived of its traditional purpose. Will this be a benefit? If one believes at all in the real values of life, the prospect at least opens up the possibility of benefit. Yet I think with dread of the readjustment of the habits and instincts of the ordinary man, bred into him for countless generations, which he may be asked to discard within a few decades. Must we not expect a general nervous breakdown?[4]

Commenting on the poor who for intellectual reasons have chosen a state of poverty, Michael Harrington has noted:

> They accept the poverty because it provides them a certain freedom. As one writer brilliantly described them, they reject the working world because it does not give them time.... perhaps it is more significant to remember that our affluent society contains those of talent and insight who are driven to prefer poverty, to choose it, rather than to submit to the desolation of an empty abundance.[5]

Changing Values
in a Transition Economy

The transition to a steady state population and economy may not be nearly so traumatic as Keynes feared. A recent psychological study found that parents do not seem to be as distressed as in the past when the last child leaves home. The study also reported that fewer than one-fourth of the middle-class middle-aged men that were interviewed considered work as an important source of current satisfaction.

With more middle-aged Americans beginning to appreciate that their work lacks meaning and, as Charles Reich has suggested, can sometimes be "mindless, exhausting, boring, servile and hateful, something to be endured while 'life' is confined to 'time off' " — it would not be too surprising if the next great wave of economic dropouts turned out to be adults with accumulated savings or early retirement options, rather than teenagers who have never experienced the drudgery of an assembly line.

For, in the final analysis, there is not just the distinction between luxuries and necessities as a reason for expecting additional income above some minimal requirement to possess diminishing marginal utility, but a rather large number of other considerations[7] that could make further growth in per capita income unnecessary or even socially counterproductive.

There is a growing feeling, for example, that work, itself, should be both meaningful and a source of personal satisfaction. If a highly organized and bureaucratic working environment does not provide such satisfaction it may not be irrational for successful individuals to partially or completely sever their relations with large corporations and seek to create a more rewarding personal service, communal, or subsistence economy of their own choosing — even if it means a substantial sacrifice of income.

Another reason for supposing that increases in the volume of consumption might provide only dwindling increments to well-being is the lack of time to fully enjoy an increase in per capita affluence. As Staffan Linder has pointed out in *The Harried Leisure Class*, consumption takes time. If technological improvements increase our ability to produce goods more rapidly than our ability to enjoy them, the growth of per capita GNP could outstrip per capita welfare. In a highly productive time-scarce society where many feel "compelled to read for profit, party for contacts, lunch for contracts, bowl for unity, drive for mileage, gamble for charity, go out for the evening for the greater glory of the municipality, and stay home for the weekend to rebuild the house,"[8] there can, as Walter Kerr has so aptly expressed it, be a decline of pleasure.

In his book on *The New Industrial State* John Kenneth Galbraith has noted:

> *Expansion in the output of many goods is not easily accorded a social purpose. More cigarettes cause more cancer. More alcohol causes more cirrhosis. More automobiles cause more accidents, maiming and death; also more preemption of space for highways and parking; also more pollution of the air and the countryside. What is called a high standard of living consists, in considerable measure, in arrangements for avoiding muscular energy, increasing sensual pleasure and for enhancing caloric intake above any conceivable requirement.*

Galbraith goes on to note that increased production as a worthwhile social goal is nonetheless very nearly absolute. It is imposed by assumption

> *things are better because production is up. . . . No society has ever before provided such a high standard of living as ours, hence none is as good.*[9]

In summing up the findings of various studies, psychologist Henry Clay Lingren has observed that despite the conviction of a great many people to the contrary, money is far from a cureall for feelings of insecurity. The notion that higher earnings or a heftier bank balance will cause problems to vanish is wishful thinking that has no basis in fact. Most problems stem from basic psychological causes that have nothing to do with money. These problems, according to Lingren, must be faced and coped with — regardless of whether income is large or small.

In an almost forgotten book published in 1924, William A. Robson observed:

> *The peculiar curse of our age is what may be called Monetary Inter-*

pretation of Welfare. . . . It is when the souls of men are dominated by mere things, and wealth is regarded as something objective and unconditional rather than as subjective and qualified, that materialism corrodes the heart of society and turns the world into a wilderness of strife and misery. It is, in short, the general identification of wealth with welfare, and in particular the confusion of private wealth not only with the common good but also with the welfare of the owner thereof, that leads men to waste their substance in a vain and rapacious scramble for the power to acquire possessions and command services that bring satisfaction neither to themselves nor to others, but which nevertheless deprive whole hosts of their fellow creatures of true forms of well-being.[10]

Per Capita Consumption

In 1971 American consumers purchased over 500 trillion cigarettes. Consumption of metals amounted to about one-half ton per person. Fifty pounds of fibers were consumed per person and paper consumption amounted to more than 566 pounds. Each person in the United States consumed about 180 bottles and glass containers each year, 5 pairs of shoes and slippers, and 14 pairs of socks and hosiery. Per capita food consumption included 125 pounds of beef, 100 pounds of sugar, 1.43 gallons of wine, 1.85 gallons of distilled spirits, and 19 gallons of beer.

In 1967, 3.7 million typewriters were sold in the United States, enough to supply almost every high school graduate with his or her personal typewriter, regardless of typing ability. During the recession year of 1970, when the number of families and unrelated individuals in the United States only increased by 1.4 million, 8.1 million new electric coffeemakers were sold.

In 1972 housing production, including mobile homes, amounted to almost 3 million units, the equivalent of almost one and one-half new housing units per person age 20 and older who was added to our adult population.

The passenger car population topped the 100-million mark in 1973 for the first time in history. (This is almost equal to one car for every two people in the United States.) The new milestone came at about the same time that the country's two-millionth traffic fatality was being recorded.

In 1973 American consumers purchased 6.8 million refrigerators, 5.3 million room air conditioners (down fairly significantly from the 5.9 million purchased in 1970), 5.6 million washing machines, and 9 million vacuum cleaners. The United States also produced or imported 17 million television sets and an unbelievable number of radios, which some sources suggest may have amounted to about 50 million units.

While producing and consuming these items, the American economy generated approximately one ton of air pollutants per person. These pollutants include almost a half ton of deadly carbon monoxide and over a quarter of a ton of acid-forming sulfur and nitrogen oxides. More than 100,000 gallons of waste water per person were discharged to our rivers and streams. Residential, commercial, and institutional solid wastes amounted to 1.25 tons per person, industrial wastes 0.5 ton, mineral wastes almost 10 tons, and agricultural wastes over 12 tons per person.

Energy Production and Consumption

In the process of producing, consuming, and disposing of waste products, the United States also used up fossil fuels with the energy equivalent of more than 10 tons of coal per person. The supply of fossil fuels is finite and will eventually be too costly to use as a source of primary energy. Whether the United States will be able to develop alternative sources of energy which are sufficiently safe, reliable, convenient, and cheap enough to preserve for thousands of years the lifestyle to which the average American has become accustomed is conjectural.

The proportion of GNP going into the production of basic energy has averaged a little less than 3 per cent since 1900. If this energy were valued at its probable replacement cost, however, and if GNP were depreciated to reflect natural resource exhaustion and expenditures necessary to offset pollution, real GNP would be from one-third to one-half less than current estimates. As Paul Samuelson has said, "most of us are poorer than we realize. Hidden costs are accruing all the time; and because we tend to ignore them, we overstate our incomes."

The rapid rate at which fossil fuels are currently being used up is particularly disturbing economically because consumers are not being charged the full social costs of increased energy consumption. When energy (or any other item) is priced at less than its marginal cost there will be underinvestment in resources that can be used to conserve energy and a tendency to use fossil fuels for purposes that do not provide human satisfaction equal to their real cost to society.

One solution to the problem of excess consumption arising from the underpricing of natural gas (regulated by the Federal Power Commission) and "old" domestic oil (under federal control even after most price and wage controls were ended in 1974) would be to immediately decontrol the prices of domestically produced energy as well as to tax gasoline and other energy consumption that produces external costs — such as pollution and traffic congestion. The government revenues could be used for education and other worthwhile social purposes besides roadbuilding. Immediate deregulation of domestic energy prices would be quite inflationary, however. It would provide windfall gains to large oil companies and would also be a severe blow to many low income families that have already been impoverished by large price increases for gas, fuel, and electricity.

In a world where inflation and equity considerations make it difficult if not politically impossible to allow the price of domestically produced energy to rise to equal the cost of imported energy, a very strong economic case can be made for the adoption of energy standards. Such standards would help to reduce and constrain energy consumption to about the level that would prevail if energy were taxed and priced enough to cover the full marginal cost to society of increased energy consumption.

Limiting Energy Consumption

Energy consumption could be limited in many ways without resorting to higher prices. For example, a limited number of coupons or rationing stamps could be issued to every family and business as in World War II. Although such a system may be necessary, if the supply of imported oil is disrupted for an extended period, it is hard to devise a coupon system that can be considered fair to families and businesses in different locations with different energy needs. A coupon system can also be costly and difficult to administer.

Assuming that the Arab oil embargo is not renewed, I would favor an expanded form of consumer protection which is not only concerned about new product safety but also sets minimum standards for product durability, required insulation, and the overall efficiency of heating equipment and energy-converting devices. A few steps are already being taken in this direction.

In 1971 the Federal Housing Administration (FHA) announced an upgrading of insulation standards for new houses. It estimated that the residential heating losses would be reduced by one-third and that the savings in heating bills would pay for the additional construction costs in one year. Additional study has shown that a further investment of $280 for a 1,500-square-foot house in Washington, D.C., would reduce the thermal losses to 50 per cent of the new FHA standards. This sum is fairly small compared to the annual heating cost for the same house without adequate insulation.

New and old homes in New York State that are being converted to gas heat are now required to have insulation in the roof, sidewalls, and crawl spaces as well as storm windows and doors. Much stiffer insulation requirements also seem in order for new homes that are to be heated with other forms of energy.

Nationwide, 24 per cent of all electricity goes for lighting. In New York City, the figure is 65 per cent. The recommended lighting levels in commercial buildings have tripled since 1952 to the point that many experts consider excessive. The excess light throws off heat, which in turn must be cooled with more energy. H. G. Stein has calculated that various design and operational changes can reduce electrical consumption to less than half of that consumed using current building standards and practices.[11] National standards in building codes would help reduce wasteful energy consumption.

Aside from lighting and space heating the biggest users of residential energy are hot water heaters, air conditioners, refrigerator-freezers, stoves, and clothes dryers. A 1972 report of the U.S. Office of Emergency Preparedness indicates that significant improvements are possible in the efficiency of these major appliances through better design. Some refrigerators and room air conditioners are more than twice as efficient as competing appliances now on the market. The OEP report recommended that the energy consumption of different appliances be stated on the name plate, on the price tag, and in every advertisement in which selling price is mentioned. The energy bill which was enacted into law in December 1975 not only requires labeling with respect to fuel consumption but also sets standards of efficiency for major household appliances.

The same law requires automobile manufacturers to build cars that get better gasoline mileage or face cash penalties. Beginning with the 1978 model year the cars of each manufacturer must average 18 miles per gallon. This standard will rise to an average of 27.5 miles per gallon for 1985 cars.

Limitations on the amount of energy that can be consumed by new houses and automobiles are of particular interest for conservation and the long-run distribution of economic well-being. The ability of poor people to conserve energy who cannot afford new houses and automobiles will be greatly limited in the long run if relatively more affluent consumers are not forced to buy durable goods that are energy-efficient. Tough energy standards for fancy homes and luxury automobiles could also serve a worthwhile social purpose by creating a national market for energy conserving innovations that are still too expensive for the average consumer.

Solar heating systems and heating pumps for residential dwelling units, as well as electronically controlled fuel injection systems for private automobiles, can help reduce our long-run dependence upon fossil fuels. They are not likely to be widely utilized, however, unless affluent consumers can be induced to buy them.

Efficiency standards for new houses, appliances, and automobiles can also be justified on other grounds such as traffic congestion and the trend toward smaller and more closely spaced housing units. The larger the car, the more difficult it will be to provide adequate parking space; the more inefficient the air conditioner, the more costly it will be for one's neighbors to cool their own home.

Finding adequate space to house and store all the appliances now available to the average consumer is already a problem for most households and is likely to be compounded in the future as the maturing baby boom moves into apartments and relatively small single-family dwelling units. Mobile homes and multifamily housing starts accounted for over half of all new housing starts in 1973 compared to about one-fifth of all new housing units in 1959.

Construction expenditures per single-family start in terms of resources used, moreover, has apparently been falling since about 1966.

The shift to smaller homes may be partly caused by differential inflation in the market for land suitable for residential development. In the 1950s and 1960s the price of land rose from 400 to 500 per cent in developing areas, compared to a 60 per cent increase in the general price level.

The shift to smaller homes may also be related to such factors as declining birth rates, differentially low productivity in the residential construction industry, fiscal zoning in suburban communities, differentially high inflation in the residential construction industry, and excessive reliance on the property tax to finance elementary and secondary education.

The problem of insufficient space to house and store all the furniture and consumer durables that American industries can now produce might in itself have been partly responsible for the economic slowdown that began in 1973, before the Arab oil embargo. This problem, combined with evidence which suggests that household demand for automobiles and more electrical appliances was nearly saturated by the end of 1973, could in turn have a deleterious effect upon economic activity and new employment opportunities if consumers are not provided with economic incentives to replace large cars and inefficient electrical appliances.

Such incentives could be provided by gradually deregulating the price of domestically produced oil and natural gas and by setting minimum efficiency standards for new housing and consumer goods. Decontrol of natural gas and petroleum prices was being discussed in the mid-70s. Congressional acceptance of a comprehensive set of national efficiency standards is needed. Such standards are particularly attractive from a balance of payments point of view, because the saving in energy consumption would help to eliminate production bottlenecks and would be at the expense of high-cost imported energy rather than at the expense of domestic job opportunities.

Charles F. Luce, chairman of the board of consolidated Edison, has suggested:

> It should become a mark of distinction that an individual consumes less than he can afford — drives a smaller car or uses public transit,

> *lives in a smaller home which he does not overheat in winter or over-cool in summer, carefully controls his diet, and otherwise exercises self-restraint in the consumption of material things. And it should become a badge of shame that an individual leaves his electric lights blazing on a bright summer day, roars down the highway at 80 miles per hour in a two-ton automobile, or otherwise is profligate in the use of limited natural resources.*[12]

Other representatives of the electrical utility industry have been more hostile to the idea of energy conservation. The following message was published in the *Wall Street Journal* (as a tax-deductible business expense) by the American Electric Power System:

> *There's no more nonsensical concept than "generate less" as a solution to our energy crisis.*
>
> *The nonsense is revealed by this evidence: it took energy to produce everything we have in this country.*
>
> *Since we produce more than any other nation, America uses 35% of the world's energy and enjoys the highest standard of living in the recorded history of man.*
>
> *Just start listening to the critics of our society, start generating less energy, and the plummet begins.*
>
> *Less production, fewer jobs, lower demand for products followed by still further diminished production and galloping unemployment until America is eventually reduced to the hard life.*[13]

The appropriate response to this line of reasoning is that energy conservation, itself, has the potential of being a very profitable growth industry. A 1974 Federal Energy Office Study examined opportunities for conserving energy in industry, transportation, commerce, and the household sectors of the economy. It concluded that over 400 billion dollars could profitably be invested in increased insulation and other energy-saving devices between 1974 and 1985.[14]   These investments would yield energy savings that can be considered cheaper and more profitable than imported oil at an assumed price of $8 per barrel in 1973 dollars. They can also be considered more profitable than new domestic supplies of energy if the equivalent cost of new domestic energy is assumed to equal $8 or more per barrel. If all the investments proposed in the study were made, the projected total savings in energy in 1985 would be equivalent to almost 15 million barrels of oil per day or nearly as much oil as was being consumed in the United States in 1973.

Energy conservation not only implies opportunities for profitable investments but also implies the creation of new jobs. Mark Seidel of the Federal Power Commission has estimated that from $50 to $100 billion could usefully be invested in increased insulation and other home improvements that conserve energy. If the investment was made over a six-to-twelve-year-period, the annual cost would be about $8 billion and almost 1 million new jobs would be created. Because most labor could be supplied by apprentices or relatively untrained people, a major conservation effort could significantly help to revive economic activity in the United States. Considering the high costs, delays, and technological difficulties that will be encountered in simply trying to halt the decline in domestic energy production which began in the early 1970s, a vigorous effort to conserve energy — instead of implying less economic production, fewer jobs, and a hard life — may well provide many of the new job opportunities that will be needed in the rest of this decade.

Notes

1. Staffan Linder, *The Harried Leisure Class* (New York: Columbia University Press, 1970), pp. 124 - 125.

2. Charles E. Silberman, "The U.S. Economy in an Age of Uncertainty," *Fortune* (January 1971), p. 75.

3. J. M. Keynes, "Economic Possibilities for Our Grandchildren," *Essays in Persuasion* (New York: Norton, 1963), pp. 371 - 372.

4. Ibid., p. 366.

5. Michael Harrington, *The Other America* (New York:), pp. 87 - 88.

6. Charles Reich, *The Greening of America* (New York: Bantam, 1971).

7. One of the more interesting sources of upward bias in measured income is new products that are first produced as handicrafts and sold at monopolistic prices to those with very high incomes. As modern technology increases the volume of the new product, costs will usually decline dramatically, permitting price reductions sufficient to generate a mass market. Because the mass market might never have materialized without the sharp decline in costs and prices, new products can sometimes increase both output per manhour and deflated GNP rapidly without necessarily increasing real income or welfare.

8. Walter Kerr, *The Decline of Pleasure* (New York: Simon and Schuster, 1965), p. 39.

9.   John Kenneth Galbraith, *The New Industrial State* (Boston: Houghton Mifflin, 1967).

10. *The Relation of Wealth to Welfare* (London: George Allen and Unwin, 1924).

11. H. G. Stein, "A Matter of Design," *Environment* (October 1972).

12. Charles F. Luce, "Marks of Distinction," *The New York Times* (October 15, 1973), p. 35.

13. *Wall Street Journal* (March 26, 1974), p. 19.

14. Mark R. Seidel, *Demand Curtailment and Conservation Scenarios* (Washington, D.C.: Federal Energy Office, 1974).

chapter 8

LEISURE

Employment statistics for production workers in different industries show that the number of hours worked by full-time employees in the United States have remained fairly constant since World War II. The average weekly hours for production workers in manufacturing, for example, was 40.4 hours in 1947. By 1973 this figure had actually increased slightly to 40.7 hours. The only major industries with a significant reduction in the average number of hours per week were retail trade and services, two industries with a marked influx of women, teenagers, and part-time workers.

The statistics on average weekly hours are clouded by the U.S. Labor Department's practice of only asking employees to report hours paid for rather than hours actually worked. Actual working hours may be less because of longer vacations and more paid holidays. An increase in hidden leisure could be more than offset in some instances, however, by a tendency for more workers either to hold two jobs or to spend relatively more time commuting to work than when the United States was less urbanized.[1] Some writers have even suggested that the reduction in average work time, after trending downward throughout most of the first half of this century, has virtually ceased since World War II.

Recent experiments with a 10-hour four-day work week that reduces commuting time by as much as 20 per cent strongly suggests, however, that many workers are concerned about the amount of effective leisure that is currently available for other purposes. Having diverted so little of the 100 per cent increase in output per manhour since 1948 to a reduction of working hours, increased leisure might have become a social issue even without the stimulus of high unemployment, an environmental movement stressing the conservation of energy and materials, and new

123

lifestyles based on a minimum consumption and popularized by such tracts as *The Greening of America.*

In this chapter I will first consider an institutional bias that encourages employers to require people to work long hours. I will then examine the goal of a four-day work week and briefly consider the tyranny of a goods-oriented society, as well as the problem of how to make work more interesting and meaningful. In the last sections I include some evidence indicating growing popularity of early retirement and will discuss such problems as job mobility and pension reforms.

An Institutional Bias

The American economy seems to be biased in the direction of encouraging and even forcing people to work long hours. Entry into the medical profession is so restricted that some doctors are probably overworked. The social security system to which most workers belong is also institutionally biased toward longer working hours and the hiring of specialists as opposed to less skilled labor.

Employers at the present time must pay into the social security system a fixed proportion of wage and salary income up to some threshhold amount. This figure has gradually been increased to a level somewhat greater than the median American family income in 1974. After the threshhold is reached employees and their employers need not make any further contributions. Profits will be maximized, other things being equal, if employers increase overtime for existing workers earning more than the threshhold amount rather than incur the extra expense of hiring new workers who have not made the maximum social security contribution.

Because this bias could help to create a situation in which a portion of the labor force is overworked while many less skilled workers remain unemployed and the recipients of public welfare, basic reforms are needed. Employers could be encouraged to hire the so-called disadvantaged worker and part-time employee by simply exempting the first $3,000 - $4,000 of a worker's income from all social security taxes. The loss in tax revenue could be made up of general revenues from the U.S. Treasury or by requiring workers and employers to contribute a fixed proportion of all additional wage and salary payments to the social security fund. These changes would help to neutralize the social security system's bias toward longer working hours and perhaps even favor part-time employment in those industries where the fixed costs of hiring and training new employees are low.

These reforms would also help to reduce poverty and improve the distribution of after-tax income. The payroll taxes used to finance the social security system have come under increasing criticism in recent years as being unfair to families with low and moderate incomes. Between fiscal 1960 and 1974 reliance on payroll taxes increased from 16 per cent of total revenue received by the federal government to 30 per cent. Social security taxes now provide the federal government with more than twice as much revenue as the corporation income tax and more than two-thirds as much revenue as the individual income tax.

Economists who have studied personal income in the United States have been surprised to discover that the degree of family income inequality has changed very little since 1950 (Table 8.1). A

TABLE 8.1
Percentage Share of Aggregate Money Income Received by Each Fifth of Families and Unrelated Individuals, Ranked by Income, Selected Years, 1950–1971[a].

Income rank	1950	1960	1970	1971
Families				
Lowest fifth	4.5	4.9	5.5	5.5
Second fifth	12.0	12.0	12.0	11.9
Third fifth	17.4	17.6	17.4	17.4
Fourth fifth	23.5	23.6	23.5	23.7
Highest fifth	42.6	42.0	41.6	41.6
Top 5 per cent	17.0	16.8	14.4	n.a.
Unrelated individuals				
Lowest fifth	2.3	2.6	3.3	3.4
Second fifth	7.0	7.1	7.9	8.1
Third fifth	13.8	13.6	13.8	13.9
Fourth fifth	26.5	25.7	24.5	24.2
Highest fifth	50.4	50.9	50.5	50.4
Top 5 per cent	19.3	20.0	20.5	20.6

Source: U.S. Bureau of the Census, *Current Population Reports*, Series P-60, No. 85, "Money Income in 1971 of Families and Persons in the United States" (1972), Table 14.
n.a. Not available.
[a]Money income includes earnings, transfer payments, and income from property, but excludes income from the sale of capital assets.

fairer and more equal distribution of net purchasing power requires further reforms in the welfare and social security systems.

One step has already been taken in this direction. In the Social Security amendments of 1972 Congress enacted a guaranteed annual income for the elderly and disabled. Under these amendments public assistance for the aged, blind, and disabled was assumed by the federal government in 1974 and renamed the Supplemental Security Income program. The SSI program is administered by the Social Security Administration but is financed by general Treasury revenues instead of payroll taxes. When the new program first went into effect it provided a guaranteed minimum income of $130 a month or $1,560 a year to an eligible individual and $195 a month or $2,340 to a married couple. Later, payments were increased systematically to compensate for inflation. Though SSI payments are not yet sufficient to lift beneficiaries over the official poverty line unless they received additional income from other sources, real benefits will probably be raised and the war on poverty will eventually be over for the aged, blind, and disabled.

The Four-Day Work Week

In the 1930s the philosopher Bertrand Russell proposed a policy of leisure growth rather than commodity growth and viewed the unemployment question in terms of the distribution of leisure:

Suppose that, at a given moment, a certain number of people are engaged in the manufacture of pins. They make as many pins as the world needs, working (say) eight hours a day. Someone makes an invention by which the same number of men can make twice as many pins as before. But the world does not need twice as many pins. Pins are already so cheap that hardly any more will be bought at a lower price. In a sensible world, everybody concerned in the manufacture of pins would take to working four hours instead of eight, and everything else would go on as before. But in the actual world this would be thought demoralizing. The men still work eight hours, there are too many pins, some employers go bankrupt, and half the men previously concerned in making pins are thrown out of work. There is, in the end, just as much leisure as on the other plan, but

*half the men are totally idle while half are still overworked. In this
way it is insured that the unavoidable leisure shall cause misery all
round instead of being a universal source of happiness. Can
anything more insane be imagined?*[2]

In 1972 school officials in Unity, Maine, conducted an 18-week
experiment with a four-day class week. The experiment showed a
gain in student achievement and savings of $18,794 in bus, food,
and upkeep costs. It also permitted teacher training in in-
dividualized instruction on Friday morning.

The four-day work week has long been a goal of organized
labor. In 1973, Howard Coughlin, president of the AFL-CIO Office
and Professional Employees International Union, predicted that
the four-day week is inevitable. "It will occur not because I say so;
but simply because it offers the most practical solution to the con-
glomerate of social and economic problems that grow worse as our
technology grows better. Such diverse problems as unemployment,
bottlenecks in service fields, conversion to a peacetime economy,
traffic jams, equipment down-time, the quality of life — all can be
ameliorated by conversions to the four-day work week."

Coughlin's plan is to use three work shifts over a six-day week,
with each shift on the job four days. Employees will work nine
hours a day for the first three days and eight hours the fourth. Such
a schedule, he believes, allows more leisure time for workers and
greater utilization of the employer's facilities with lower costs
because of little or no overtime work. "We are convinced that the
four-day work week is the next big step forward in white-collar
and professional labor relations and that we will see it go into
effect in this decade."

Not everyone is enamored with this kind of four-day work
week. Many state laws would have to be changed to permit women
to work longer hours. In those industries that customarily operate
three or more shifts per day it would not be possible to go to a
longer work day without a chaotic restructuring of work schedules
that might create more confusion than benefits. Longer working
hours in some industries, moreover, would not be consistent with
increased safety and productivity.

Dr. Austin Henschel, a consultant of the National Institute of
Occupational Safety, has noted that most people reach an efficiency peak during the third hour of the morning and the third hour of
the afternoon. After that, efficiency declines as much as 25 to 30

per cent. Dr. Henschel also notes the correlation between increased strain and safety.

It is now almost 40 years since the five-day, 40-hour work week became "standard." Though I am not optimistic about the chances of a four-day work week quickly becoming a standard, I do think that Congress should pass a law which allows everyone that is willing to accept a proportionate cut in weekly pay the right to work only four days per week, without discrimination in promotional opportunities, retirement, and other benefits such as health and unemployment insurance.

If part-time employees were not denied fringe benefits, as is often the case, older employees might take unscheduled vacations or in other ways share their jobs with younger workers during economic recessions and periods with prolonged layoffs.

The Tyranny of a Goods-Oriented Society

Though some goods are necessary to sustain life, in a larger sense an overemphasis upon those things which are associated with material well-being can master and even improverish human beings. Some people become so involved in the acquisition and care of goods, for example, as to actually be enslaved by their own possessions.

Power and prestige are usually associated with higher levels of income and consumption. In striving to become economically, socially, or politically successful, many Americans may feel impelled to earn more money and consume a great many things that provide little or no satisfaction except as being representative of high social status.

In a predominantly free-enterprise economy characterized by a rapid rate of economic growth, many people have been able to acquire social status by being industrious and working long hours. If it is true, however, that the United States is already adjusting to a steady state economy, the opportunities for obtaining fame and fortune by working hard may not be nearly as favorable in the future as in the past two centuries. Stiff inheritance taxes and the steep upward rise in property taxes that finance education and services provided by local government, moreover, have made it far more difficult and costly for families that have acquired wealth to hang on to their property and maintain social status by engaging in a life of conspicuous consumption.

Under these adverse circumstances, high social status is becoming less closely identified with income and consumption. Such a blurring of the relation between income and status would seem particularly likely in a world where janitors, coal miners, and garbage collectors may obtain union contracts which put them on a financial par with teachers and white-collar professionals. If income ceases to be a fairly reliable measure of social status, then the stage might well be set for an even more dramatic change in public attitude about work and leisure.

Professors Harrod and Linder suggest that goods are an imperfect substitute for time in consumption, and that an increasing scarcity of time for servicing and maintaining consumption goods might eventually lead to a voluntary consumption maximum. Sweden, in many respects, is probably the closest of all the more industrialized nations to a steady state economy in which almost all workers are relatively affluent. Absenteeism at Volvo's Torslanda plant is reported to be about 18 per cent. To cope with absenteeism, 800 extra workers must be kept on the payroll. As one worker expressed it, the common attitude among workers is: "They live for the day. They know life is so short. People have so many things. They want to enjoy these things."

In the harried American "leisure class," it becomes increasingly clear that too little time — for love, for wise decisions, for reading good books, for friendship, for exercise, for excellence in the arts, for health care, for raising children, for relaxation, for appreciating history, for conservation of cultural artifacts, for the repair and improvement of spiritual well-being, for understanding public issues, and for appreciating natural and social environments — is a serious problem which may justify public intervention in behalf of less work, more leisure, cultural enrichment, and a slower growth in economic activity.

In *The New Industrial State*, Professor Galbraith has suggested:

> *The employed person should be accorded a much wider set of options than at present as between work and goods on the one hand*

and leisure on the other. The way should be opened for the individual who wishes to satisfy his needs for food, clothing and simple houseroom with ten or twenty hours of labor a week to do so. We should look with interest and hopefully with admiration on inventive use of the remaining time.[3]

But the options for leisure, Galbraith believes, should not be confined to the work week, since this is a poor unit for organizing leisure time. He notes that it has long been customary for persons with high social, educational, or financial position to plan their holidays, travel, and tasks in terms of months and years rather than days and weeks. He also suggests that all individuals, in return for lower annual pay, should have such options as a shorter work week, extended leaves of absence, and several months of paid vacation.

Flexible working hours, now a way of life in West Germany and the Scandinavian countries and becoming widespread in Canada, are a step in this direction. Occidental Life Insurance of California has recently allowed its workers to choose individual starting times between 7 and 9 a.m. in quarter-hour increments. It has led to improved employee morale and is also helping to reduce traffic congestion. Occidental's vice president in charge of personnel, Robert Condon, has said that "In some areas there has been greater productivity, and there have been no reports of a decline in productivity. Tardiness has almost disappeared."[4]

Senator Jacob Javits has pointed out that absenteeism on grounds of illness increased at an average annual rate of 2.8 per cent between 1957 and 1972. A 1973 Gallup poll showed that the number of workers that were satisfied with their jobs had declined by 10 per cent since the same question was asked in 1960. Younger workers under the age of 30, moreover, were substantially more dissatisfied with their jobs than older workers.

Greater freedom in the number of hours worked per week as well as the time of work might help to reduce worker dissatisfaction and increase labor productivity, particularly among younger workers who are not locked into expensive lifestyles or saddled with the responsibility of educating more than one or two children.

If every worker was guaranteed the right to work no more than a regular four-day week, if they so desired, a 32-hour work week might become a status symbol that unions and the general population would accept as a goal, even if it meant some sacrifice of real take-home pay.

Interesting and Meaningful Work

A 15-year study for the U.S. Department of Health, Education and Welfare has shown that the greatest single factor in aging is the extent to which a person's job is satisfying.[5] Job satisfaction was found to have a far greater effect on life span than diet, exercise, medical care, and genetic inheritance.

In 1972 General Motors was struck for 174 days at its new highly automated Lordstown Plant in Ohio, where the average worker's age was under 25. The issue was not pay or financial benefits but "dehumanized" working conditions. Though the spread of what *Business Week* has labeled "the Lordstown syndrome" has been reduced to some extent by rising unemployment, a younger and more highly educated labor force may eventually bring about reforms that will make work more interesting and meaningful.

In a 1974 survey of young people between 16 and 25, a Yankelovich poll found that young blue-collar workers rated job security (with a 51 per cent response) 15 percentage points below interesting work as a job criterion. Out of a list of 35 possible criteria, making a lot of money ranked among the bottom 10.

In the early 1970s Motorola set up a major operation in which each assembly worker puts together and tests an entire product. The result was a "turned-on group of individuals who enjoy their work and have a great deal of pride in their product." Motorola found that individual assembly requires 25 per cent more workers, as well as a more detailed training program, but the greater cost is nearly offset by higher productivity, the need for less inspection, and by lower repair costs.

It has been suggested that employers should place the same emphasis on the design of work as the physical plant design:

> In the long-range interests of the enterprise, they should be as innovative and concerned about the needs and feelings of the workers as they are with their profits. A broad spectrum of experiments

should include: basic changes in the production process; improving health and safety conditions; more attractive surroundings; reduction of special privileges and greater equity in amenities; consideration of more flexible work schedules; use of work teams; and more decentralized decision-making. New designs in the work place can more nearly satisfy the needs of workers while they enhance overall vitality of the organization.[6]

Before leaving the U.S. Department of Health, Education and Welfare Elliot Richardson released a report on *Work in America*, which also stressed the need to upgrade job satisfaction. "The design of jobs," according to Richardson, "appears to be lagging markedly behind the enormous gains in educational attainments of the work force, and the elevation in credentials required of the worker has not been accompanied by an elevation in the content of work. If anything, it is more routinized and bureaucratized, leaving less to the imagination and control of the worker."[7]

In a General Foods pet food plant at Topeka, Kansas, blue-collar workers are now allowed to perform every major job in the plant, from unloading with a forklift truck to making complex tests in the quality control laboratory. While it may never be economical to eliminate completely the drudgery associated with assembly lines, it may still be possible in many instances to redesign work to make it more challenging and also permit enough variations to at least make employment less boring as well as a more enjoyable means to other ends.

Several Scandinavian countries seem to be more advanced than the United States in redesigning jobs and conducting experiments to make work more challenging and satisfying for workers. Volvo has replaced its assembly line with a hexagonal plant in which teams of production workers can set their own pace and get some variety in their jobs.[8] Declines in absenteeism and costly labor turnover are two immediate company benefits.

Serious consideration should also be given to the possibility of creating national job exchanges to assist ordinary workers who are locked into company pension systems to trade houses, jobs, and perhaps even salaries from, for example, three months to one full year. In those industries and professions where work is either dull or rather routine, an opportunity for periodical changes in locations and surroundings might do much to relieve boredom and increase employees' job satisfaction.

Early Retirement

It has often been assumed that employers' and employees' interests are best served by establishing pension plans that put a high premium on staying with one firm. This philosophy, according to the American Assembly in its report on the changing world of work, "is incompatible with the need for flexibility, mobility, and individual freedom in our society. Nor does it serve the best interests of the firm. In too many enterprises, executives, middle managers, and rank and file workers have left the firm mentally but will not leave physically until they retire."[9]

Private retirement systems now cover nearly half the private work force, more than double the proportion for 1950. However, more than half of all the workers covered by such plans received few, if any, benefits before the enactment of a new law governing private pension systems in 1974. Half the American labor force, in addition, is without any private pension plan coverage.

Bankers Trust Company of New York has reported that since the 1960s a marked trend has developed toward company policies permitting retirement at the age of 55. A similar study of some 180 corporations by social scientists at the University of Oregon has found that at least half of all employees retire before the mandatory age, often with reduced benefits. Two-thirds of the companies surveyed allowed retirement at age 55. Since Chrysler Corporation adopted its now famous "30 and out" retirement scheme in 1966, more than 60 per cent of all its workers have been retiring before age 60.

When the social security retirement system was first revamped to permit workers to retire before 65, only a handful took advantage of the change. By 1973, however, more than half the workers on social security rolls were retiring before they reached 65, even with lower benefits. In 1953, 87.9 per cent of men aged 55 - 64 were in the labor force; by 1973 this figure had dropped almost 10 percentage points to 78.3 per cent.

These trends suggest that the "early retirement ethic" has not only captured the minds and imaginations of company executives and trade unionists, but the average worker as well. The statistics also show that we still have a long way to go before the dream of an early retirement on a comfortable income can become a reality for nearly all workers that might aspire in that direction.

Although inflation may have dealt a rather severe blow to some plans for early retirement, I believe that the trend toward early retirement will resume and be even more popular as our population approaches a steady state equilibrium. A steady state population will be about ten years older, on the average, than the present population. The population structure, moreover, will be less triangular and more rectangular up to about age 55. Because the age pyramid will no longer be roughly congruent with what Herman Daly has called the "pyramid of authority in hierarchical organizations,"[10] there will be relatively fewer opportunities for rapid promotion to challenging positions and perhaps a greater tendency at middle management levels to seek personal achievement and success outside formal employment. Assuming a reasonable success in finding satisfaction in other areas, the tendency toward early retirement is likely to increase even more.

Pension Reform

Since the 1965 presidential study popularly known as the "Cabinet Committee Report," there have been extended congressional hearings and a continuing public debate over private pension reform. The three main issues are vesting, funding, and insuring pension plans.

Vesting means the conferring or giving to an individual employee the right to a future receipt. If vesting occurs before retirement, the rights to benefits will not be forfeited by termination of the employment through which they were earned. Vesting of pension rights before an individual's retirement was not required by law or regulation until 1974.

The 1974 law requires employers with pension plans to adopt one of three vesting options. Under the *gradual vesting option*, each participant is vested for at least 25 per cent of his or her accrued benefit from the employer's contributions after five years of service. An additional 5 per cent must be vested for each of the next five years of service, and an additional 10 per cent for each succeeding year. Under this option workers are entitled to 100 per cent of their pension rights after 15 years with a company.

A second option provides employees with full pension rights after 10 years' service. Under the third option, *the rule of 45*, a worker is entitled to at least 50 per cent vesting when the sum of his years of service and age total 45. Vesting then increases by 10 per cent for each additional year. The rule of 45 applies only after an initial five-year period of service, but full vesting is assured after fifteen years of employment regardless of age.

Workers now have the right to be admitted to a plan when they reach age 25 or have one year of service, whichever is later. Credit of up to three years is allowed for service before age 25, once the worker qualifies for participation.

The pension reform bill requires companies to make contributions to their pension plans in an orderly way by setting aside enough money to cover liabilities for both current payments and the accrual of past credits toward pensions. Companies or unions with pension plans that are not adequately funded have up to forty years to catch up with their accrued pension liabilities.

To protect workers with an interest in an underfunded pension plan, the new law requires companies and unions with pension funds to purchase insurance from a new federal agency modeled after the Federal Deposit Insurance Corporation. The new Pension Benefit Guarantee Corporation is empowered to pay as much as $750 monthly in retirement benefits to an individual worker if a company goes out of business or terminates its pension plan, and there are insufficient assets in the pension fund to cover vested benefits.

Workers who do not participate in either company or union pension plans may now contribute up to 15 per cent of their annual income or $1,500 a year, whichever is less, to a special retirement account. Taxes on both the contributions to and the earnings of the account may be deferred until the money is withdrawn at retirement. Self-employed workers are allowed to set aside as much as $7,500 a year in special retirement accounts, with taxes deferred until the benefits are collected upon retirement.

The new law does not require all firms to have pension plans. The very rapid price inflation in the United States since the Vietnam War has seriously eroded the purchasing power and real income status of many retired persons living on fixed private pension benefits. However, the financial burden of inflation has been reduced to some extent by a social security system that is now "indexed" or automatically adjusted upward for changes in the consumer price index. It seems likely that indexing to provide inflation protection will soon be an important collective bargaining issue in most private, state, and local government retirement systems.

Young people are often not as concerned about pension benefits as older workers. Reasonably generous pension plans with adequate vesting and suitable provisions for early retirement could be in the best interest of nearly everyone, however, by opening up jobs for young men and women who might otherwise be unemployed or forced to accept inferior jobs. A better, more comprehensive system of public and private pension benefits that enables all workers to retire on comfortable incomes at age 55, if they desire, could, I believe, be an important instrument for helping to achieve a condition of reasonably full employment in the remainder of this decade.

To achieve this goal the minimum benefits currently available under social security, I believe, should be raised to a level which will permit anyone 55 or over who has been in the system at least ten years to retire and receive enough income so that the retiree and his or her spouse will not fall below the official poverty line.

Teachers, college professors, and some other professionals might find considerable merit in pension plans that actually force some early retirements. In exchange for a pension system that permits early retirement with comfortable incomes, educators might be required to allow the question of tenure, or continuing appointments, to be reopened, for example, every five years after a teacher reaches age 50. At that age, a teacher should not be forced to retire unless evidence can be presented to show that he or she is doing an inferior job. After the age of 55, however, it might be argued that only those teachers who are average or above average should be allowed to continue in their chosen profession.

If a modified tenure system along these lines were coupled with a reasonably generous retirement system, it would provide a humane solution to the fairly common problem of misfit teachers and professors who have either become lazy or lost their sense of rapport with students or with the subject matter. Knowing that the question of tenure will eventually be reopened, teachers would have greater incentives either to keep up with their disciplines and remain successful, or to switch to alternate careers.

Actual retirement should often be preceded by a period of semi-retirement in which the worker takes time off to prepare for a life with greater leisure. A four-day work week could be an important instrument for helping some people to adjust to retirement.

Extra leisure is not always a blessing. As some critics have pointed out, a four-day week could give some workers more leisure than they can handle. A revamped educational system might make leisure more worthwhile. In thinking ahead to future economic possibilities, John Maynard Keynes remarked that:

> for the first time since his creation man will be faced with his . . . permanent problem — how to use his freedom from pressing economic cares, how to occupy the leisure which science and compound interest will have won for him, to live wisely and agreeably and well.

This, in the final analysis, may very well be the most significant challenge of American society in the next 100 years.

Notes

1. For a historical overview of work and leisure in the United States and other countries see Juanita M. Kreps, *Lifetime Allocation of Work and Income* (Durham, N.C.: Duke University Press, 1971).

2. Bertrand Russell, *In Praise of Idleness and Other Essays* (London: George Allen and Unwin, 1935), pp. 16 - 17.

3. John Kenneth Galbraith, *The New Industrial State* (Boston: Houghton Mifflin, 1967), pp. 365 - 367.

4. Janice Neipert Hedges, "New Patterns for Working Time," *Monthly Labor Review* (February 1973), pp. 3 - 8.

5. For perhaps the best overview of this subject see Sar A. Levitan and William B. Johnston, *Work Is Here to Stay, Alas* (Salt Lake City: Olympus, 1973).

6. "The Changing World of Work," Report of the Forty-third American Assembly (November 1 - 4, 1973), p. 5.

7. *Work in America* (Cambridge: MIT Press, 1973).

8. Agis Salpukas, "Swedish Auto Plant Drops Assembly Line," *The New York Times* (November 12, 1974), p. 31.

9. "The Changing World of Work," op. cit.

10. Herman Daly, *Toward a Steady-State Economy* (San Francisco: Freeman, 1973), p. 22.

chapter 9

EDUCATION

In 1863, German economist Heinrich von Thunen noted that a moral timidity seems to keep authors and everybody else from thinking about what a man costs and the amount of capital that is invested in him. The human being is considered so superior to other animals and inanimate objects that it would seem a disgrace to involve him in considerations of this kind. Adam Smith, however, was not adverse to drawing an analogy between machines and human capital:

> When any expensive machine is erected, the extraordinary work to be performed by it before it is worn out, it must be expected, will replace the capital laid out upon it, with at least the ordinary profits. A man educated at the expense of much labor and time to any of those employments which require extraordinary dexterity and skill, may be compared to one of those expensive machines. The work which he learns to perform, it must be expected, over and above the usual wages of common labor, will replace to him the whole expense of his education, with at least the ordinary profits of an equally valuable capital. It must do this too, in a reasonable time, regard being had to the very uncertain duration of human life, in the same manner as to the more certain duration of the machine.[1]

Until about the mid-1950s economists still tended to neglect the study of human wealth. T. W. Schultz, then chairman of the Department of Economics at the University of Chicago, suggested that:

> The answer is that we cannot easily rise above our values and beliefs; we are strongly inhibited from looking upon men as an investment, except in slavery, and this we abhor. . . . Our political and legal institutions have been shaped to keep men free from bondage. . . . Thus it is understandable why a study of man, treating him as if he were wealth, runs counter to deeply held values, for it would

seem to reduce him once again to a material component, to something akin to property, and that would be wrong.[2]

Such economists as Kuznets, Abramovitz, Kendrick, and Solow, however, have shown that a large part of the secular increase in measured national income, perhaps as much as 50 per cent, can not be accounted for by increases in such conventional factors of production as land, manhours of work input, and investment in commercial facilities and industrial plant and equipment. This "mystery," and the encouragement of Professor Schultz, has made it quite fashionable for younger economists to study the financial returns that have been associated with different amounts of education.

In this chapter I will first examine some of the financial benefits of education, the relationship between education and economic growth, and the extent to which education can be substituted for other resources. The remaining sections consider such problems as sex education and how to make education more valuable for its own sake.

Much of the pleasure as well as many of the cultural benefits to be expected from a liberal education are intimately related to the use of leisure time for reading. Many kinds of reading materials are now in danger of being priced out of existence. In the concluding section we will examine the survival of reading from an ecological perspective.

The Returns to Education

The pecuniary returns of education, in some instances, have been nothing short of spectacular. The mean income of American males, aged 25 and over with four or more years of college was 54 per cent greater than the income of high school graduates in 1946, 52 per cent greater in 1957, 53 per cent greater in 1968, and 55 per cent greater in 1972. These and other data are consistent with the hypothesis that average income, at any given time, is roughly proportional to educational attainment; that is, a person with a high school education can expect, on the average, to receive nearly half again as much income as a person with only eight years of schooling, while a person with a college education can expect to obtain, on the average, twice as much income.

Assume for a moment that these differences in income measure improvements in the quality of the work force that can be attributed to education. One could still postulate an end to economic progress on the grounds that the costs of higher education are a rapidly increasing function of the number of years of schooling, and that at some point the extra costs of increased schooling will be greater than the economic benefits. By *costs*, an economist usually means direct educational outlays for schools, books, and teachers plus foregone earnings that could have been obtained by the student if he or she had sought employment rather than remained in school.

Schultz has estimated that the economic cost of a year of elementary education was $280 in 1956; that a year of high school cost $1,420, and that a year of undergraduate college education cost $3,300. The rapid increase in costs led him to postulate that "the differences in earnings between those who complete elementary schooling and those who acquire more schooling, although they are large in absolute amounts and still imply a favorable return on the additional investment, are not large enough to produce on the much larger costs a rate equal to the high rate realized on what is invested upon completion of the elementary grades."[3]

Data on occupation and median earnings of males age 25 to 64 compiled from the 1960 census indicate that most persons with one to three years of college do not earn significantly higher incomes than those with only four years of high school, when occupations are the same. Persons with some college education have higher average earnings than high school graduates, but only because they seem to be more successful at becoming managers and effecting entry into better paying occupations. About a quarter of those persons with a college degree, moreover, do not earn more income than an average high school graduate without college training.

Both the pecuniary returns and employment opportunities for younger men with college educations have noticeably declined in recent years. In 1967 the mean difference in income for men 25 to 34 years old with only four years of college and those with twelve years of school and no college education was estimated by the U.S. Census to equal $2,281 per year. By 1970 this difference had increased to $2,756. It has since declined, however, to $2,102 in 1972.

In 1949 Professor Seymour Harris, in *The Market for College Graduates*, predicted an oversupply of persons with bachelors' degrees. The sharp decline in the relative income status of younger men with only four years of college education would strongly suggest that Professor Harris's prediction may have simply been published about twenty years too soon.

The image of education as a factor of production has also been tarnished somewhat in recent years. More detailed evidence shows tremendous variation in the returns for different occupational classes with the same education. High rates of return in some professions, such as medicine, may result from restrictions on the number of students admitted to medical schools, which have enabled doctors to charge monopoly prices for their services, rather than improvements in labor productivity.

Recognizing that the direct benefits from a college education might be small or even negative in some instances if it encourages a student to become interested in the humanities and enter a low-paying profession, some economists have emphasized the possibility of spillover benefits to the public or economy as a whole. It has become increasingly clear, however, that rates of technological change by country[4] and by industry[5] do not seem to be correlated with educational investment.

Expenditures per pupil enrolled in elementary and secondary education have historically been significantly greater in Scotland than in England. The proportion of Scottish youth obtaining a university education has for many years been nearly double that of England and Wales. The emphasis on higher education would appear quite justified because the incomes of Scottish professionals have also been greater. It turns out, however, that the higher incomes are largely caused by the exporting of intellectuals to England and other areas.

Although the benefits to the rest of the world may have been substantial, it is doubtful that the spillover effect has benefited Scotland. Until the recent discovery of North Sea oil the Scottish economy generally remained backward — growth was retarded, and average Scottish wages and salaries remained lower than could be obtained by migrating to England.

The example of England and Scotland might be considered unique, yet a close parallel can be found in the United States. In 1950, Utah had the largest percentage of college-educated adults and the next to the smallest percentage of functional illiterates, yet it ranked in the lower half of all states in per capita income.Education, it would seem, can be a rather poor substitute for a dearth of other resources.

Education and Other Resources

In the United States — with its heretofore abundant supplies of iron ore and large deposits of fossil fuels costing one-tenth to one-twentieth of the effort required to produce their caloric equivalent in grain — it is not necessary to operate a tractor many hundreds of hours per year to reduce the cost of a horsepower of work output to less than a nickel per hour. A mature adult capable, on the average, of delivering a tenth of a horsepower of sustained effort and earning $2 per hour would, by way of contrast, cost four hundred times as much.

The gap between what a man is worth in terms of repetitive working effects and what he is paid is both large and significant. Among other things, it helps to explain the dramatic substitution of inanimate energy for animal power, a rise of almost chronic unemployment within the young and unskilled labor force, and a renewed interest in education and training.

The remarkable substitution of mechanical horses for human beings is especially impressive considering the technical efficiencies involved. A healthy person or work animal can convert about 35 per cent of the food energy it consumes into work, which is more energy-efficient than the gasoline engine that converts less than 25 per cent of the fuel it consumes into work, and compares favorably with the diesel engine. The remarkable efficiency of the human being suggests that the substitution of inanimate energy for animal power must be caused by other factors than technical efficiency, such as the use of lower-priced energy and the weight advantage of inanimate prime mover.

Work animals are, on a pound for pound basis, about as energy-intensive as aluminum. Though steel is much less energy-intensive than aluminum, the most important savings of energy in the fabrication of mechanical horses stem from the fact that a one-horsepower tractor weighs only about a tenth as much as a live draft animal. As one moves from farm tractors to airplane engines, the savings in weight are truly phenomenal.

Though formal education may have been an aid in helping inventors develop prime movers that can convert energy into work with nearly the same technical efficiency as the human being, it is doubtful whether these developments would have proceeded very far without materials which could be fabricated into mechanical horsepower at a fraction of the energy required to raise an equivalent amount of animal power or without an energy source requiring less effort to produce than carbohydrate food energy.

Even today, with the emphasis on chemistry and electronics, it is difficult to find processes and machines that require operators and repairmen with a college education. James Bright has found that automation does not necessarily result in higher work force skills and may even tend to require less operator skill after certain levels of mechanization are achieved.[6]

Computer programming originally required the services of a competent mathematician. With the development of Fortran and other simple languages, the rudiments of programming can be taught the year a student is first acquainted with the new elementary school math.

Though simplified computer language in no way disparages the importance of a good elementary and secondary education, it does illustrate that most economic progress depends on inventions and production processes that are only partly understood by workers and in some cases may not even be fully understood by their creators or discoverers.

The general ignorance about chemical and mechanical processes is vividly illustrated by the tremendous amount of experimentation involved in perfecting missiles and aircraft. In 1953 Hollis B. Chenery noted that the complete analysis of the chemical change involved in making cement had not been worked out and that a similar condition existed for most mechanical operations in which the laws of mechanics limit the design of machines but do not describe their function completely. If everyone had to understand the laws of thermodynamics to drive an automobile, traffic congestion would probably not be a problem.

In the United States, with its large deposits of fossil fuels and surplus of agricultural products which can be exported to the rest of the world, it has been easy to neglect and even minimize the importance of nonhuman resources. Having observed employment in agriculture and mining decline from over 50 per cent of the employed labor force to less than 5 per cent in about 100 years, economists have tended to ignore natural resources and turned to intangible explanations of economic growth. Because most economists are teachers, they have understandably emphasized the importance of education as a source of such growth.

Although a teacher may be able to gain some satisfaction from believing that all we have we owe to formal education, some flaws in this attitude are apparent. One of the most serious dangers in overinflating our own egos about the economic importance of education is that underdeveloped countries will be advised to compensate for a lack of other resources with an overemphasis on higher education. This approach to economic development is likely to be extremely disappointing. Higher education is expensive, even in poor countries. Preparing people for teaching and other job opportunities that do not exist is not only bad economy but could lead to a great deal of frustration and disillusionment.

In stressing the possibility of diminishing and even negative returns to investment in education, I do not mean to imply that education is unimportant or that it is something an ambitious person can afford to be without. The trend toward more general, lengthy, and, I hope, better education is, without doubt, one of the most impressive features of a progressive economy. But the college graduate's best protection against possible disappointment will probably continue to be the intangible values that have inspired countless individuals to pursue a higher education without regard for pecuniary returns. If the economic benefits from a college degree are minimized, then higher education must be a superior consumption good, at least for some people.

Such studies as the Carnegie Commission report *A Degree and What Else?* suggest that higher education may be valuable for its own sake. College graduates, for example, appear to have happier marriages and are less likely to go through the traumas of divorce. Marital success may be partly the result of the fact that college-educated persons tend to marry later, are more mature, and in a better position to know their own values and goals in life. Marital success may also be related in part to the fact that persons with college educations earn higher average incomes.

Because the economic advantages to be expected from a college education are increasingly uncertain, educators might find it prudent to reorient the college curriculum in ways that make it a little less vocational and more valuable for its own sake. If life expectancy eventually increases to 75 years and if the average worker retires after thirty years or less of full-time employment, the average high school graduate can look forward to almost as many years outside the labor force as spent on the job. Not only higher education, it seems to me, but education at all levels could help to make those years more rewarding and worthwhile.

In the remainder of this chapter I will mention a few areas in which changes either are taking place at the present time or might take place in the future which will enable people to adjust better to a steady state economy.

Sex Education

Progress in achieving zero population growth has been impeded to a considerable extent by the reluctance of many parents, communities, and school systems to provide young people with adequate sex education. A major nationwide survey in 1974 shows that youths endorse the principle of sexual freedom more today than was the case in the 1960s, at the time of the so-called "sexual revolution." The survey also showed that the revolution is spreading from college campuses to young blue-collar workers and other working high school graduates, plus dropouts and graduates who stay at home.

Though much has been written about the need for sex education we still have a long way to go if all babies are wanted and planned for. A 1971 study found that nearly half of all unmarried women had sexual intercourse by age 19. Three out of ten teenage American girls who have had premarital intercourse, moreover, have become pregnant. Unwanted babies are not confined to just the "poorer" segments of society. Nor are they likely to simply disappear because of the "overall sophistication" of today's youth compared to previous generations.

The birth rate among adolescents went up 250 per cent in the twenty-three years before 1970 according to the Commission on Population Growth and the American Future. In 1972, induced abortions performed on girls between the ages of 10 and 19 accounted for over one-third of those done in upper New York State.

The need for more sex education is not limited to teenagers. A national fertility study conducted in 1970 found that despite advances in birth control techniques that have sharply lowered the nation's birth rate, more than a third of the married women who practiced birth control over a five-year period became pregnant anyway. The problem, in many instances, was the use of ineffective techniques. The study found that the education of the wife did not seem to be a significant factor in the failure rate. Nearly 25 per cent of all pregnancies in the United States in 1974 are estimated to have been terminated by abortion.

A common objection to sex education and especially the provision of contraceptive devices to teenagers is the parental fear of increased promiscuity and a further breakdown of the American family. Such fears have been bolstered to some extent by the behavior of many celebrities.

In 1971 more than three times as many Hollywood celebrities obtained divorces as became married. A major factor was the growing number of people who simply live together rather than march to the altar only to pay divorce attorney fees a few years later. Alimony and lawyer fees were not the only savings to be expected from a practice of living together without the benefit of marriage. In the Tax Reform Act of 1969 Congress unwittingly placed a heavy burden on married working couples. Congress's aim was to quiet the complaints of single taxpayers who had long protested about the tax advantages married couples have in filing joint returns. The new tax law, however, turned out to favor working couples who live together without the benefit of matrimony.

Though living together has become quite fashionable on some campuses and will no doubt spread to other segments of society, I believe that sociologists will be able to detect a major revival of interest in marriage as an institution, even in California, long before the end of this century. Persons that do marry, or at least stay together, seem to be happier, take better care of themselves, and also tend to live longer.

Many goods that are produced and consumed in the home have some of the characteristics of a public good that can be expected to yield benefits proportional to the number of persons in the household. Though two adults may not be able to live as cheaply as one, living together is cheaper than maintaining two separate households, provided they have similar values. It seems likely, therefore, that most couples who live together for an extended time will discover that they are better off and that for the sake of the children or for the prospect of better social insurance benefits will eventually decide that they ought to get married. The new sexual freedom, far from destroying family life, will in the end, I believe, lead to fewer mistakes of an enduring nature, stronger marriages, and a significantly lower divorce rate.

About 25 per cent of the marriages of the mid-1970s are remarriages. Remarriages seem to be as successful, if not more successful, on the average, than first marriages. A high divorce rate, in other words, doesn't mean that more people are discovering that they prefer to live alone or are unwilling to try to compensate for past mistakes and make the institution of marriage work for them.

A good program in sex education would emphasize the need for compatible value systems as well as the compromises and adjustments that may be necessary to make a marriage successful. It might also go a long way toward dispelling such myths as the idea that the best way either to get married or to save a rocky marriage is to have a baby. The steady state economy, in my view, will be something less than ideal if all babies are not wanted and planned for by both parents.

D. H. Robertson, a distinguished British economist, once asked the illuminating question: What is it that economists economize? His answer was "love, the scarcest and most precious of all resources."

Alternative Lifestyles

The economist Arthur Cordell has noted:

Because different people are increasingly viewing reality with a different mind set they are coming to different conclusions. Their perceptions are changing.

As Gail Steward notes in a recent paper the change in perception can have a profound impact on the individual. She notes that for people who experience the shift in perception it is like "going through the looking glass," or "turning the world inside out." It constitutes almost a visual shift which embraces the whole environment including oneself. This may be an exhilarating or a frightening experience, since much that was formerly considered trivial may

assume great importance. People are critically looking at
themselves, their behavior patterns, attitudes and, life-styles. New
insights relating to human behavior are emerging . . . . Old truths are
questioned and many are found to be false; their widespread accep-
tance was useful so that the system could function. Continued accep-
tance is no longer tenable, however, since a wide variety of un-
desirable consequences both to the individual and to society are
now beginning to be perceived.

Thus value sets are changing in very profound ways. Even to say
that bigger is no longer better implies a change since this view would
have gone unquestioned by most even a decade ago.[7]

Junior colleges have always emphasized the value of practical
knowledge. In the future I expect many colleges and universities
will also give college credit for such mundane subjects as consumer economics, automobile mechanics, electric wiring, plumbing, and home repairs — not with a view to making persons
professionally competent in these areas, but to better prepare
students to manage their own personal affairs. The *Wall Street
Journal* has reported that as distasteful as it may be to them, many
communes have been forced to turn to business techniques. Their
survival often depends on being able to cope with the nitty-gritty
problems of finances. Most longer-lived communes in this country
appear to have been the result of stressful times and religious
persecutions. Though I do not believe that a steady state economy
in an affluent country like the United States will be characterized
by radically new or substantially different lifestyles, it does seem
to me that communal ventures are worthy of greater study as well
as greater tolerance than might be suggested by a recent Supreme
Court decision which upheld the authority of a Long Island village
to bar six unrelated college students from sharing a rented one-
family house. Ron Roberts, who has provided a fairly balanced
picture of *The New Communes*, concludes that:

The next decade in America is likely to see a great proliferation of
communal ventures founded by "the gentle people." Those of us
with humanistic values should applaud the few groups that manage
to survive the rigors of communal pioneering. For the large majority
of groups that can be expected to fail, one is reminded of the advice
given Charles Nordhoff by a member of the Icarian commune. It was
1878, and the French Icarians were on the brink of defeat after
nearly forty years of utopian socialism in the new world.

"Deal gently and cautiously with Icaria. The man who sees only
the chaotic village and the wooden shoes, and only chronicles those,

will commit a serious error. In that village are buried fortunes, noble hopes, and the aspirations of good and great men."

Even if most current utopists fail in their immediate communal ventures, society will be no worse off than before. If they succeed even partially in their objectives, they could become the vanguard of a new age. It is, therefore, the duty of the concerned social scientist to consider the intellectual premises as well as the internal dynamics of modern utopian movements.[8]

The Doctor of Arts Degree

In a 1971 *Faculty Senate Bulletin*, Chancellor Boyer of the State University of New York noted:

The ancient Chinese utterance, "May you live in interesting times," double-edged in meaning, seems especially appropriate to the contemporary higher education scene. . . . What I've said suggests that forces beyond our immediate, personal control are vigorously pressing in upon our educational system. In response, we must think more creatively about the ultimate benefits which it presumably confers. We must examine with care such basic questions as who should go to college; what should be the curriculum; when, where, and for how long should the student study? Once we raise such questions, however, we must be prepared to act effectively upon the answers and conclusions which follow. Too often we raise the right questions, but are unwilling to accept the novel answers, even when they are clear.

From this year on, all of us in higher education will be living in more interesting times. We face both crisis and opportunity, and the success of the outcome depends very largely on the quality of our response.

In 1968, the U.S. Office of Education was still clinging to the belief that "faculty shortages (in higher education) have existed, do exist, and will continue to exist as far into the future as men can see." To improve the quality of college teaching and to also ease what was feared might be a continuing shortage of qualified academic personnel, the Carnegie Corporation provided grants to ten universities in 1971 to plan a Doctor of Arts Program that would allow graduate students to specialize in college teaching. In retrospect it now seems clear that the D.A. degree could not have been implemented at a less propitious time. The New York State

Education Department has estimated that two-thirds of the private colleges in New York could go out of business in the next fifteen years.

Although the future demand for college teachers was greatly exaggerated at the beginning of this decade, there would still appear to be a need for a new type of doctorate program that encourages persons with a master's degree to continue their education and make learning a lifetime enterprise.

To facilitate this objective, John Heim and I have proposed that major colleges and universities institute a new type of doctor of arts degree which would be automatically awarded only to people over 40 who had completed the equivalent of 90 semester hours of undergraduate and graduate work beyond the bachelor's degree. This degree, not limited to teaching, would not require a dissertation, an oral, or any major field exams that might limit or restrict the number of degrees awarded.

The need for a doctor's degree in "continuing education" can best be appreciated in the context of several studies that show that student performance on various kinds of tests appears to be significantly related to a teacher's level of educational attainment. The empirical evidence, in other words, strongly suggests that efforts to improve the average level of teacher education in a school are not only likely to be more effective in improving student performance but far less costly, other things being equal, than reducing class size or hiring teachers with more experience.

A paradoxical consequence of the recent decline in the demand for new elementary and high school teachers is that relatively more college graduates with bachelor's degrees in education are now going directly after the master's degree. The assumption is that it will eventually be needed anyway, and might be helpful in entering their chosen profession. Though further study might help to make them better teachers, it could also pose a longer run problem since most of these students will no longer have a realistic goal or incentive for continuing their education if they are hired as teachers.

Yet in those areas where knowledge is increasing, or where history is continuing to be made, continuing education is a major vehicle through which breakthroughs on the frontiers of knowledge are transmitted to many people. A reduction in the incentive for continuing education could increase the time lag between discovery and widespread implementation of such breakthroughs. A new type of doctor of arts degree that creates a higher personal goal and provides increased recognition for teachers that continue their education beyond the master's degree would help to solve this problem.

With this degree, junior colleges could better deal with the problem of tenured faculty who have considerable teaching experience but who need refresher courses beyond the master's degree to keep up with developments in their disciplines,. Such people usually could not expect to satisfy all the requirements for an ordinary Ph.D. at a prestigious graduate school.

Our proposed D.A. degree might also be attractive to some corporate and government executives with a master's degree who would like some additional courses to update and round out their education or to better prepare them to enjoy early retirement. A D.A. degree requiring supervised teaching experience, or a Ph.D. requiring a research dissertation, would in most instances be an unsuitable goal for successful administrators who can afford to go back to school.

In a thought-provoking speech, Dr. William McGill, the president of Columbia University, has urged that universities "contemplate fundamental reform generating a more rational relation between occupational ladders and parallel education ladders, thus permitting free movement back and forth between the university and the profession."

Some private colleges are now being forced to close because of declining enrollments; enrollments at public colleges and universities are also expected to decline in a few years. This will tend to create excess capacity that could be put to good use by opening college dorms, campus facilities, and classrooms to older students and perhaps even retired persons who are seeking a more stimulating environment.

In an age of rising concern about the quality of our environment, colleges and universities, which have historically engaged in relatively low-polluting, mental activity, could do a little market innovating. Providing attractive, nonprofessional advanced degrees without research requirements might allow higher education to compete more effectively with expensive automobiles, air travel, motor boats, fancy packaging, and electrical gadgets which add to our environmental woes.

Sesame Street and the success of "informal schooling" in Britain strongly suggest that education can be both effective and fun.

In a country where highly educated people are already in surplus supply, however, and where increased leisure is not only possible but highly desirable if it does not put too much strain on the environment, it makes sense to de-emphasize the pecuniary value of knowledge, make its acquisition less like work, and strive to create a climate that is more favorable to continuing education, not only in the classroom, but also in the home.

The Survival of Reading

Radio and television have increased the productivity of some entertainers and at the same time lowered the demand for skilled musicians and many other performing artists. These inventions, combined with rising costs and differentially low productivity in the publishing industry, also seem to be threatening the survival of other socially desirable activities such as reading.

In the last decade or so more than 160 magazines either failed or were merged into oblivion. In 1972, *Life*, the last of the great picture magazines, slipped away. Its demise is sad not only culturally but also economically, because a great deal of consumer surplus (value that is received but not paid for) can be lost when a unique publishing venture dies. Anyone who has ever sat in a doctor's office, flown on an airplane, been to a library, or grown up in a house with picture magazines will appreciate that almost everyone will be poorer, as a result of the passing of *Life*, whether they were subscribers or not.

To remain in business most publishers of mass circulation magazines must rely upon advertising for about two-thirds of their revenue. Rising costs of paper, printing, and postage, however, have increased the cost of distributing advertising messages in periodicals. With advertising revenue leveling off or being transferred to radio and television, which benefit from free public airways, publishers have had to charge higher subscription prices to cover increased costs. Costs have now reached the point where many periodicals are in danger of being priced out of existence.

To create an environment which is more favorable to the survival of reading and continuing education the environmental movement should shift its emphasis from recycling waste paper to the recirculation of magazines. This would encourage multiple readership, increase the cost-effectiveness of magazine advertising compared to television commercials, and help to conserve natural resources. It would also reduce the cost of publication and lessen the amount of solid wastes that must be disposed of each year. A magazine which may cost a dollar or more to produce has a waste paper value of less than a penny a copy and is simply too valuable to be read only once.

There are numerous ways to promote recirculation. For example, publishers and the U.S. Post Office could encourage two or more families to subscribe to the same magazine. (The price for the magazine would be somewhat higher but not double that for a single suscriber.) The first family would be expected to read the magazine fairly quickly, cross out their own name and address, and redeposit the periodical in a mailbox to be delivered to the next family on the subscription list attached to the publication.

This system for encouraging the recycling of slightly used magazines would have several advantages. It would provide publishers with an objective indicator of multiple readership, which should be helpful in bargaining for the increased advertising revenue necessary to keep magazines financially solvent. (The advertising revenue received by mass circulation magazines reached an all-time peak in 1969 and has since declined.) It would also tend to make magazine publishing more profitable by reducing the cost of paper and printing, which currently accounts for over 40 per cent of the expenses associated with publication. The Post Office, which has been in deep financial trouble for more than a decade could also expect to benefit from recirculation.

Relatively few activities are as important to a free society as reading. In recent testimony before the House Subcommittee on Postal Service, Norman Cousins, then editor and president of *World Magazine*, discussed the financial risks and problems in starting a new magazine. He fears that with rapidly rising postal rates and subscription prices, magazines may cease to serve the traditions of an open society by facilitating the fullest possible circulation of ideas and information. Some magazines will no doubt continue to be born, but if they can only survive by serving the professions, special interests, and other elites, the United States will have lost an important cultural bridge that has helped to inform and bind various socioeconomic and ethnic groups together.

Notes

1. Adam Smith, *Wealth of Nations* (New York: Dutton, 1910), vol. 1. pp. 88 - 89.

2. Theodore W. Schultz, "Investment in Man: An Economist's View," *Social Service Review* (June 1959), pp. 109 - 117.

3. Theodore W. Schultz, *The Economic Value of Education* (New York: Columbia University Press, 1963), p. 59.

4. Edward F. Denison, *Why Growth Rates Differ: Postwar Experience in Nine Western Countries* (Washington: The Brookings Institution, 1967).

5. Joseph Froomkin and A. J. Jaffee, *Technology and the Labor Force* (New York: Praeger, 1968).

6. James Bright, "Does Automation Raise Skill Requirements?" *Harvard Business Review* (July 1958), pp. 85 - 87.

7. Arthur J. Cordell, "The Socio-Economics of Technological Progress," a paper prepared for the Faculty of Science Lecture Series on the Human Environment — Problems and Prospects, Carleton University (February 23, 1972), pp. 11 - 12. (Gail Steward, "Gone Today and Here Tomorrow," *Public Policy Concern*, Ottawa, October 1971.)

8. Ron Roberts, *The New Communes* (Englewood Cliffs, N. J.: Prentice-Hall, 1971), p. x. (Charles Nordhoff, *The Communistic Societies of the United States,* New York: Harper and Brothers, 1875, p. 339.)

PART FOUR

Zero Growth and
the World Economy

chapter 10

THE MALTHUSIAN SPECTRE

The population of the world is now increasing at an average annual rate of almost 2 per cent. In the United States and many other industrialized nations the growth rates are less than 1 per cent per year. Annual growth rates that exceed 3 per cent are not uncommon, however, in Latin America and some other developing areas that are located near the equator.

In such densely populated areas as India, Bangladesh, Pakistan, and Sri Lanka, where population growth rates are still above the world average, there is virtually no unused farm land. One reason for supposing that the population growth rates in these countries cannot continue is the behavior of crop yields in the United States.

In this chapter I will first discuss the possibility of increasing food production in the United States and the rest of the world. I then go on to consider such topics as the possibility of a new ice age, "lifeboat ethics," and hunger in America. In the concluding section some estimates about the probable increase in population in various regions of the world are presented.

Crop and Livestock Yields

The sustained increase in American agricultural yields is a comparatively recent phenomenon. The record-breaking crop yields of 1912 were not exceeded until 1937, a period of twenty-five years in which aggregate evidence in support of technological progress was offset by the necessity of bringing into production about 70 million acres of marginal land to feed the expanding population. Without the invention of automobiles, trucks, and farm tractors, which helped to bring about a near demise of the horse population, the United States would have been hard pressed to feed its expanding population. Not until after the end of World War II were per acre yield increases in the United States more than sufficient, on the average, to meet the food requirements of a growing population.

Between 1942 and 1958 the U.S. Department of Agriculture's index of crop production per acre in the United States increased at an average annual rate of about 1.4 per cent, or somewhat less than the average percentage growth in the population. From 1959 to 1963 four successive new crop records were established (Table 10.1). The average annual gain in crop yields amounted to 2.4 per cent from 1958 to 1963, or one full percentage point more than in the preceding sixteen-year period.

In the 1963 - 1972 period the average annual growth in crop yields was only 2 per cent. Crop production per acre remained

TABLE 10.1
Record-Breaking Crop Years (1967 = 100).

Years	Crop production per acre	Length of record (years)
1912	61	—
1937	62	25
1941	64	4
1942	70	1
1946	71	4
1948	75	2
1956	76	12
1957	77	1
1958	86	1
1960	89	2
1961	92	1
1962	95	1
1963	97	1
1965	100	2
1968	105	3
1969	106	1
1971	112	2
1972	115	1

Source: U.S. Department of Agriculture.

about the same in 1973 as the number of harvested acres was allowed to expand by over 9 per cent. Bad weather reduced crop yields about 10 per cent in 1974, the largest decline since 1936. Though American farmers may be able to achieve some new records by the end of the 1970s, the average improvement in crop yields will probably never equal the 1956 - 1972 rate.

In 1962, James Bonner analyzed the factors regulating photosynthetic efficiency. He found that the upper limit "is already being approached today in those regions with the highest level of agricultural practice — in parts of Japan, of Western Europe, and of the United States."[1] Reservations about the ease of making further improvements had been expressed by agronomists much earlier. In 1954, R. W. Jugenheimer noted:

> It is becoming more and more difficult to develop hybrids definitely superior in all characteristics to the better ones now available in the corn belt. Therefore, corn belt hybrids of 1965 may not be radically different from those of today. I believe, however, that there will be considerable improvement in hybrids adapted to other areas of the United States and in many other sections of the world.[2]

In 1975, the National Academy of Sciences issued a rather pessimistic report, "Agricultural Production Efficiency," which concluded that biological ceilings will soon constitute a severe if not impenetrable barrier to further increases in yields per acre.

Agriculture is one area where technological progress is well understood. Yields can be increased by making plants and animals disease-resistant, by reducing pests, moisture, and nutrient constraints, and through mutations, proper care, and selective breeding. None of these techniques is open-ended. After natural constraints have been eliminated and the genetic characteristics of plants and animals altered to take advantage of a more favorable environment, progress can be painfully slow.

It has been possible to boost grain yields fairly dramatically since the 1930s partly because a high proportion of carbohydrate food energy production does not increase a plant's chances for survival in a natural environment. However, the opportunities for further improvements as a result of selective breeding are often quite limited. Speed, for example, is a characteristic that has helped many animals to outdistance predators.

In 1875 the world speed record over a one-mile distance for a man on horseback was 1:41.25, set by an unidentified fellow on a horse named Kadi. The present record for a mile by a horse (named Dr. Fager) is 1:32.2. In the space of about 100 years there has been less than a 10 per cent improvement. Human speed also has limits. In 1875 the world one-mile record for a man on foot was 4:24.5, set by Walter Slade of England. The 1975 record of 3:49.4 was set by John Walker of New Zealand.

Even those characteristics of plants and animals which are not very important for survival are subject to diminishing returns. For example, the U.S. Department of Agriculture bred eight generations of unculled, unselected Holstein-Friesian cows to proved bulls. The herd's yearly butterfat production increased from an average of 530 pounds per cow to 703 pounds by the fifth generation, but increased to only 711 pounds in the last three generations.

The most disturbing aspect to yield technology is not the logic of an upper limit but the difficulty of sustaining high yields. Consumption of DDT has trended downward for more than a decade, partly as a result of Rachel Carson's *Silent Spring*, but also because some insects have developed greater resistance. In 1960 a California committee noted:

> Perhaps the most pressing aspect of the pesticide problem, in the present absence of any effective alternate control technology, is that of growing resistance of insects of public health importance to many of the formerly effective insecticides and the never ending need to shift to new insecticides. This is increasingly significant owing to predictable increases in the mosquito, fly, gnat and other vector problems in response to increasing population, water resources development, industrial expansion, agricultural changes, and recreational area growth.[3]

In 1970 drought and an extension of the southern leaf blight, a fungus disease, reduced corn yields in parts of the northern corn belt by more than 25 per cent.

Running hard simply to stand still is a problem that is not limited to crop production, disease, and pest control. Culling cows that produce a less-than-average amount of milk may even reduce average herd performance, since exceptional producers are not always able to transmit preferred characteristics to their offspring.

The Green Revolution

Between 1939 and 1973 the United States was able to double its farm output by engaging in an extensive program of plant breeding and by increasing the consumption of fertilizer and limiting materials more than tenfold. I expect some new production records in the years ahead as more marginal land is brought back into cultivation, as still more fertilizer is applied to crop land, as farmers replace conventional wheat with new hybrids, and as high-yielding plant varieties are made more disease-resistant and better adapted to less than ideal growing conditions. It doesn't seem likely, however, that farm production in the United States, Canada, Europe, the Soviet Union, China, and Japan will ever double again. Whether food production in the rest of the world can be doubled is less certain.

After the development of high-yielding varieties of miracle rice and wheat in the mid-1960s it appeared as if many of the poorer, more overpopulated countries might be able to avert starvation and achieve rapid economic growth without resort to extraordinary population control measures. New plant varieties and the concomitant rapid growth in fertilizer use produced yields per acre in some developing countries about double those from older varieties of wheat and rice.

In 1966 India had to import more than 8 million tons of wheat and sorghum to avert a serious famine. By 1972 rice production had increased almost 20 per cent. American grain exports to India at the same time declined to less than 200,000 tons. In 1973, however, India had to import almost 3 million tons of grain from the United States to compensate for abnormal weather.

Crop production in Southern Asia was even more seriously affected by drought, flooding, and other adverse weather conditions in 1974. The Food and Agricultural Organization of the United Nations estimated that 460 million people were threatened with starvation in 1974, and that the developed countries of the world would have to divert an additional 7 to 11 million tons of food to Bangladesh, India, Pakistan, Sri Lanka, and Tanzania to prevent widespread famine.

About 20 per cent of the rice land outside China has now been planted with new varieties. To double this percentage and stave off widespread hunger for another five to ten years will not only require large additional investments in chemical fertilizer, which is currently in short supply, but will also require several billion dollars for new investments in irrigation facilities to provide adequate and controllable water supply. Without such investments, the new varieties of wheat and rice are not superior to older varieties. Looking beyond a further doubling of the acreage planted to miracle rice, it becomes questionable whether there is sufficient water that can be made available to sustain the so-called green revolution.[4]

Even before the Soviet crop failure of 1972 and the floods, drought, and storms which reduced food production in many countries in 1974, it was becoming increasingly clear that the green revolution would not be a good substitute for family planning and policies of population control.

The Population Explosion?

In Chapter 5 we noted that the fertility of women in the United States has already declined to somewhat below the replacement level. If fertility remains at that level and if net immigration is halted in the near future, the total population of the United States can still be expected to increase from 30 to 40 per cent.

The fertility of women in most of the poorer nations of the world is still far above a replacement level. Even at replacement levels, the population of some of these countries would more than double, because children and young adults are a much larger fraction of the total population than in the United States.

Because of this high proportion of the population that has not yet replaced itself, it follows that less developed nations should begin to limit the size of families long before the limit to crop production is reached. However, most governments do not think about establishing such national policies until after malnutrition and starvation have become a serious problem.

In 1974, the United Nations sponsored a world conference on population. Of the 149 participating countries, 85 viewed their population growth rates as satisfactory, 22 perceived their growth rates to be deficient, and only 42 countries considered overpopulation to be a domestic concern of any consequence.

In 1972 Prime Minister Indira Gandhi assured an Indian journalist, "I don't consider the population problem with grave anxiety." Just days before the 1974 World Population Conference, however, she told her countrymen bluntly for the first time on nationwide broadcasts that India has a serious problem of over-population. She later sent a letter to every *sarpanch* (headman) in India's more than 570,000 villages informing them of the government's concern and urging them to encourage birth control. In India's new five-year plan, funds for family planning were increased 85 per cent — an encouraging step, but not nearly sufficient.

Greater efforts to control population would seem especially imperative because many climatologists believe that the global climate is now returning to a harsher and more normal state than the unusually mild weather of the first half of the twentieth century.

A New Ice Age?

The mean temperature of the earth appears to have increased from around 1885 until about 1945. In the last thirty years the mean surface temperature has dropped by one-third to one-half a degree centigrade (Figure 10.1), the longest continued downward trend since surface temperature records began.

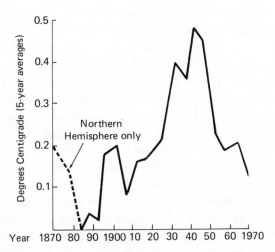

FIGURE 10.1
Mean Surface Air Temperature Changes, 1870–1970.
Source: National Center for Atmospheric Research.

Reid Bryson, director of the Institute for Environmental Studies at the University of Wisconsin, has suggested that alternate warming and cooling of polar icecaps strongly influence the world's climate. When the icecaps cool, as they are now doing, droughts, early frosts, heavy rains, and widespread flooding result. The same phenomenon, he argues, may account for the southern shift of the monsoon rains that has left widespread sections of Asia dry in the normally wet rice-growing season.

Bryson is a leading spokesman for the view that man-made atmospheric pollution has changed the global climate. Fossil-fuel burning, mechanized agricultural operations, accidental forest fires, and the slash-and-burn land clearing method practiced in the tropics, he believes, have increased the amount of dust in the atmosphere and caused more sunlight to be reflected into space, lowering the earth's temperature.

The warm conditions that have prevailed during most of the earth's history have been periodically interrupted by glacial periods or ice ages. Large amounts of atmospheric dust originating from increased volcanic activity can lower the earth's temperature, perhaps initiating ice ages. Once polar icecaps have expanded, additional cooling can be expected because the extra ice and snow will make the earth's surface more reflective.

As water from the oceans is deposited on the polar icecaps, however, some carbon dioxide, which was formerly dissolved in the ocean, will be released to the atmosphere. Carbon dioxide is believed to have a "greenhouse" effect on surface temperatures. Its build-up in the atmosphere eventually can be expected to warm up the surface temperatures enough to perhaps reverse the glaciation. As the ice pack begins to melt accumulated dust will be exposed and the reflective capacity of the polar ice reduced, leading to a further contraction in the amount of land covered by ice and snow. As the extra carbon dioxide in the atmosphere is reabsorbed in the ocean the stage may then be set for another ice age.

Although several other theories have been proposed to explain the expansion and contraction of the polar icecaps, the possibility that man-made pollution may be disrupting worldwide weather patterns is a good reason for cleaning up air pollution. Because most industrialized nations are located in the more temperate regions of the northern hemisphere, they have the most to lose from early frosts and more erratic weather patterns.

Whether the global climate is now returning to a harsher and perhaps more normal state is uncertain. The climatic disasters that have struck the food-producing regions of Africa, Asia, and North America in recent years, however, do seem to have ushered in a new wave of pessimism on the part of many knowledgeable persons concerned with population and the world's food resources.

Lifeboat Ethics

Philip Handler, president of the National Academy of Sciences, has suggested that the developed world may decide to forget the countries of South Asia, "to give them up as hopeless." Only a massive program of aid and development can help these countries, Handler believes. Unless total support is supplied, he thinks it would be better to do nothing because a lesser effort would be counterproductive, encouraging continued population growth and more deaths later. "Cruel as it may sound, if the developed nations do not intend the colossal all-out effort commensurate with the task, then it may be wiser to let nature take its course as Aristotle described it: 'From time to time it is necessary that pestilence, famine and war prune the luxuriant growth of the human race.' "

In times of war or disaster medical personnel have often been forced to adopt the ethics of *triage*, in which aid is first given to those casualties which have the best chance of survival. The Paddock brothers have suggested that the United States and other developed countries may soon be forced to practice triage ethics on a relatively widespread and nonwar basis.[5]

Garrett Hardin, has likened this predicament to a lifeboat with a capacity of only 60 people. If 100 others are swimming in the water outside the lifeboat begging for admission or a handout:

> We have several options: we may be tempted to try to live by the Christian ideal of being "our brother's keeper," or by the Marxist ideal of "to each according to his needs." Since the needs of all in the water are the same, and since they can all be seen as "our brothers," we could take them all into our boat, making a total of 150 in a boat designed for 60. The boat swamps, everyone drowns. Complete justice, complete catastrophe.[6]

India has a population of over 600 million, which increases by about 15 million each year, Hardin notes. This population already puts a huge load on an improverished environment. India's forests are now only a small fraction of what they were three centuries ago, and floods and erosion continually destroy much of the remaining farm land. Every life saved through medical or nutritional assistance from abroad will continue to diminish the quality of life for those who remain for subsequent generations. He then asks:

> If rich countries make it possible, through foreign aid, for 600 million Indians to swell to 1.2 billion in a mere 28 years, as their current growth rate threatens, will future generations of Indians thank us for hastening the destruction of their environment? Will our good intentions be sufficient excuse for the consequences of our actions?

The United States could do much to alleviate the possibility of world hunger and starvation in the next decade or so. By reducing our animal herds and by diverting to human consumption part of the ton or more of grain now produced per person in the United States that is largely fed to livestock, we could clearly feed a much larger population. Professor Jean Mayer, a nutritionist at Harvard University, has noted that "the same amount of food that is feeding 210 million Americans would feed 1.5 billion Chinese on an average Chinese diet."

Norway is apparently the first country to try to curb the eating of meat. Professor Norum of the University of Oslo has argued that the meat from grainfed animals is harmful to health as well as wasteful of the world's limited grain supply. Norwegian statistics show that a 40-year-old man today has less chance of living to 70 than was the case at the start of this century. More than half of the deaths in Norway are now from heart disease. At the end of World War II, when grainfed animals were extremely scarce, such deaths were rare.

A large amount of protein is currently consumed in the United States by pets. In 1974, Secretary of Agriculture Earl Butz apparently backed off from an earlier suggestion that if Americans would get rid of half their dogs and cats most of the world's food problems would be solved — a suggestion not warmly received by the public. Butz later declared, as he posed for photographers with two beagles on his lap, that "Americans have always been pet lovers and will continue to be."

About 15 per cent of the fertilizer used in the United States goes into such nonfood applications as improving lawns, cemeteries, and golf courses. Senator Hubert Humphrey has proposed that Americans limit the use of fertilizer for such purposes, since that much fertilizer could increase the wheat crop of India by 2 or 3 million tons.

Whether the United States and other affluent nations will make an heroic effort to keep others from starving in less-developed parts of the world by eating less meat, by owning fewer pets, and by reducing nonagricultural fertilizer consumption is uncertain. The magnitude of food aid will no doubt greatly depend on the weather in the United States as well as in those countries which can afford to import large quantities of grain if their own output is insufficient to satisfy domestic demand.

From 1964 to 1966 when American wheat surpluses threatened to exceed current production, the United States shipped nearly a fifth of its wheat crop to India to forestall famine. Most of this grain was given away in exchange for local currency that was never spent by the United States government.

International food reserves were substantially depleted in 1972 and 1973 as a result of bad weather. At the 1974 World Food Conference in Rome, Senator Clark of Iowa proposed that the United States double its food aid to needy nations under Public Law 480 from 1 to 2 million tons. This increase is rather small in comparison to the more than 8 million tons of grain that was shipped to India in 1966 and was initially rejected by the Ford Administration.

A resolution was passed at the World Food Conference, however, calling for an annual 10-million-ton food aid program for needy nations, enough food to keep about 50 million people from starving. Because about 80 million people are added to the world's population each year, such aid — a third of which would probably come from the United States — might not go very far toward solving the food problem. Before embarking on such a task many people would probably argue that we ought to first try to solve the problem of hunger in the United States.

Hunger, USA

A 1968 report, Hunger USA (by the Citizen's Board of Inquiry into Hunger and Malnutrition in the United States), alleged that at least 10 million Americans were suffering from chronic hunger or malnutrition. It listed 256 counties in 20 states as "hunger areas" involving "desperate situations." Federal outlays for various food assistance programs at that time amounted to less than $1 billion annually. The thought of millions of people suffering from hunger in the most affluent nation of the world struck a responsive chord in Congress. By 1973 federal outlays for food assistance programs had been increased more than fourfold to $3.7 billion.

Food stamps alone have increased from an expenditure of $187 million in fiscal year 1968 to more than $4 billion in 1975. Although the United States has not enacted a guaranteed annual income, the food stamp program has been transformed, without much public notice, into a guaranteed annual income for food. It is essentially a negative income tax earmarked for food, with national standards of eligibility depending only on the income of the family and its size. By 1975 about 19 million people were receiving food stamps. The average family of four with a net income of $330 per month received $1,800 in food stamps for which it paid $1,140 — additional purchasing power of $660.

Not all low-income families have taken advantage of food stamps, however. Presumably all the 25.6 million persons officially below the poverty line in 1971 were eligible, but fewer than half participated. Some may not know that they are eligible for food stamps; others may be inhibited from using food stamps because of the rather large initial cash outlay or because of the embarrassment of paying for food with stamps rather than money.

The very rapid increase in food prices since 1972 has been especially hard on families with low and moderate incomes. In Senate hearings on nutrition and human needs in 1974, it was suggested that perhaps as much as one-third of all the dog and cat food sold in city slums is being eaten by human beings. Nancy Amidei told the committee: "Adequate income means never having to eat dog food."

The United States government has the resources to end such indignity. It could increase the value of food stamps, publicize their availability, and even make them available on installments or easy-credit plans. Or the existing food stamp program could be replaced with a negative income tax. In 1974 former Health, Education and Welfare Secretary Caspar Weinberger proposed that food stamps and the maze of other federally sponsored public assistance programs be scrapped in favor of a proposed new welfare program guaranteeing poor families a minimum annual income of $3,600.

One advantage of a guaranteed income program is that it would not encourage those low-income farm families with gardens or access to other food supplies to overeat. Obesity and overeating is probably a far more serious health hazard in the United States as a whole than starvation.

Millions of people in the United States, however, are not eligible for either food stamps or a negative income tax. They include an estimated 5 million people who are now living in this country illegally. Many of these immigrants are from Mexico where the annual population growth rate is about 3.5 per cent. It is estimated that illegal residents now hold about 1 million jobs that could be filled by United States citizens. Their presence is another indication of the worldwide population problem that the United States cannot ignore altogether.

Is the Population Problem Hopeless?

The total population of the world is estimated to have been nearly 4 billion in 1974. From 1963 to 1972 the average annual growth rate was about 2 per cent. At that rate total population would double in the next 35 years and equal about 18 billion by 2050. Though past efforts to control the growth of population in less developed countries offer little grounds for optimism, it does not seem likely that the world's population will ever double again. I would guess that the world population will eventually peak at between 6 and 7 billion and gradually decline to a figure that is substantially less than the world's present population. In the first column of Table 10.2 the estimated 1974 population is broken down into five regions. In column 2 I present an educated guess about the minimum population increase that can be expected in the different regions. The high estimate in column 3 will probably not be exceeded in the future. The estimates in Table 10.2 were made before I read Lester Brown's strategy for stabilizing world population. The low increase of 2,020,000,000, however, is almost exactly equal to the 2,040,000,000 increase advocated by Brown as being both feasible and In the Human Interest.[7]

TABLE 10.2
Population Estimates and Projections for the World and
Different Regions (in Millions).

Region	Estimated population 1974	Projected population increases	
		Low estimate	High estimate
North America, Europe, and the Soviet Union	1,000	250	400
Japan and China	925	350	500
Rest of Asia	1,315	700	1,000
Africa	400	400	600
Latin America	320	320	500
World total	3,960	2,020	3,000

About a quarter of the world's population currently lives in North America (excluding Mexico and Latin America), Europe, and the Soviet Union. The population growth rate for the Soviet Union was about equal to the United States rate from 1963 to 1972 (Table 10.3). Canada had a somewhat higher growth rate, much of which was caused by immigration that has since been restricted. Because European growth rates are generally lower than the United States and Soviet rates, a conscientious effort to limit fertility and reduce the number of unwanted babies might be sufficient to keep the total population of countries in temperate regions of the northern hemisphere from increasing by more than about 250 million. Without such efforts, I believe, the increase in population would probably not be more than 40 per cent or about 400 million.

Slightly more than half the world's population is located in Asia. China, with more than 800 million people in 1972, has the largest population. The Chinese government has made very substantial progress at improving agricultural yields and at reducing widespread hunger and malnutrition. Chinese scientists were apparently able to develop new high-yielding dwarf varieties of "miracle rice" even before the International Rice Research Institute was established in the Philippines. Much Chinese effort has gone into the development of controllable water supplies. Some 800 backyard fertilizer factories turn coal and water into nitrogen fertilizer that supplements organic wastes and commercial fertilizers.

Though China's agricultural accomplishments are impressive, U.S. Department of Agriculture statistics show that China imported about 6 million metric tons of wheat and corn in 1973 — a figure that was only partly offset by the export of 1.3 million tons of

TABLE 10.3
Population Estimates and Growth Rates for Countries with More Than 20 Million People.

Country	Estimated populations 1972 (millions)	Annual percentage of increase 1963–1972	Population density per square kilometer 1972
Egypt	34.8	2.5	35
Ethiopia	25.9	1.9	21
Nigeria	58.0	2.5	63
South Africa	23.0	3.2	19
Zaire	22.9	3.9	10
Canada	21.8	1.6	2
Mexico	52.6	3.5	27
United States	208.8	1.1	22
Argentina	23.9	1.5	9
Brazil	98.9	2.9	12
Colombia	22.5	3.2	20
Bangladesh	53.2[a]		
China	800.7	1.8	83
India	563.5	2.2	172
Indonesia	120.4	2.1	81
Iran	30.6	3.0	19
Japan	106.0	1.1	287
South Korea	32.5	2.1	330
Pakistan	56.1	2.4	70
Philippines	39.0	3.0	130
Thailand	36.3	3.1	71
Turkey	37.0	2.5	47
North Vietnam	22.0	2.3	139
France	51.7	0.9	95
West Germany	61.7	0.8	248
Italy	54.3	0.7	180
Poland	33.1		106
Romania	20.8	1.1	87
Spain	34.5	1.1	68
United Kingdom	55.8	.4	229
Yugoslavia	20.8	1.0	81
Soviet Union	247.5	1.1	11

Source: United Nations Yearbook, 1972.
[a]Data are for 1963.

rice. Although progress at improving food supplies has been substantial, it doesn't seem likely that Chinese farm production will
increase as rapidly in the remainder of this century.

China's population increased at an average rate of 1.8 per cent
from 1963 to 1972. The fertility of women is nearing a replacement
level, however. My guess is that China's population will not be
allowed to increase by more than about 50 per cent in the future. In
Japan, with 106 million people in 1972, the population growth rate
was 1.1 per cent from 1963 to 1972, about the same as in the United
States and the Soviet Union. For Japan and the Soviet Union I expect a total population increase of not more than 500 million people and, with a little more emphasis on population control,
perhaps only 350 million.

The population outlook for the rest of Asia is not as favorable.
The biggest problem is India with a population of 563.5 million in
1972 and a growth rate that is still above the world average. The
Club of Rome, in "Mankind at the Turning Point," has proposed
that the industrialized nations of the world invest $250 billion per
year in the developing countries until 2000. If such massive
assistance were provided on a per capita basis, India's population
would probably double in the next 50 years.

The real value of United States economic aid to other countries has trended downward since 1966, however. India will no
doubt continue to receive some food and development assistance,
if for no other reason than to discourage it from exploding more
atomic devices and spreading such technology to other less
developed countries. I rather doubt that there will be enough outside aid, however, to enable India to double its population.

Pakistan, Bangladesh, and several other heavily populated
countries in Asia must either adopt strict measures to reduce the
birth rate or accept chronic malnutrition and widespread famine.
With stringent measures to reduce human fertility the increase in
Asian population outside China and Japan might be kept to about
700 million. Without such measures starvation and disease, I
suspect, will keep the total population from rising by more than
about a billion people.

Latin America now has a population of about 320 million, and
Africa approximately 400 million. Keeping the population of these
two continents from doubling will not be easy. Population growth
rates are often very high; the leaders of some African and Latin
countries even think they are underpopulated. Most of Africa and

Latin America is either too dry for intensive agriculture, however, or is covered by tropical jungle with lateritic soil that quickly bakes into an unproductive bricklike material if the natural vegetation is removed.

The information on average caloric intake in various regions of the world shows that most of Africa suffered from famine in 1974 and that most people in Latin America had either inadequate or only minimally adequate food supplies. If no effort is made to control population growth, hunger and disease will probably restrict the total population of these continents to something less than 1 billion each.

Whether the less-developed nations of the world will be able to control the growth of their populations enough to avoid a Malthusian solution to the population problem is uncertain. Kingsley Davis has noted that our mores were formed when human societies could only survive with a birth rate about three times as great as the modern death rate. "Built into the social order, therefore, are values, norms, and incentives that motivate people to bear and rear children. These cultural and institutional inheritances form the premises of our thinking. Respected leaders of society are not about to disavow them, nor is the general public likely to do so."[8]

Davis also notes that the most spectacular declines in birth rates have occurred in those less-developed countries which are more advanced and on the verge of becoming more urban and industrialized, which may have been more the result of changing social and economic conditions rather than of family planning policy. He suggests that it is hard to escape the conclusion that the kinds of official programs which have been adopted around the world may have little to do with the trend of the birth rates. If the public wishes to limit births, a way will be found to get the means, but if it does not wish to limit births, "no official program for providing services will lead it to do so."

Very few governments have made serious efforts to control population growth, however. Only about $250 million was being spent around the world in 1974 by both public and private sources to spread the message of family planning. Poor people in most countries of the world, including the United States, simply do not have free access to a wide variety of effective contraceptive devices. This problem could easily be overcome at a rather modest cost to most governments.

In 1973, the U.S. Supreme Court barred states from interfering with the decision of a woman and her doctor to end a pregnancy within the first three months. Although this decision may have been somewhat ahead of the social mores at that time, recent polls suggest that a majority of Americans now favor legalized abortion.

To promote zero population growth in an "overpopulated area," the Puerto Rican government is now carrying on a vigorous program of offering free — but voluntary — sterilization for both men and women. In 1974 Puerto Rico's population density was 871 persons per square mile, more than twice the density of India and Japan. The death rate was 6.5 per 1000 inhabitants in 1973, whereas the birth rate was 23.3. With a natural annual growth rate of 2 per cent Puerto Rico's population density could reach 1,300 persons per square mile by the year 2000 if the free sterilization program and other efforts to lower the birth rate are not successful. A government study indicates that about 83 per cent of the population endorse the idea of free sterilization.

This finding is encouraging. I hope that it implies that we are now on the verge of a major revolution in public attitudes about population growth which will help to avert hunger and starvation both at home and abroad.

A rise in the average age at which young people marry in the United States has helped to lower fertility. In 1974 the median age at first marriage for men was up about six months to 23.1 years compared to the mid-1950s. For women the average age at first marriage was up a full year to 21.1 years.

In some parts of Europe with very low fertility rates men and women customarily do not marry until they are between 25 and 35. If the average age at first marriage in most underdeveloped countries could be raised to this range, it would allow more time to raise food supplies to support an expanding population even if people's attitudes about the desired number of children did not change.

In The Meaning of the Twentieth Century, Kenneth Boulding has suggested somewhat facetiously that countries with an overpopulation problem should issue a limited number of marketable licenses for the privilege of having babies. An alternative approach might be to require young people and their parents to pay marriage taxes. High enough taxes would tend to discourage both early marriage and large families.[9] It would probably be even more effective if the proceeds were used to finance a system of old age insurance for unmarried individuals, married couples, and widows or widowers with two or less children. It would not be so necessary then for poor people to have large families to provide themselves with income security in their old age.

To be both equitable and maximally effective the tax should probably be composed of two parts. The first part should consist of, say, a 10 to 20 per cent levy on the total wealth owned by the parents of both the bride and groom. The second part would be a lump sum financial payment that would be the same for every couple. It should be high enough so that young people from families that do not have much taxable wealth might have to work several years to accumulate enough financial resources to pay the tax.

One problem with such a tax system is that there are not enough jobs available in many developing nations to keep the existing labor force fully employed. Among the poorer countries of the world only China seems to have been highly successful at providing sufficient job opportunities. The Chinese approach resembles the Civilian Conservation Corps, which was created in the United States in the 1930s to provide "make-work" jobs for unemployed youth. If the United States increases its food assistance to needy nations, it might require that a large part of this aid be used to sponsor labor-intensive conservation and development projects for unmarried young men and women.

Our food and development assistance could probably be redirected in other ways that would help to defuse what Paul Ehrlich has described as "the population bomb."[10] Lester Brown of the Overseas Development Council in Washington has noted that birth rates usually do not decline unless a certain minimum level of living is reached that includes an assured food supply, literacy (if not an elementary school education), at least rudimentary health services, and reduced infant mortality. "What we may witness," according to Brown, "is the emergence of a situation in which it will be in the interest of the rich countries to launch a concerted attack on global poverty in order to reduce the threat to our future well-being posed by continuous population growth."[11]

The costs of doing so, he believes, are not as formidable as one might think. The United Nations Educational, Scientific and Cultural Organization (UNESCO) has estimated that it only costs approximately $8 to enable a person to become literate in a developing country. At an annual cost of only $1 or $2 billion, to be shared by several wealthy nations, the number of illiterates in the world could be greatly reduced. Brown suggests that this might be a very cheap price to pay to achieve one of the preconditions for a major slowdown in global population growth.

The Chinese experience in providing health services, including family planning, to the countryside has also been instructive. By using limited available resources to train paramedical personnel, the Chinese have apparently succeeded in providing at least rudimentary health services to almost everyone even though individual incomes only average about $150 annually.

By redirecting economic assistance programs away from large, capital-intensive development projects toward satisfying more basic human needs, the United States could probably do much to help establish some conditions for a major slowdown in global population growth. Not much progress can be expected, however, without the cooperation of public officials in the less-developed nations.

In 1963 Harold Barnett and Chandler Morse wrote that: "In general, it should be expected that societies will attempt to control their population numbers when the social gains of such action — or the costs of unlimited expansion — pose a clear threat to social welfare."[12] During the 1950s and the 1960s the leaders of the less-developed nations really didn't have to worry about widespread famine because they could count on the United States government with its huge grain reserves to bail them out. Those reserves have now been used up. The deaths of several million Africans and Asians from starvation in the last few years show that time is running out. Before very long these countries will either have to limit human fertility or accept a condition of chronic malnutrition and recurring famine. I am inclined to believe that they will opt for population control and that the problem of widespread hunger and starvation will be largely solved in the next 100 years.

The final choice is not ours, however. Aside from making food and development assistance more conditional upon local efforts to establish some of the necessary preconditions for a rapid decline in population growth rates, about all we can do is echo the sentiment of John Stuart Mill:

A population may be too crowded, though all be amply supplied with food and rainment. It is not good for man to be kept perforce at all times in the presence of his species. A world from which solitude is extirpated is a very poor ideal. Solitude, in the sense of being often alone, is essential to any depth of meditation or of character: and solitude in the presence of natural beauty and grandeur, is the cradle of thoughts and aspirations which are not only good for the individual, but which society could ill do without. Nor is there much satisfaction in contemplating the world with nothing left to the spontaneous activity of nature; with every rood of land brought into cultivation, which is capable of growing food for human beings; every flowery waste or natural pasture ploughed up, all quadrupeds or birds which are not domesticated for man's use exterminated as his rivals for food, every hedgerow or superfluous tree rooted out, and scarcely a place left where a wild shrub or flower could grow without being eradicated as a weed in the name of improved agriculture.

If the earth must lose that great portion of its pleasantness which it owes to things that the unlimited increase of wealth and population would extirpate from it, for the mere purpose of enabling it to support a larger, but not a happier or better population, I sincerely hope, for the sake of posterity, that they will be content to be stationary, long before necessity compels them to it.[13]

Notes

1. "The Upper Limit of Crop Yield," *Science* (July 6, 1962), pp. 11 - 15.

2. R. W. Jugenheimer, "Tomorrow's Hybrid Corn," *Crops and Soils* (November 1954), p. 14.

3. *Report on Agricultural Chemicals and Recommendations for Public Policy.* State of California (December 30, 1960), p. 13.

4. Walter P. Falcon, "The Green Revolution: Generations of Problems," *American Journal of Agricultural Economics* (December 1970), pp. 698 - 710.

5. W. and P. Paddock, *Famine — 1975!* (Boston: Little, Brown, 1967).

6. Garrett Hardin, "Lifeboat Ethics: The Case Against Helping the Poor," *Psychology Today* (September 1974), p. 40. See also "The Tragedy of the Commons," *Science* (vol. 162, 1968), p. 1243.

7. Lester R. Brown, *In the Human Interest* (New York: Norton, 1974).

8. Kingsley Davis, "Zero Population Growth: The Goal and the Means," in *The No-Growth Society*, ed. Mancur Olson and Hans H. Landsberg (New York: Norton, 1973), p. 21.

9. Many interesting variations are possible. One approach would be to collect a very high tax when the bride and groom are quite young and gradually reduce the amount of the tax, perhaps phasing it out altogether if both are over 30.

10. Paul R. Ehrlich, *The Population Bomb* (New York: Ballantine, 1968).

11. Lester Brown, "Rich Countries and Poor in a Finite, Interdependent World," *The No-Growth Society*, pp. 153 - 164.

12. Harold J. Barnett and Chandler Morse, *Scarcity and Growth* (Baltimore: Johns Hopkins Press, 1963).

13. John Stuart Mill, *Principles of Political Economy* (London: John W. Parker, 1847), vol. 2, p. 326.

chapter 11

INFLATION

As a steady state economy is approached, improvements in output per manhour can be expected to decline and perhaps be negative. This, in turn, will make it more difficult to fully offset natural resource scarcity without a rise in the relative price of many raw materials. Both these harbingers of a stationary economy — the decline in the growth of productivity and the differential rise in natural resource prices — can be expected to aggravate the problem of inflation.

In this chapter I will first examine the behavior of prices and wages in the United States from 1961 to 1974. Their behavior indicates that inflation is a worldwide problem that can occur in this country as a result of food shortages and pricing decisions in other countries. Without some cooperation from other nations it may not even be in our own best interest to try to halt inflation. Some wage and price controls, however, may create a climate in which expansive monetary and fiscal policies can be used to ensure a condition of reasonably full employment.

The Behavior of Prices and Wages

I have assembled some data (Table 11.1) on the percentage changes in prices, earnings, and output per manhour for the private nonfarm economy for the 1961 - 1974 period, and on the wholesale price index, the consumer price index, government spending, and the national money supply. The percentage changes in the consumer price index, the wholesale price index, and the implicit price deflator for the private nonfarm economy (the price index that is used to convert the current dollar value of nonfarm income into real GNP) have tended to move together, but the rates of inflation as measured by the different indexes in some years show sizable disparities.

From 1959 to 1964 there was virtually no change in the wholesale price index. The consumer price index (CPI) during the same time increased at an average annual rate of about 1.25 per cent, which might be described as "normal inflation" resulting from differential improvements in labor productivity in different industries. If output per worker and wages in industry and agriculture increase at an average annual rate of, for example, 3 per cent, and if improvements in labor productivity in government and some service sectors of the economy are only about 0.5 per cent, then prices in these sectors will have to be raised about 2.5 per cent annually to provide workers with the same increase in wages that are obtained in industry and agriculture. If employment in both the more progressive and less progressive sectors of the economy is about equal, the average rate of price increase will be about 1.25 per cent. This, in a somewhat oversimplified way, describes much of the inflation in the CPI during the late 1950s and early 1960s.

In 1965 the United States became heavily involved in the Vietnam War. Unemployment, which had averaged more than 5 per cent per year from 1958 to 1964 fell to an average rate of only 4.5 per cent. Labor shortages enabled workers to obtain an average increase in adjusted hourly earnings of 3.7 per cent, compared to an increase of only 2.8 per cent in 1964 (see column 1, Table 11.1). Higher wages and a shortage of some raw materials helped boost the wholesale price index 2 per cent and the consumer price index 1.7 per cent.

Labor and some basic commodity shortages became even more acute in 1966 as the United States escalated its involvement in Vietnam and continued to fight poverty at home without raising taxes. Government spending, which had increased only 6.6 per cent in 1965, jumped 13.6 per cent in 1966. Price inflation, as measured by changes in the CPI, increased by 2.9 per cent in both 1966 and 1967. Some of the largest and strongest unions were locked into long-term wage agreements. Adjusted hourly earnings in the private nonfarm economy increased only moderately from 3.7 per cent in 1965 to 4.1 per cent in 1966 and 4.8 per cent in 1967.

The modest increase in wages compared to the nearly 3 per cent increase in consumer prices eroded the real purchasing

TABLE 11.1

Percentage Changes in Average Annual Prices, Earnings, and Output per Manhour for the Private Nonfarm Economy and for Wholesale Prices, Consumer Prices, the Money Supply[a] and Total Government Spending in the United States, 1961–1974.

Year	Data for the private nonfarm economy				Data for the total U.S. economy			
	Adjusted hourly earnings (1)	*Output per manhour* (2)	*Col. (1) minus Col. (2)* (3)	*Implicit price deflator* (4)	*Wholesale price index* (5)	*Consumer price index* (6)	*Nation's money supply* (7)	*Total government spending* (8)
1962	3.3	4.5	−1.2	.9	.3	1.1	1.5	7.3
1963	2.9	3.1	−.2	1.2	−.3	1.2	3.7	4.4
1964	2.8	3.7	−.9	1.3	.2	1.3	4.6	5.1
1965	3.7	2.9	.8	1.4	2.0	1.7	4.6	6.6
1966	4.1	3.5	.6	2.2	3.3	2.9	2.4	13.6
1967	4.8	1.6	3.2	3.3	.2	2.9	6.6	14.4
1968	6.3	2.7	3.6	3.5	2.5	4.2	7.9	11.3
1969	6.6	−.2	6.8	4.5	3.9	5.4	3.5	6.5
1970	6.6	.5	6.1	5.0	3.7	5.9	6.1	8.6
1971	7.1	3.8	3.3	4.3	3.2	4.3	6.3	8.8
1972	6.5	3.6	2.9	2.4	4.6	3.3	8.7	9.4
1973	6.4	2.3	4.1	4.1	13.1	6.2	6.1	9.6
1974	8.0	−2.7	10.7	11.4	18.9	11.0	4.4	13.0

[a]The change in the money supply is from the beginning of the year to the end of the year in question rather than an average annual change.

power of the wage increases received by workers. With unemployment lower than 4 per cent, many unions were successful at obtaining sizable "catch up" wage increases. In the next three years, from 1968 to 1970, adjusted hourly earnings in the private nonfarm economy increased by more than 6 per cent annually.

Annual price inflation, I believe, might have remained at levels of about 3 to 4 per cent if improvements in labor productivity in the private nonfarm sector had not slumped to less than half the 1966 level in 1967, recovered moderately in 1968, and then fallen to almost negligible levels in 1969 and 1970 (see column 2, Table 11.1). This combination of higher wages and below-average increases in labor productivity created a classic condition of "cost-push" inflation, which forced businessmen to raise their prices at accelerated rates from 1966 to 1970 to finance the higher wages.

In 1966 and again in 1969 the monetary authorities became disturbed about the problem of inflation and slowed the growth rate for the nation's money supply (see column 7). This helped to dampen the growth rates for the gross national product and for total employment in 1967 and 1970 but did not moderate inflation as measured by changes in the consumer price index. By 1970 the rate of inflation in the CPI had jumped to 5.9 per cent and was less than one percentage point below the 6.6 per cent increase in adjusted hourly earnings. The narrowing spread between increased wages and prices led to a condition of great unrest among workers. In the first half of 1971, despite rising unemployment and a comparatively stagnant growth rate for real GNP, some unions were successful at obtaining very sizable wage increases.

The unexpected surge in wages after the prolonged economic recession brought on by relatively restrained monetary and fiscal policy led Arthur Burns, chairman of the Board of Governors of the Federal Reserve, which controls the growth of the money supply, to question the effectiveness of monetary and fiscal policy as a means of controlling inflation and to talk about the need for an incomes policy. President Nixon and his principal economic advisers were strongly against the idea of wage and price controls.

In October 1969, Nixon noted that his first job in government had been with the old Office of Price Administration during World War II. "From personal experience let me say this: Wage and price controls are bad for business, bad for the working man, bad for the consumer. Rationing, black markets, regimentation — that's the wrong road for America and I will not take the nation down that road."

Nixon's policies for controlling inflation did not seem to be working, however. The stock market remained in the doldrums throughout 1970; unemployment and prices were rising. George Meany and other representatives of organized labor began to listen to John Kenneth Galbraith, a staunch advocate of controls, and suggested that wage and price controls be used to regulate the economy. Even many businessmen began to recommend government intervention. Congress responded by providing the administration with the authority to impose controls. On August 15, 1970, President Nixon said, "I have previously indicated that I do not intend to exercise such authority if it were given to me. Price and wage controls simply do not fit the conditions which exist today." The president then signed the Price Stabilization Act that gave him the authority to freeze prices and impose wage and price controls.

On June 29, 1971, Treasury Secretary John B. Connally repeated the president's position that he was not going to invoke wage and price controls. On numerous occasions during the summer of 1971, however, the president told the public that "this is an activist administration" and if the "economy is not moving as fast as it should move to deal with the unemployment problem then we will act." The deficit in the international balance of payments soon became so unfavorable that the president was forced to act. On August 15 he announced a 90-day freeze on prices and wages to be followed by the system of controls commonly called "Phase II."

In retrospect, Phase II probably could not have been implemented at a more propitious time for taking advantage of natural forces that reduce the rate of inflation. Large increases in labor productivity are more easily achieved when the economy is recovering from a recession, when capacity utilization is low, and when total output is increasing rapidly. During the five quarters from the fourth quarter of 1971 when Phase II was implemented through the fourth quarter of 1972, output per manhour in the private nonfarm economy increased at an average annual seasonally adjusted rate of more than 4 per cent. The consumer price index, which had been increasing at a 5.9 per cent rate in 1970 and a 4.3 per cent rate in 1971, increased by only 3.3 per cent in 1972.

The inflation record was so good between the middle of 1971 and the end of 1972 that it looked as if the battle against price increases had been won. In January 1973 the President's Council of Economic Advisors concluded that controls were a success and persuaded the president that Phase II should be replaced by a more relaxed set of controls, dubbed "Phase III."

An altogether new phenomenon soon forced the president to abandon Phase III, however, and initiate Phase IV. The change in policy had little to do with the American economy directly but was mainly caused by a sharp fall-off in the rate of agricultural output abroad, particularly in the Soviet Union, which led to unprecedented price increases for many agricultural products. Wheat on the world market was $1.38 per bushel when the Russians came to buy approximately one-fourth of the United States wheat crop in June 1972. It rose to $5.37 in 1973. This unpredictable increase created a whole new ball game in 1973.

What William Nordhaus and John Shoven have described as "a combination of devaluation, bad weather, and bad politics" helped to cause the first commodity inflation in over two decades. The food component in the CPI increased 14.5 per cent in 1973, causing the CPI as a whole to increase 6.2 per cent. The price index for farm products and processed foods and feeds increased 30 per cent, which raised the wholesale price index for all commodities by 13.1 per cent on an average annual basis.

The rapid rise in food and other commodity prices may have also helped to encourage Saudi Arabia to embark upon a policy of "oil diplomacy." American inflation, of course, was not the only reason for such a policy. Crude oil from the Middle East that had sold for only $1.90 a barrel in July 1972 rose to over $15 per barrel in January 1974, before settling down to about $11 per barrel when delivered in the United States.

The huge increase in the price of imported oil more than offset sizable declines in the price of some farm products and helped to create a condition of double-digit inflation in both the consumer and wholesale price indexes. With most prices rising at twice the recommended rate of increase for wages under Phase IV, organized labor gave virtually no support for continuing existing controls. On April 30, 1974 almost all price and wage controls were allowed to expire. The Emergency Petroleum Allocation Act of 1973, however, allowed the president to keep crude oil and refinery products under controls.

In retrospect, it appears that price and wage controls could not have been removed at a less propitious time. Though the economy was not operating at full capacity, many goods and materials were still in short supply, partly because of a very strong demand for United States exports, which in turn was partly caused by the devaluation of the American dollar. When controls were lifted some industries, such as the paper, cement, and steel industries, were able to raise their prices by very large percentages. The price explosion was further exacerbated because the control system had been fairly successful at suppressing normal profit margins in industries that were not operating at full capacity.

When the prices of farm products and raw materials rise, food processors, fabricators, wholesalers, and retailers tend to raise their prices by more than the increased cost of basic materials and other purchased inputs. Because controls had kept many companies from responding normally to higher commodity prices, it is not surprising that the price explosion after controls were lifted reached such proportions that inflation became the primary economic problem by mid-1974.

The problem was considerably compounded by the behavior of output per manhour, which either declined or was very flat from the first quarter of 1973 through the fourth quarter of 1974. If productivity declines without a corresponding decline in the growth rate for hourly earnings, businessmen experience a cost-price squeeze that forces them to raise prices even faster to offset part or all of the resulting profit loss.

The percentage changes in output per manhour have been subtracted from the percentage changes in adjusted hourly earnings in Table 11.1 (column 3). When these differences are compared to the percentage changes in the implicit price deflator for private nonfarm GNP (column 4), it becomes quite clear that there is a fairly close relation between changes in wages, productivity, and prices and that a decline in output per manhour will tend, other things being equal, to add to the problem of inflation. This was particularly true in 1969 and 1970, as well as in the latter part of 1973 and during 1974.

The surge in prices that resulted from sagging improvements in output per manhour and the decontrol of prices and wages was particularly unfortunate because it helped to further erode the savings and purchasing power of many consumers. At the time of President Ford's national summit conference on inflation in

September 1974, it was already apparent to many economists that the erosion of consumer income had helped tip the American economy into a major recession.

With prices still rising rapidly, unions had little choice but to demand large, catch-up wage increases. The net result was a renewed wage-price spiral in the midst of a serious recession, or what some economists have labeled a condition of "stagflation."

International Inflation

Inflation is not limited to the United States. The percentage rates of increase in wages and prices in most other countries were higher than in the United States in 1974. It is questionable, moreover, whether significantly lower rates of inflation are in the best long-run interest of the more industrialized nations of the world.

Harold Cleveland of the First National City Bank has suggested a parallel between what happened in Germany in the 1920s and what happened to the price of oil in 1974. The Allies tried to exact reparations from a defeated Germany but the Germans fooled them by inflating their economy and making the payments in marks of steadily depreciating value. Cleveland suggests that the oil-producing countries are likely to be similarly frustrated, to some extent, in their attempt to obtain more real goods for their oil by unilaterally raising prices.

Like Germany's reparations creditors, the oil-producing countries have had to finance the oil-consuming countries' added cost of oil — in part, by buying more of their exports, but also by investing oil revenues that cannot be spent currently in financial assets denominated in the currencies of the industrial countries.

Higher prices for imported oil have spread to other energy prices, including the prices of oil, gas, and coal. The rise in energy costs has raised costs directly in transportation and in energy-intensive industries. The resulting rise in living costs has tended to push up wages.

These more or less direct effects of the oil price rise, Cleveland suggests, could raise the general price level in leading industrialized nations by 3 or 4 per cent. This, in turn, might lead to an accelerated game of wage and price increases that would more than offset most if not all the interest on the financial assets acquired by the oil-producing countries in exchange for high-priced petroleum.

The United States and other industrialized nations have found it very difficult to control price and wage increases even if price and wage stability are perceived to be in the national interest. If the general perception that inflation is bad should change to a feeling that more inflation is desirable, there is simply no telling how rapid the worldwide rate of inflation might be.

Without wage and price controls industrialized countries like the United States may not be able to moderate a general surge in wages and prices brought on by a steep rise in the price of food and other national resources. Reduced government spending is one way to reduce inflationary pressures. The growth rate for total government expenditure (including outlays for social security) increased every single year between 1970 and 1974, however. President Ford and his economic advisors did advocate a reduction in federal spending in late 1974. That idea was quickly abandoned, however, as the economy plunged into a serious recession. The recession has moderated the sharp upward growth in prices, but at a rather enormous cost in terms of unemployed resources.

Monetary policy is another instrument often used to control inflation. Percentage changes in the money supply during the 1962 - 1973 calendar years (Table 11.1, column 7) can be compared to the average annual increase in the consumer price index (column 6). These percentages tend to move together somewhat, but the changes in growth rates from year to year are not very well correlated. There have only been four years in the 1963 - 1974 decade when the growth rate for the money supply was allowed to decrease. In each of these years — 1966, 1969, 1973, and 1974 — the growth rate for the consumer price index actually increased. Tight monetary policy, in other words, has not been very successful at bringing about a speedy end to price inflation.

It has been very successful, however, at bringing about a subsequent contraction in the growth rate for real GNP (Table 11.2). The contractions in real output are usually equal to or greater than the percentage point contractions in the money supply growth rate in the preceding year. The data, in other words, help to reinforce the hypothesis that a tight money policy is far more successful at deflating the growth rate for real output than the growth rate for prices in general.[1]

TABLE 11.2

Contractions in the Growth Rate for Real GNP Following
Contractions in the Monetary Growth Rate, 1951–1974.

Money supply contraction period	Percentage contractions in the annual growth rate		Real GNP contraction period
	Money supply	Real GNP	
1951–53	−4.5	−4.5	1952–54
1954–57	−3.4	−8.7	1955–58
1958–60	−3.2	−4.5	1959–61
1961–62	−1.6	−2.6	1962–63
1965–66	−2.2	−3.9	1966–67
1968–69	−4.3	−3.1	1969–70
1972–74p	−4.3	−9.1	1973–75

p = preliminary estimate.

If inflation is assumed to be mainly the result of wage increases in excess of improvements in labor productivity a tight
money policy may be less effective at reducing inflationary
pressures than a more moderate policy of easier credit. For example, if the initial effect of tight money is to reduce the growth in
real output, the evidence in Chapter 1 on the interrelation between
year-to-year fluctuations in labor productivity and real output
suggests that labor productivity is reduced. If wages remain the
same and labor productivity is reduced, businessmen experience a
cost-price squeeze, which may force them to raise prices to offset
part or all of the profit loss resulting from a decline in the growth
rate for labor productivity.

Additional factors such as cost of living escalators, which tie
wage increases to increases in the consumer price index, and
heavy debt loads may also force businessmen to either raise prices
or risk bankruptcy if sales decline. In 1960 nonfinancial corporations raised only $12.9 billion in external funds to finance
sales growth. Total external financing, mostly in the form of bank
loans and new corporate bonds, rose to a seasonally adjusted annual increase of $105.7 billion in the third quarter of 1973 — a
sevenfold increase in debt accumulation compared to an increase
of only about 150 per cent for corporate sales.

In an age of wage agreements tied to the CPI and high
overhead expenses, including debt and other fixed costs that cannot be quickly reduced in response to a decline in sales, it is

reasonable to suppose that tight money might be counterproductive. It might simply accelerate the game of price and wage increases compared to the inflation that would prevail if monetary policy were sufficiently liberal to permit some improvement in both total output and output per manhour.

The behavior of prices during the economic slowdowns and recessions of 1966, 1970, and 1974 have indeed made this type of scenario so plausible that many business economists have begun to lose faith in the idea that monetary constraints help to reduce price inflation. The economic declines following periods of tight monetary policy, in any event, have usually forced the monetary authorities to relax their stringency and allow the money supply to grow at faster rates.

Unemployment Versus Inflation — A Modest Proposal

The key lesson to be learned from the behavior of prices in 1973 and 1974 is that inflation is now a worldwide problem. It can occur as a result of food shortages and pricing decisions in other countries. Without cooperation from the oil-producing nations, there may not be much advantage for the United States to even try to halt a fairly rapid upward rise in prices and wages. Without international agreements to stabilize the price of petroleum at reasonable levels, I believe, public policy should be directed not so much at the problem of controlling prices and wages but at the problem of ameliorating some of the most undesirable side effects of inflation. This could be accomplished by raising social security and welfare benefits to provide reasonable protection to those individuals who are unable to work or find jobs that benefit from inflationary wage increases.

If there is an international agreement to stabilize the price of imported oil (see Chapter 12), I favor a system of domestic controls that endeavors to reduce inflation by controlling the growth of above-average incomes. If inflation is to be controlled, there will have to be some losers, at least in a relative sense. The losers, in my judgment, should not be poor people, workers with low incomes, and retired persons living on a pension with fixed benefits, but individuals and corporations with above-average incomes.

Wages and salaries, for example, might be limited to 2 per cent plus x cents per hour for every percentage point increase in the consumer price index. The "x cents per hour" would be the same for every worker; low-income workers would then be able to bargain for wages that improve their real incomes while persons with above-average incomes might not be able to fully offset high rates of inflation.

The "x cents per hour" increment opens up the possibility of more than full protection for those workers with low and moderate incomes who need inflation protection the most. Workers with above-average incomes would tend to lose in a relative sense, and those with very high incomes might see their real incomes decline. The smaller the increment, the more likely it would be that persons with very high incomes would lose real purchasing power. But by the same token, the more likely it would be that the rate of wage and price inflation would be quickly reduced to a level not much greater than the 2 per cent rise in wages which everyone is permitted to bargain for.

Congressmen and others with relatively high wages and salaries, knowing that they are going to be losers anyway, would then have an economic incentive to keep the "x cents per hour" adjustment factor low, which would speed up the painful business of winding down wage and price inflation. Such a goal would probably seem even more desirable if the formula limiting the growth of wages and salaries was automatically scheduled to terminate once the average increase in wages was reduced to, for example, 3 per cent per year.

Assuming that this system of reducing wages and salaries was accepted, my recommended solution to the problem of controlling corporate income would not be to control most prices, but to limit increases in corporate dividends to the same basic 2 per cent per year permitted for all individuals.[2] Any profits earned in excess of the permitted increase in dividends would have to be invested in new plant and equipment or used to reduce corporate indebtedness. (A reduction in corporate indebtedness would tend to free funds for reinvestment in housing and public facilities.)

Because most technological advances are embedded in new plant and equipment, it follows that a fairly sizable increase in corporate profits that are plowed back into new investments, instead of increasing inflationary pressures, might actually help to boost labor productivity and bring about a speedier end to wage and price inflation.

When price and wage controls were eliminated in 1974, many economists felt that they had failed. Statistical studies measuring the influence of raw material prices and other variables on consumer prices over the fairly long and rather turbulent period from 1947 to 1973 suggest, however, that wage and price controls may have been more effective than is commonly supposed.

The most telling argument in behalf of wage and price controls, however, is not that they are all that effective at solving the problem of inflation. The main benefit of the 1971 controls was a climate that allowed monetary and fiscal authorities to forget about inflation and concentrate on the problem of expanding domestic output enough to reduce unemployment significantly. In the 32-month period from August 1971 to April 1974 more than 6.5 million new jobs were created in the civilian sector of the economy, by far the best record of employment gains for any three-year period in the history of the United States.

Widespread unemployment, in the final analysis, is a far more serious problem than inflation. If all prices and incomes were to increase by the same percentage, and that percentage was not so great as to cause people to leave work early to spend their money more quickly, no one would be appreciably worse off as a result of fairly rapid inflation. Because some prices and incomes will increase at a slower than average rate there are likely to be some losers as a result of inflation. Their losses will be largely offset by gains to someone else. With appropriate social security and welfare programs, however, those persons with low incomes that would otherwise suffer the most from inflation can be compensated for their losses. And if some of those who are not compensated for the losses caused by inflation turn out to be petroleum-exporting countries that have invested in financial assets of the United States government, the nation might be better off as a result of rapid inflation.

To employ such traditional remedies for inflation as tight monetary and fiscal policy when the domestic economy is not operating at or near full employment, on the other hand, could mean substantial real losses not only to individual Americans but to other countries that export goods and services to the United States.

In early 1975, after the industrial output of the United States had declined by more than 10 per cent, the prices of non-petroleum commodity exports had declined by as much as 50 per cent. As a result of declining prices and lower demand, the export income of the oil-importing developing countries was expected to drop about $8 billion. This was equivalent to about two-thirds of all the official development assistance received by these countries from the more industrialized nations during 1975. At a meeting of the Organization for Economic Cooperation and Development, smaller countries criticized the United States, West Germany, and Japan for not acting quickly enough to revive their economies.

The National Industrial Conference Board estimates that the moderate economic growth and continuing high unemployment rates projected by the Ford Administration in 1975, to control inflation, will cost the economy $320 billion to $350 billion in lost real output by 1980. The projections assume that the unemployment rate will remain above 6 per cent until the end of the decade. Many economists believe that this is too high a price to pay for a policy that might not be successful at preventing a revival of inflation if world weather conditions are not very favorable.

Notes

1. Changes in the money supply, under ordinary circumstances seem to be a much better predictor of changes in real output than changes in consumer prices. The average annual percentage change in real GNP in the years since 1957 has either been under or about 3 per cent plus the annual (or December to December) change in the money supply in the previous year minus the *annual* change in the consumer price index in the previous year. See Daniel Egy and Edward Renshaw, "A Simple Variant of Quantity Theory Predicts Real GNP," *Money Manager* (October 15, 1974), pp. 8 - 13.

2. If an industry is believed to possess a significant amount of monopoly power, then a stronger case can be made for price controls as well as a constraint on incomes that are paid out in the form of dividends.

chapter 12

THE PRICE
OF IMPORTED OIL

Economists have reacted to the monopolistic prices now being charged by members of the Organization of Petroleum Exporting Countries with uncertainty and even bewilderment about the stability and future of economic activity in the United States and the rest of the world. The mammoth increase in the price of oil is likely to be particularly disastrous for less-developed oil-importing countries. The World Bank has calculated that the additional oil import bill exceeded the entire amount of foreign aid forty-one such countries received in 1974.

Rising concern about the impact of higher prices on the world economy and international monetary system has led the United States and other oil-consuming nations to work toward a cooperative action program for sharing energy resources in an emergency. It has also led the United States government to advocate a price roll-back. Although it would be unrealistic to suppose that the price of imported oil will be rolled back to the pre-embargo level of October 1973, a mutually beneficial compromise might be worked out between the oil-producing and consuming nations. Such a compromise, it seems to me, requires that the oil producers realize that the United States and other industrialized nations do have some weapons that might reduce their monopoly profits. Consuming nations must also appreciate that most naturally occurring petroleum should be priced at fairly high levels to reflect its scarcity value and discourage wasteful consumption.

Inflation

In Chapter 11 I noted that rapid inflation is already being used by the consuming nations to reduce the long-run cost of petroleum

193

imports. The gains to be realized from inflation are related to the sizable accumulation of liquid assets by the petroleum-exporting nations.

Saudi Arabia and other petroleum producers, with relatively small populations and more oil revenues than can be wisely spent at the present time on commodity imports and internal development projects, could easily turn out to be the big losers in a game of hyperinflation. It can be argued, therefore, that it may be in the producers' best interests to stabilize oil prices in exchange for cooperative inflation control efforts in consuming nations. In exchange for the roll-back, the consuming nations might agree to provide an automatic "cost-of-living escalator" for future deliveries of oil that would be based on the prices of manufactured goods and commodities that the oil-producing countries import. On November 11, 1974, the Ministry of Information and Tourism of Iran ran a full-page ad in *The New York Times* supporting the Shah's proposal to link the price of crude oil to the prices of some twenty to thirty other basic commodities needed by OPEC members and developing countries. This idea, I believe, is constructive. But without corresponding concession in oil prices, it may not be in the long-run interest of the oil-consuming nations to agree to such a link.

Recycling Petrodollars

The petroleum-exporting nations received about $60 billion more in revenues from the sale of oil in 1974 than they spent on imported goods (Figure 12.1). About 4 per cent of this surplus was loaned to developing nations. Most of the surplus, however, was either deposited in commercial banks, invested in international financial institutions, or used to buy government securities and other financial assets from the more industrialized nations. The International Monetary Fund has estimated that these liquid assets or "monetary reserves" of the oil-producing nations might total from $300 to $600 billion by the end of this decade. More recent estimates by the U.S. Treasury suggest that the build-up of petrodollars will be less spectacular but could still equal between $200 and $250 billion by 1980, or about twice the total gold and foreign exchange reserves of the entire world in 1973.

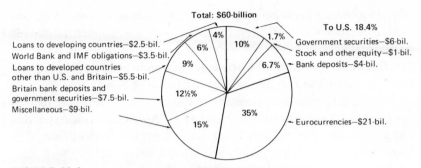

FIGURE 12.1
Disposition of Surplus Oil Revenues by Organization of
Petroleum Exporting Countries in 1974.
Source: U.S. Treasury Department.

The huge increase in monetary reserves has already helped to
fuel worldwide inflation and has also raised the possibility of a
major collapse of world trade and the international financial
system. The capacity of commercial banks and international financial institutions to absorb additional petrodollar deposits without
risk of financial insolvency — should businesses and governments
with deficits in their balance of payments default on their bank
loans — is rapidly being approached. If bank failures are to be
avoided, new institutional mechanisms will have to be created to
channel the increased savings of the oil-producing nations into
profitable investments.

The present system of dealing with the flow of petrodollars is
particularly precarious. In 1974 and 1975 most petrodollars were
used to finance oil consumption rather than new investments that
might reasonably be expected to pay for themselves. In the short
run it may be desirable for the importing nations to borrow
publicly to maintain oil consumption. In the long run, however, oil
consumption must either be cut back or exports expanded enough
to pay for the oil consumed.

A sharp cutback in oil consumption would tend to lower the
revenues of the oil-producing nations and retard the economic
development of those petroleum-exporting nations with large populations. It also might have a deleterious effect on total international trade and keep the world economy from quickly recovering from the recession of 1974 - 1975.

The large increase in monetary reserves could be an international blessing if the increased savings of oil-producing nations

were channeled into increased investments in other countries. But higher oil prices have greatly decreased the opportunities for profitable new investments, especially in some more affluent industrialized countries that are most dependent upon oil imports and that have the biggest balance of payments deficits.

To avoid economic stagnation Italy, France, and Japan will simply have to increase their exports — if not to the oil-exporting nations, then to other countries that are more self-sufficient in basic energy and can profitably absorb large amounts of new capital investments. In other words, developing nations, not the more industrialized countries, should be incurring large deficits in their balance of payments. Unless most petrodollars can be quickly recycled into long-term investment projects in Mexico, Brazil, Algeria, Egypt, Nigeria, and many poorer developing nations that desperately need new capital investments if they are to avoid a Malthusian trap, the world could easily get caught up in a negative dynamic that will not be to the long-run benefit of either the oil-consuming or producing nations.

The United States and other industrialized nations with multinational corporations could help the oil-producing nations in providing investment guarantees and in recycling petrodollars to less developed countries. However, such help would not necessarily be in our own best interest unless cooperative arrangements can be worked out to stabilize the market for imported oil at reasonable prices that do not disrupt economic growth and investment opportunities in the rest of the world.

Without such arrangements, the United States should strictly limit the investment of petrodollars in this country to bank deposits paying a limited return, tax-exempt bonds of state and local government, federal securities, and the stock and bonds of a few large multinational corporations with at least a third or more of their assets invested overseas. The oil-producing nations should not be allowed to invest in domestic real estate or the stock and bonds of domestic companies that might reasonably be expected to provide a financial return in excess of the general rate of inflation.

Such restrictions, it seems to me, would have several advantages. By making financial investments in this country either unprofitable or riskier the oil-producing nations would be encouraged to spend their revenues faster, thus helping to increase the exports of the more industrialized nations directly. It would also encourage the oil-producing nations to invest their excess revenues directly in other countries or international financial institutions that make loans to developing nations, which would lead to an indirect increase in the value of world exports. If the petroleum-exporting nations elected to buy government securities, then the United States should become more heavily involved in recycling petrodollars to those countries of the world — including perhaps China and the Soviet Union — which most need American exports to finance investment projects.

Taxes

Taxes are another area in which it might be possible to reach some mutually beneficial agreements. A matching tariff or coordinated system of excise taxes on refined petroleum products equal to the average monopoly profits or export taxes collected by exporting nations can be highly effective at reducing monopoly profits and increasing the domestic welfare of importing countries.[1]

In 1974 the United States was almost the only "oil-poor" industrial nation that did not levy a large tax on gasoline of 50 cents or more per gallon to limit the demand on imported oil. Drivers in other countries, as a consequence, had a greater incentive to buy smaller cars, organize car pools, drive at lower operating speeds, utilize mass transit, and generally help to conserve energy.

High gasoline taxes, perhaps more than any other factor, helped to restrain the growth of demand for oil and prevent OPEC, which was organized in 1960, from raising prices during its first decade. Not until 1970, when oil production in the United States began to level off, was the growth in demand for petroleum imports sufficient to enable the producing nations to raise their prices.

Until very recently the United States did not use the proceeds from the federal excise tax on gasoline for purposes other than roadbuilding. Emulating the tax structure of other importing nations would probably be sufficient to seriously weaken the international oil cartel in the next few years as American automobile drivers increasingly switch to small cars and as expanded supplies of coal and uranium begin to replace high-cost petroleum as a source of energy for other purposes than vehicle propulsion.

Excise taxes on gasoline are a particularly interesting weapon to employ against the cartel because they might be highly beneficial in their own right. In a thought-provoking paper on the theory and measurement of the private and social costs of highway congestion, Alan Walters has argued that a minimum fuel tax of at least 33 cents a gallon ought to be charged in most urban areas of the United States to bring private costs, at the margin, into approximate equality with the marginal social cost of traffic congestion.[2]

Higher gasoline taxes might also help to reduce air pollution, reverse the downtown deterioration of some cities, and lessen the need for federal support for urban renewal and mass transit subsidies.

In 1973 President Nixon signed a bill that for the first time allowed money from the Highway Trust Fund to be spent for mass transit improvements. Nixon at that time was opposed to federal operating subsidies and later threatened to veto a bill that would have provided $800 million in operating assistance to local transit companies over a two-year period. The president changed his mind in early 1974 and supported a plan that would have made $700 million in federal funds available in fiscal 1975 for either capital investment or operating assistance. The bill, which was eventually signed into law, provides local governments almost $12 billion over a six-year period for both operating subsidies *and* new capital construction. This can be regarded as a major breakthrough. Mass transit subsidies that cover only capital costs have been criticized by the Brookings Institution and others as being wasteful and inefficient:

> If the federal government is paying two-thirds of the cost of new equipment, but nothing toward repair and maintenance, local transit officials will naturally replace buses very quickly, long before they should be scrapped. The total cost of providing mass transit will rise sharply, and a large part of the subsidy will serve not to benefit riders but to cover the costs of inefficient decisions.[3]

Transit subsidies of a more general character can be justified on the grounds that they will help to conserve gasoline, can be expected to reduce air pollution, will lessen traffic congestion,[4] and, because operating subsidies may be necessary in some instances, to help preserve large amounts of consumer surplus that might otherwise be lost if existing transit systems went out of business.[5] Because gasoline taxes also tend to reduce air pollution and lessen traffic congestion, they can be considered an especially good source of financing for mass transit subsidies.

A serious objection to higher gasoline taxes is that they hurt the poor relatively more than those with above-average incomes. This problem could be solved in several ways, however, by using the proceeds to provide increased services or disproportionate tax benefits to families with low and moderate incomes. West Virginia, which pioneered the revival of food stamps in 1961, began experimenting with transportation stamps in the mid-1970s. Its Transportation Remuneration and Incentive Program (TRIP) helps to finance low-cost public transportation for poor and elderly citizens and also provides the transportation industry with customers and revenues needed to keep mass transportation functioning.

An alternative way to offset the regressive impact of higher gasoline taxes is to use the proceeds to raise Social Security benefits and reduce payroll taxes. Wage earners and retired persons who do not belong to the social security system could be given tax credits of about equal value to the reduction in payroll taxes that could then be either applied against federal income taxes or refunded by the Treasury in cash.

The overall progressiveness of this shift in the tax structure could be increased by raising social security benefits by the amount of tax credit and by using the bulk of the proceeds to exempt, for example, the first few thousand dollars of wage and salary payments from social security taxes.

Such a system could be implemented quickly, with little loss of consumer buying power, and would tend to benefit poor families and middle-income groups that endeavor to conserve gasoline proportionately more than rich families. A 1969 - 1970 survey by the Census Bureau found that families earning $4,000 a year drive only 148 miles a week, on the average, compared to a national average of 223 miles for all income groups. Families with an annual income of $15,000 or more average 288 miles.

If the United States raised the taxes it collects on gasoline and other petroleum products to a level nearly equal to those in other importing nations, it might then be possible to vary the amount of taxes collected on petroleum imports so that the total collected by all consuming nations is about equal to the monopoly profits currently being earned by petroleum exporters. The stage might then be set for reducing both export and import taxes. A mutual reduction in all taxes, especially excise taxes on gasoline (which have been raised to over $1 per gallon in some countries), could turn out to be particularly advantageous to petroleum exporters in maintaining a high level of export earnings in the years ahead when petroleum will be increasingly replaced by other energy sources in industry, home heating, and the generation of electric power.

Long-Run Energy Self-Sufficiency

In commenting on the estimated costs of imported oil in 1974, former Treasury Secretary George Shultz noted:

> I believe we must be driven to the conclusion they are simply not realistic. At the prices used in these calculations the consuming countries will not — and in some cases probably cannot — import such large volumes. In the more developed countries the combination of consumer choice and government controls is bound to restrict consumption of imported oil substantially, even in the short run.
>
> Increasingly over time, imports will fall even further behind earlier forecasts, not only from reductions in consumption, but also from increases in production from alternative energy sources which have become economic by comparison. With the economic incentives which now exist, I suspect we shall all be surprised by the new ways of producing and of saving energy which "come out of the woodwork."[6]

One good thing about higher energy prices is that some formerly wasted energy sources are now being utilized. For example, before the recent energy pinch New York City was actually flaring some of the methane produced by its sewage treatment plants. That is not likely to happen again.

Agricultural wastes are another potential source of energy. Conversion of all animal wastes generated in the United States could supply enough methane to equal about half the current rate of natural gas consumption. Much of these wastes are too widely dispersed for practical methane production. One of the nation's largest beef cattle feedlot operators though, has built a plant to manufacture methane from animal wastes. Such plants will also help to reduce water pollution in some areas.

Environmentalists have long known that from 75 to 90 per cent of the material in ordinary garbage is essentially equivalent to low-sulfur coal and oil. It was not until the oil embargo, however, that large cities, some states, equipment manufacturers, and electrical utilities such as the Tennessee Valley Authority began to consider turning trash into electricity. Connecticut expects to recover enough steel from trash and garbage by 1985 to build 20,000 automobiles, enough glass to make 450 million bottles, enough aluminum for 23,000 tons of products, and enough fuel to generate 10 per cent of its total energy needs.

Dumping used oil from internal combustion engines into rivers and harbors is another serious pollution problem that higher energy prices will probably help to solve. In 1974 the House Ways and Means Committee was considering the repeal of a 6-cent tax on each gallon of recycled oil, to make its price more competitive with new oil and provide service stations with a greater incentive to save used oil.

Many lives have been lost in coal mine explosions from escaping methane. Higher energy prices may make it profitable to capture some of this wasted but relatively clean natural gas *before* new mines are put in operation and at the same time improve the safety of coal mining operations. Several processes are also being developed to recycle old tires for oil — another environmental breakthrough of sorts.

In 1972 more than 13 million bicycles were sold in the United States, pushing their sales over that of automobiles for the first time since the early part of this century. Since the 1973 oil embargo, many cities no longer regard the bicycle as just a source of recreation, but as an important factor in commuting patterns and possibly a solution to such urban ills as congestion, pollution, fuel shortages, and flabby muscles.

In *Stress*, Walter McQuade and Ann Aikman have pointed out that the machine age is very hard on the human body. The body was designed for physical use and "is probably the only piece of equipment in life that improves with work." In the remainder of this century, I would expect a continued revival of bicycling, hiking, running, folk dancing, camping, home tinkering, arts and crafts, and other social activities that increase the expenditure of human energy relative to inanimate energy.

Fuel shortages have also helped to relax "gateway" restrictions that force trucking companies to detour out of their way to pass through certain cities. Regulations necessitating empty backhauls when cargo was available for a return trip also appear doomed.

American efforts to reduce auto emissions is another area where industry was, in a sense, moving in the wrong direction before the oil embargo. The more than 90 million tons of carbon monoxide and unburnt hydrocarbons produced by transportation vehicles each year are, after all, a potential energy source that should not be wasted with afterburners and expensive catalytic converters. It now seems likely that auto makers will begin to pay more attention to Honda's stratified charge system, diesel engines, and other control systems that promise not only to meet the original 1975 air quality standards but be more reliable than earlier control systems and also save energy.

The Congressional Research Service of the Library of Congress has reported that an *emulsified* blend of water and gasoline can improve engine performance. The water also cuts down pollutants in the exhaust. The report noted that a mixture of gasoline and water may someday eliminate the need for pollution controls as well as the gas economy penalty that some of these controls cause.

In 1970 the Edison Electric Institute estimated that at least 10 per cent of the nation's railroad track, carrying about 50 per cent of all freight traffic, could profitably be electrified and obtain its power from coal or nuclear energy rather than imported oil. In 1974 a government-industry task force headed by William Loftus of the Federal Railroad Administration recommended that the U.S. Transportation Department help finance railroad electrification, even though electrifying the 20,000 miles of track might cost $2 billion or more.

More than half the energy consumed in households and commercial buildings is for space heating. The Advanced Cooler Manufacturing Corporation of Troy, New York, has shown that it is now possible to design cost-competitive buildings that are so well insulated as to not require a furnace in a climate with winter temperatures as cold as Albany, New York. The four inches of urethane foam insulation used to keep buildings warm in the winter also reduces the need for air conditioning equipment in the summer.[7]

The United States had about 140 oil-fired electric power plants in 1974 that provided about 20 per cent of the base-loaded electrical capacity of plants that are operated around the clock. In 1974

President Ford urged American utilities to convert all these power plants to coal by 1980.

Though the United States has only about 5 per cent of the world's proven petroleum reserves, it may possess up to half the world's most accessible coal and nonpetroleum resources. With higher gasoline taxes, greater emphasis upon investments to conserve energy, and shifts from oil to other energy sources for electricity production, process and comfort heat in energy-intensive industries, the United States could realistically curb its growing appetite for imported oil and eventually become much more self-sufficient in basic energy.

Though quickly reversing the downward trend in domestic petroleum production which began in 1971 may not be easy, the United States does have a great deal of unexplored acreage along the outer continental shelf. In 1972 approximately 11 per cent of the oil and natural gas produced domestically was extracted from offshore wells, compared to approximately 5 per cent in 1965. Less than 5 per cent of the outer continental shelf area to a depth of 200 meters, however, had been leased for exploration and development. Presidential directives have been issued that greatly increase the annual offshore acreage leased for exploration.

Economists associated with the Massachusetts Institute of Technology have suggested that oil production from the previously untapped North Sea could reach 6.4 million barrels per day in 1980, and that production in other non-OPEC countries could increase from 15.7 to 27.6 million barrels per day by 1980. They estimate that these increases would be more than sufficient to satisfy the probable growth in world demand for oil without any increase in supplies from OPEC countries. With these other sources, they conclude, the price of imported oil is more likely to fall in the next few years than to rise.

Before the Arab oil embargo was lifted, the United States was the world's largest producer of petroleum. It is still the largest consumer of oil and is now the second largest oil importer in the world.

Though it is not clear whether the United States will actually become self-sufficient in basic energy, Congress will probably appropriate the funds necessary for developing the technology to establish such a capability. A policy of greater self-sufficiency could put a great deal of downward pressure on the price of imported oil.

If the United States and other industrialized nations were to agree to import either the same amount of oil or a specified amount of oil at a mutually agreed-on price for, say, the next two decades, this might well be worth more to the producing nations in the long run than the economic and financial chaos which might result from trying to maintain an unreasonable price in the short run. With an assured market for at least as much oil as is currently being exported, the producing nations could then industrialize and diversify their economies without the risk of crude oil price erosion or a shrinking market for oil as new supplies are discovered and substitutes developed.

Exchanging Technology and Markets for Imported Oil

World trade, in the final analysis, is a two-way street. The long history of quotas on oil imported into the United States suggests that if OPEC is not to reawaken protective forces that will eventually ensure self-sufficiency, its pricing policy must be reasonably in line with the longer run cost of obtaining liquid hydrocarbons from alternative sources.

Though there may be a temporary advantage in maintaining a monopoly price for imported oil and working out bilateral agreements in which oil is exchanged for advanced technology, it will not be advantageous in the long run for the producing nations to develop the capability to become major exporters of petrochemicals and then discover that there is no market for such exports except at distressingly low prices. France and Japan, which are more dependent upon imported oil than most other nations and perhaps more inclined to accept bilateral trade arrangements, are likely, for this same reason, to be the least willing and least able to pay for manufactured products from the producing nations once they have their new manufacturing plants in place.

If there is to be a large market for other products besides crude oil, the producing nations will need assurances from the United States and other consuming nations that are not so dependent on imported oil, that OPEC-manufactured products will not be banned from international markets.

The best way to obtain such assurances, it seems to me, is

through a crude oil pricing policy that allows the oil-importing nations to finance their purchases of oil and other goods and continue to achieve economic progress. A monopolistic pricing policy that brings about a worldwide recession or prolonged economic stagnation would almost certainly set in motion protective forces which would virtually preclude most of the oil-producing nations from obtaining a significant foothold in other markets besides crude oil.

In exchange for a pricing policy more in line with the long-run cost of obtaining liquid hydrocarbons from other sources, the United States and other industrialized nations might agree to reserve an expanding share of their own markets for some petrochemicals. The nitrogen fertilizer market is a particularly good example of an industry where it might be economically advantageous for the United States to expand imports rather than domestic production.

Higher food prices have made it more profitable for American farmers to apply massive doses of fertilizer to wheat, corn, and other crops. The surge in fertilizer demand, moreover, comes at a time when declining reserves of low-cost natural gas have made it very costly to expand domestic production. (Each of the 68 anhydrous ammonia plants in the United States is totally dependent upon natural gas as a process feedstock.) A recent study by M. W. Kellogg, one of the world's major designers and builders of chemical processing systems, suggests that it will be less costly for the United States to import ammonia from the Carribean in the future than to manufacture it from other raw materials in the United States.

An accelerated shift of ammonia production to the oil-production countries has several other advantages. It would enable them to use low-cost natural gas, which in some cases is either being flared or otherwise wasted. It is less dangerous, more convenient, and economical to ship liquid ammonia long distances than to liquify and transport natural gas by ship. A cooperative agreement to rapidly expand ammonia production outside the United States would also help to relieve a worldwide fertilizer shortage that experts believe might last for several more years.

A rationalization of the world fertilizer market would be particularly helpful to the oil-importing developing countries that were being priced out of the United States fertilizer market in

1975. New varieties of wheat and rice and the concomitant rapid growth in fertilizer use have made it possible for some developing nations with large populations to boost crop yields per acre dramatically in recent years and keep abreast of population growth. If the green revolution is not to be prematurely aborted and followed by mass starvation, it seems essential to overcome fertilizer supply shortages quickly and emphasize least-cost supplies.

A Fair Price For Imported Oil

Before the Arab oil embargo, Jahangir Amuzegar, chief of the Iranian mission in Washington, suggested that the oil producers and consuming nations must be willing to compromise. He noted that the oil-exporting countries want "full pay" for their oil, which they regard not as a perpetual source of income but as a depleting asset, changing its form from crude to cash:

> They consider "full pay" as the true scarcity value of oil in terms of production costs in other parts of the world, equivalent price for competing sources of energy, or costs of replacement.
> They want their oil incomes adjusted for price inflation where their oil is sold (and windfall profits made).
> They want to have adequate say through ownership or participatory arrangements over the way their resources are utilized (e.g., level of production, size and direction of exports, reinvestment policies, and conservation measures).
> They want appropriate access to Western technology, engineering, marketing and distribution in order to develop their domestic resources most efficiently.
> They would like to insure lasting benefits for their future (and probably oil-less) generations during the brief period in their long history when market conditions are in their favor.
> They are searching for reasonably safe and productive outlets in the West for their surplus investable funds, and complete freedom of control over their foreign exchange reserves.[8]

Henry Wallich has suggested:

> Should efforts to break producer cartels succeed, we shall have to remember that the lowest possible price is not necessarily the right price. Exhaustible natural resources have a scarcity value that may

well exceed the present cost of bringing them above ground. A
rational approach to this scarcity price might form the basis of a
mutually beneficial compromise with the oil producers.[9]

When the question of price is approached from this perspective it becomes increasingly clear that the probable cost of obtaining substitute oil from shale or coal (not the dollar or so cost of
producing oil in the Middle East) is a fair and reasonable price for
the oil-producing and more affluent consuming nations to strive to
maintain in the decade ahead. A significantly higher price would
have the disadvantage of providing the United States with an
economic incentive not only to develop the capability to become
self-sufficient in energy production but also to implement such a
goal. It would also have the disadvantage of giving the United
States, which is already more self-sufficient in energy production
than most other industrialized nations, an unfair advantage in
world trade.

Setting the price near the longer run cost of obtaining oil from
coal or shale would have another advantage: because the United
States is one of the world's largest oil producers it would probably
have a vested interest in helping OPEC to maintain that price by
varying domestic production, taxes, and imports if necessary.
Former Treasury Secretary George Shultz has suggested: "We as a
nation are not for free trade in oil, despite what economists used to
believe, and we might as well say so."

Not all monopolies are equally bad. Oil that is retained in the
ground for use by our grandchildren can reasonably be expected
to appreciate in value (even at today's inflated prices) and be
worth more a generation or two later than at present. Wise investment of increased revenues by the oil-producing nations could be
an important instrument for achieving economic development in
their own countries as well as in other developing nations. What is
needed, it seems to me, is not a drastically lower price for all imported oil, but a greater measure of distributive justice.

Walter J. Levy, a leading oil industry expert, has suggested that
the oil-producing and oil-consuming countries agree on a two-tier
pricing system for crude petroleum: oil would go to the poorer, underdeveloped countries at a lower price, while the rich industrial
nations would be expected to pay a higher price. Both price levels
would be negotiated, and thus, administered, rather than being

arrived at by competitive, narrow bilateral arrangements between oil producers and consumers.

Failure to establish such a pricing system, Levy believes, could lead to an "erosion of the world's oil supply and financial systems comparable in its potential for economic and political disaster to the great depression of the 1930s." A two-price system would appear to have considerable international merit. It could help to revive economic growth in resource-poor developing nations without discouraging increased conservation in the more affluent consuming nations.

Assuming that the income and price elasticities of demand for imported oil are higher in developing nations than in the more mature industrialized nations, a two-price system could also help the oil-producing nations maintain stable and expanding revenues as oil production is increased in other parts of the world in the next decade or two.

Notes

1. Edward F. Renshaw, "A Note on Some Alternative Strategies for Dealing with the International Oil Cartel," Albany Discussion Paper #10, Department of Economics, State University of New York at Albany (February 1974).

2. Alan A. Walters, "The Theory and Measurement of Private and Social Cost of Highway Congestion," *Econometrica* (October 1961), pp. 676 - 699.

3. Charles L. Schultze and others, *Setting National Priorities: The 1974 Budget.* (Washington, D.C.: The Brookings Institution, 1973), p. 244.

4. Edward F. Renshaw, "A Note on Mass Transit Subsidies," *National Tax Journal* (December 1973), pp. 639 - 644.

5. Edward F. Renshaw, "A Justification for Operating Subsidies," *Traffic Quarterly* (April 1974), pp. 197 - 207. Consumer surplus is value that is received by consumers in excess of the price they pay for goods.

6. George P. Schultz, "Oil Users Must Join to Reduce Risk and Insure Against It," *The Money Manager* (January 28, 1974), p. 13.

7. Tom McPheeters, "Energy Crisis: A Troy Firm That Was Ready," *The Times Record*, December 8, 1973, p. 1.

8.   Jahangir Amuzegar, "Oil Producers, Consumers Must be Willing to Compromise," *The Money Manager* (August 6, 1973), p. 13.

9.   Henry C. Wallich, "Beyond Shortages," *Newsweek* (February 4, 1974), p. 70

PART FIVE

*The Economy of
the Future*

chapter 13

ECONOMIC ORGANIZATION

American historian Walter Webb has noted that before the discovery of the New World, Europe was "closed" with "very little freedom." When "an enormous body of wealth without proprietors" became available in the New World, an important "by-product of this wealth was freedom and our peculiar modern institutions and values," such as individualism and democracy. Webb goes on to suggest that "we must admit that the individual, this cherished darling of modern history, attained his glory in an abnormal period when there was enough room to give him freedom and enough wealth to give him independence."[1]

In commenting on how to prevent some common resources, such as air and water, from being overused and overpolluted, political scientist William Ophuls suggested that "The Great Frontier is no more: The New World has been filled up, the wealth has been appropriated, and our basic institutions need reexamination."

Increasing distrust of the free market mechanism and "the slow, evermore entangling web of regulations by which the power of decision is being transferred from the board room to federal agencies in Washington" has led Reginald Jones, chairman of the General Electric Company, to question the future for the investor-owned corporation. The possibility that capitalism may not be able to survive the adjustment to a steady state economy raises an even more basic question: can freedom itself be expected to survive?

Both Nobel laureate F. A. Hayek and Milton Friedman have argued that a predominantly free enterprise economy is a necessary if not a sufficient condition for the preservation of political as well as personal freedom. If we are to benefit from the promise of government while avoiding the threat to freedom, Friedman suggests that the scope of government activity should be limited:

> Its major function must be to protect our freedom both from the enemies outside our gates and from our fellow-citizens: to preserve law and order, to enforce private contracts, to foster competitive markets. . . . By relying primarily on voluntary cooperation and private enterprise, in both economic and other activities, we can insure that the private sector is a check on the powers of the governmental sector and an effective protection of freedom of speech, of religion, and of thought.[2]

Reasonable men will differ as to the importance of free enterprise as a mechanism for preserving basic freedoms that are often taken for granted in this country. The important point, it seems to me, is that a steady state economy, even with a level of per capita GNP somewhat higher than at present, does not necessarily imply that the world will be a better place. It may have the potential for being a better world, but unless we are vigilant and as concerned about preserving basic economic, social, and political freedoms as, for example, the goal of maximizing per capital income, it could be a pretty miserable world in which to live. One recent, sobering bit of evidence suggests that such vigilance may be lacking. A series of opinion polls in the early 1970s found that if the Bill of Rights were up for adoption, a majority of Americans would vote it down.

Though I am not optimistic about the prospects for maintaining a predominantly free-enterprise economy, it does seem to me that basic freedoms and a reasonably competitive economy might both be preserved by (1) a somewhat greater dispersal of government power and by (2) eventually converting many private corporations into nonprofit institutions that can be presumed to function in the public interest. In this chapter I will first consider some industries in which government activity is likely to increase as a steady state economy is approached, and then go on to consider some advantages that might result from public interest corporations.

The Railroads

The kinds of activities which are most likely to be taken over by government in the near future appear to be in such basic areas as health, materials, energy production, transportation, and such infrastructure development as water, light, and power utilities. Many private firms that operate in these areas are either regulated monopolies or have some monopoly power. Firms that are subject to economies of scale over the entire range of public demand and those which for other reasons are allowed to be dominant suppliers of particular products pose special problems for which there are no easy solutions.

Though public monopoly might be as bad as or even worse than private monopoly, I suspect that most consumers would find it preferable to the thought of paying unearned rents to private stockholders, many of whom are far more wealthy and need less additional income than the average consumer. Public regulation of private monopolies, however, can sometimes be subverted into imposing on the public a higher degree of economic waste than would have been the case had an industry been left unregulated.[3]

A federal report on railroad productivity in 1973, for example, has estimated that regulatory policies have cost shippers and consumers from $4 to $10 billion annually. Most of this waste was caused by inefficient and idle use of transportation resources, especially railroad cars. Such waste is particularly unfortunate because many railroads are now in a very precarious financial condition.

In public transportation, where rising costs and small improvements in labor productivity have made it difficult for buses and streetcars to compete with private automobiles, there has already been a significant transfer of private assets to public ownership, in practically all major cities. A similar fate may be in store for most railroads.

In 1970 Congress began taking over unprofitable railroad operations with the passage of the Rail Passenger Service Act. The National Railroad Passenger Corporation, commonly called Amtrak, was intended to be a profitable operation. Overnight, Amtrak was able to do what railroad managements had been trying unsuccessfully to do for years. In one fell swoop it eliminated more than half the existing passenger trains, from 547 to 243. Amtrak hoped that the remaining trains, still being operated under contract by private railroads, would capture enough passengers from discontinued trains to make the remaining trains profitable. The general taxpayer, however, supported Amtrak's operations with a subsidy of nearly 5 cents per passenger mile in fiscal 1974.

Since the creation of Amtrak it has become clear that passenger service is not the only unprofitable aspect to some railroad operations. In 1973 Congress passed the Regional Rail Reorganization Act to establish two new federal corporations to finance and run the Penn-Central and six other bankrupt railroads in the Midwest and Northeast. If the railroads (or their bankruptcy judges) elect to join the new system, the United States Railway Association will purchase their best lines, largely by issuing new common stock to the railroads' creditors. The rail lines that the new corporation does not want — possibly 10,000 or more of the 30,000 miles involved — will be abandoned unless states or local communities put up 30 per cent of the cost of the line's losses. If the corporation turns out to be profitable, control of the rail system will eventually pass from government hands back to private enterprise through this stock ownership.

These reorganization efforts will probably not solve the financial problems of the Northeast and Midwest railroads. The Penn-Central merger produced relatively little savings in operating costs and, in retrospect, appears to have simply set the stage for an even bigger financial disaster. If net national product is to be increased rather than reduced as a result of government involvement, there will have to be a major infusion of new capital investments, particularly for roadbed and track improvement, to reduce derailments and increase operating speeds to the point where trains are reasonably competitive with trucks, buses, automobiles, and short-distance airplanes. A 1970 study by the U.S. Department of Transportation, the *Northeast Corridor Transportation Project Report*, suggests that a large amount of new capital investment would be profitable but that the privately owned railroads are not likely to make such investments without public support.

In 1974 Amtrak sent Congress a five-year plan calling for $1 billion in grants for track reconstruction on twelve corridor routes and for $263 million in new equipment so that Amtrak can nearly double its seating capacity by 1979. The New York - Washington Metroliners have top speeds exceeding 110 miles an hour but average only 75 miles an hour. Track improvements to permit an average speed of 110 miles an hour would take nearly an hour off today's three-hour running time. The time savings on the tortuous New York - Boston run would be considerably greater.

Average BTUs of energy consumed per passenger mile are considerably less for trains than for private automobiles and only about a tenth as great, on the average, as for airplanes. If the federal government is unwilling to make the necessary investments to make our railroads more competitive, it seems likely that state governments will be forced to intervene and take over much of the responsibility of maintaining and improving track in much the same manner that they have been responsible for maintaining and improving local roads and highways.

Some steps have already been taken in this direction. In 1974, New York State voters approved a $250 million Rail Preservation Bond Act to provide capital funds for intercity passenger, freight, and commuter service facilities, and for innovative high-speed trains in the New York City - Albany - Buffalo corridor.

The interstate highway system will soon be completed. Opening up the Highway Trust Fund to encompass improvements in the nation's railways as well as highways should be seriously considered. The Northeast, with its relatively stagnant population, does not need many new highways, but it and the rest of the nation can ill afford to be without a viable, interconnecting local railroad system.

Public Utilities

The energy crisis has already had an interesting impact on the electrical utility industry. In 1974, the New York State Legislature voted, with unusual haste, to buy two partially completed power plants from the Consolidated Edison Company. Without this sale, Consolidated Edison would have faced bankruptcy. If the utility had gone into receivership, New York City might have lost hundreds of millions of dollars in real estate taxes. The threat of such losses helped to expedite the purchase of these two plants.

The power plants are to be operated by the New York State Power Authority with much of the electricity being resold to Consolidated Edison. The Power Authority will also finance the construction of a large new nuclear power plant through the sale of $700 million in tax-exempt revenue bonds. This power will be sold to both public and private utility companies.

In 1974 the voters of Massena, a town in upstate New York, approved a $4.5-million bond issue to acquire part of the electrical distribution system of Niagara Mohawk Power Company. The referendum was triggered by consumer unhappiness over rate increases of 7.5 per cent followed by a company request of another 16 per cent. If the purchase goes through, Massena will join forty-two other New York municipalities and rural electric cooperatives that own their own distribution facilities and buy power from the New York State Power Authority. One of the largest customers of the Authority is Plattsburg, where 1,000 kilowatt hours of electricity cost consumers only $9.95 compared to about $21 in Massena.

Federal Power Commission data for 1971 indicates that the 2,920 publicly owned power systems in the United States sell electricity at rates 33 per cent less to residential users and 16 per cent less to commercial and industrial users than do private power systems. Most if not all these savings are in taxes that would otherwise have been paid out by the power companies and the holders of their securities to the federal government.

In the early 1960s when interest rates were much lower, when fuel prices were stable, and when the demand for electricity was still increasing rapidly, the common stock of private utility companies was generally selling at prices above the book value of the net assets owned by the companies. Institutional investors have since become so disenchanted with the earning and growth prospects of utility companies, however, that the common stock of many companies is now selling below book value. Pension funds that own electrical utility stocks as well as other investors under these circumstances would benefit if the assets of the utility companies were simply sold to public utilities or to state power authorities at book value prices. The possibility that stockholders as well as consumers might benefit from converting private utilities into public enterprises makes it rather unlikely that the recent trend toward greater government involvement in the production and distribution of electricity will be reversed.

In 1974, the governor of Massachusetts created a Public Power Corporation Study Commission to examine the feasibility and benefits of establishing a public enterprise to undertake construction of all new electric power plants. This commission was apparently a device to delay action on a bill that would require state takeover of all basic production facilities for electricity in the state.

The high cost of electric power in Massachusetts and other New England states may be one cause of the almost steady erosion of manufacturing jobs in the Northeast since the end of World War II. The dramatic rise in the price of imported oil will exacerbate the problem of industry shifting to the South and West, where electricity is cheaper, if efforts are not made to take advantage of tax-exempt financing and also build large-scale plants which may be too big for small electric companies to operate economically.

As fossil fuels are used up and nuclear energy production increases, the arguments favoring public involvement in electricity production are likely to be even more persuasive. To increase safety in the event of a cooling system failure, it is highly desirable either to locate nuclear power plants in remote locations or at least to bury them in relatively safe underground locations. Both these measures will raise the cost of power and weaken the competitive position of densely settled regions unless the government intervenes to minimize the cost of power.

Another problem that utilities will face in a decade or two is the expense of "decommissioning" or safely disposing of nuclear plants once their useful life is over. The high cost of getting rid of radioactive facilities that no longer produce revenue could easily encourage many private utilities to sell their remaining assets to public bodies.

Although I expect most assets of private power companies eventually to be acquired by state and local governments, there may be a strong case for greater federal involvement in the location of very large nuclear power plants and in the construction of a national power grid. Various studies have suggested that capital savings of $10 billion or more could be achieved by properly interconnecting all the electric power systems in the United States. Even greater savings can be expected from interconnection as fossil fuel use declines and dependency on nuclear power increases.

Basic Materials

Private enterprise has been quite effective at exploiting new frontiers that imply profitable investment opportunities. It has not been so good, however, about shouldering such terminal costs as tearing down old structures and refurbishing obsolete production plants in areas where cheap supplies of energy and mineral resources have been used up, or in cities where reconstruction is often more costly than relocating production facilities on undeveloped suburban land. As we move from an era of industrial expansion to a steady state economy in which preservation and replacement are emphasized, government will become more involved in locating and financing business investment.

The steel industry is perhaps the classic example of a basic industry where increased government involvement may be necessary to achieve modernization, reduce energy consumption per ton of steel, and protect our balance of payments.

Output per manhour in the Japanese steel industry in 1966 was only about half the United States level. By 1972 productivity had increased to about the United States level. At the same time, German steel industry productivity increased to 80 per cent of the American level and French productivity to about two-thirds. The American productivity edge is more than offset by lower wages abroad.

In the 1966 - 1972 period annual output per manhour in the United States steel industry increased at an average rate of 1.2 per cent for all employees compared to an average rate of increase of 1.7 per cent for the longer 1947 - 1972 period. The National Commission on Productivity has suggested that to be competitive with Japanese and German industries, the United States steel industry will have to improve its unit labor cost position through substantial increases in output per manhour while striving for lower material and energy costs and improved marketing practices.

Labor and management in the American steel industry have begun a pioneering joint drive to improve plant productivity and eliminate labor contract uncertainties. Under the agreement, management meets with union representatives to discuss ways to make more efficient use of production time and facilities, to cut spoilage, and to reduce absenteeism. Both sides, moreover, have agreed to arbitration of labor disputes, which will eliminate prenegotiation inventory buildups and costly postsettlement shutdowns. If successful, the steel experiment could become a model for cooperative approaches to improve labor productivity in other industries.

Achieving substantial improvements in labor productivity, however, will require sizable investments in new facilities. In some steelmaking areas of the Northeast, many existing steel mills are old and obsolete and in danger of being closed down without being replaced. Rather than risk a further loss of high-paying jobs in steel and manufacturing, such states as New York or Pennsylvania might be induced to build modern steelmaking plants by issuing tax-exempt bonds. These plants could be either operated with government employees or leased to the steel industry.

As state and local governments become more involved in the business of separating glass and metals from ordinary garbage to produce heat and power, there would appear to be an even greater likelihood that some governmental units will become directly involved in financing and reprocessing such basic materials as iron and steel.

Housing

A serious problem facing some older, more congested cities is how to prevent structually sound older buildings from being inadequately maintained and prematurely abandoned. In his now-classic analysis of slum housing, George Sternlieb has pointed out that most slum tenements are owned by absentee white owners. "These owners are not merely absentee from the slums per se, they are also absentee, at least as residents, from the city in which they own property." He believes that, "the single most basic variable which accounts for variations in the maintenance of slum properties is the factor of ownership. Good parcel maintenance typically is a function of resident ownership."[4]

Sternlieb suggests that cities ought to consider a homestead tax rebate for resident landlords if the rebates are used to improve the rental property: "It is the resident landlord, and only the resident landlord, who is in a position to properly screen and supervise the tenantry. No one-shot wave of maintenance and a paint-up, sweep-up campaign can provide the day-to-day maintenance required in a slum area."

An alternative approach would be to have cities, counties, and local housing authorities buy up properties that are in danger of being abandoned, make necessary improvements, and then resell the properties on easy credit terms to resident landlords or low-income families.

Several nonprofit organizations are already in the business of refurbishing abandoned structures that are basically sound. Once they are restored to a livable condition, the properties are then sold to families with low and moderate incomes. An important constraint on this type of urban renewal is a lack of financing, which could be ameliorated by having the government provide more low interest loans to nonprofit housing organizations.

Philadelphia and several other cities sometimes give abandoned properties to individuals if they agree to live in the property for a period of, for example, five years and bring it up to municipal standards within a designated time. For people with limited assets who are willing to spend long hours at cleaning and fixing, this "urban homesteading" can provide the opportunity to own their own homes which in turn can lead to increased pride and personal accomplishment.

In Chapter 7 I noted that between $50 - $100 billion could be profitably invested in existing houses to conserve energy. For an investment of about $1,500 an average homeowner could save about $200 per year in annual heating costs. If this investment were amortized over fifty years the net return would be over 13 per cent annually. If the homeowner could borrow money at 10 per cent interest, the investment would pay for itself in a little less than fifteen years. If home improvement loans were for ten years, however, the homeowner could only expect to break even on an annual basis if the cost of borrowed money was a little less than 6 per cent annually.

Installing storm windows, increased insulation, and many other heat-conserving devices on almost all properties that can reasonably be expected to last fifteen years or more seems socially desirable. A fifteen-year payback period is sufficiently remote, however, that some owners of older property would probably not make such investments unless low-interest, long-term credit is available. Elderly homeowners with low incomes, families with fully mortgaged properties, and owners of basically sound housing in deteriorating neighborhoods may find financing impossible.

Because private credit markets are imperfect, and because the social benefits from energy-conserving investments for older houses are likely to be greater than the private benefits, it would appear to be in the national interest to have city and county governments borrow for the purpose of making cost-effective investments in home insulation and simply charge property owners a price (or special tax) sufficient to amortize the various investments over their expected life. Energy conservation, in the final analysis, is simply too important to be left entirely to the discretion of the private marketplace.

If local governments assumed more of the financial burden of raising capital for energy-conserving improvements, property owners and their tenants would then find it less risky and more advantageous to make other improvements and do a better job of maintaining the residential property. This, in turn, would help to increase a community's tax base and greatly reduce the problem of premature abandonment.

Housing is one area where it might be possible for the United States to resist an accelerating trend in the direction of outright public ownership. Owner-occupied housing units have increased dramatically since World War II. Ownership has been fostered to a considerable extent by a tax policy that allows mortgage interest to be deducted from gross income before computing income taxes. Taxpayers who plan to live in a particular area for an extended time usually find home ownership more economical than renting.

To enable apartment residents to take advantage of this tax loophole, and to better maximize their own profits, many builders are now making provisions for eventual conversion of multifamily housing units into individually owned "condominium" apartments. In a hundred years or so, when differences in family incomes may be narrower and when most multifamily residences may be condominiums, nearly all families may be property owners whether they want to or not.

Health

In 1972 Senator Edward M. Kennedy noted:

Even though we are a nation that places a high value on health, we have done very little to insure that quality health care is available to all of us at a price we can afford. We have allowed rural and inner-city areas to be slowly abandoned by doctors. We have allowed hundreds of insurance companies to create thousands of complicated policies that trap Americans in gaps, limitations, and exclusions in coverage, and that offer disastrously low benefits which spell financial disaster for a family when serious illness or injury strikes. We have allowed doctor and hospital charges to skyrocket out of control through wasteful and inefficient practices to the point where more and more Americans are finding it difficult to pay for health care and health insurance. We have also allowed physicians and hospitals to practice with little or no review of the quality of their work, and with few requirements to keep their knowledge up to date or to limit themselves to the areas where they are qualified. In our concern not to infringe on doctors' and hospitals' rights as entrepreneurs, we have allowed them to offer care in ways, at times, in places, and at prices designed more for their convenience and profit than for the good of the American people.

When I say "we have allowed," I mean that the American people have not done anything about it through their government, that the medical societies and hospital associations have done far too little about it, and that the insurance companies have done little or nothing about it.

I believe the time has come in our nation for the people to take action to solve these problems.[5]

From 1950 to 1972 the consumer price index rose 74 per cent, while the medical care component rose by 145 per cent. Total health care costs during the same period rose from 4.6 per cent of GNP to 7.6 per cent. The average hospital cost per patient day increased more than 500 per cent, from $16 in 1950 to $103 in 1972. Much of the increase in costs has occurred since the federal Medicare and Medicaid programs went into effect in 1966. Medicare covers the major costs of hospital and physicians' services provided to the aged under social security, and Medicaid pays for the costs of hospital and physicians' services provided to people who are either on welfare or eligible for such services as a result of liberalized programs in some states.

Herman M. Somers has described the system of health care in this country "as a technically excellent product thrown into a Rube Goldberg delivery contraption which distorts and defeats it, and makes it more expensive than it need be." A report to the Secretary of the Department of Health, Education, and Welfare suggests that "the key fact about health service as it exists today is the disorganization . . . fragmentation and disjunction that promotes extravagance and permits tragedy."

In 1967, 45 countries had more hospital beds per capita than the United States and 9 countries had more physicians per capita. In 1968, 44 countries had lower crude death rates than the United States; 10 had lower infant death rates. The mortality rate of blacks and other nonwhites in the United States is more than double that for whites. The highest infant death rates have been consistently found in low-income southern states. The death rates are closely related to the geographical distribution of physicians. In 1967, when the United States as a whole averaged 158 active physicians for each 100,000 people, Mississippi had a low of 28 and New York had a high of 228.

Proportionally, there are twice as many surgeons in this country as in England and Wales, and American surgeons perform twice as many operations. No evidence suggests that this extra surgery is necessary. One study of 246 hysterectomies performed in three states at 10 different hospitals showed that about 33 per cent of all patients operated upon either had no disease of the organs removed or else another disease was found which indicated that the hysterectomy operation was useless or even harmful.

Kansas Blue Cross Association records for 1969 appear to support a medical version of Parkinson's law: patient admissions for surgery expand to fill the available beds, operating suites, and surgeon's time. Dr. John Knowles, president of the Rockefeller Foundation, faced censure for pointing out that 30 to 40 per cent of American physicians "are making a killing in their practice of medicine through incredible amounts of unnecessary surgery."

Physicians also prescribe an enormous quantity of drugs that are unnecessary or even harmful. The quality of medical care is deficient not only because of unnecessary operations and drugs but because of a lack of continuous training. At least half of all general practitioners seldom, if ever, participate in medical updating programs. Because of the rapid growth in medical knowledge, a physician can easily become outdated after a few years of practice.

The median income of office-based physicians increased from $32,000 in 1967 to $42,700 in 1972. Incomes of $80,000 or more are not uncommon. The higher incomes have not necessarily helped to make doctors happier; the suicide rate among physicians is double that of most other professions. Higher incomes, moreover, can divert a doctor's attention to investment and money management problems at the expense of keeping better informed about new medical developments.

The high cost of medical care makes it almost certain that Congress will eventually pass some form of national health insurance which will be available to all families, regardless of age or income. If hospitals and physicians do not hold down costs and improve the quality of medical service, Congress might go so far as to restructure the delivery of health care services in the United States along European "socialized medicine" lines.

The Synthetic Fuels Industry

The Energy Policy Project of the Ford Foundation has noted that the federal government is in a unique position to shape future patterns of national energy policy through control of publicly owned energy resources. With the Interior Department as custodian, the American people own the bulk of the remaining fossil fuel resources in the United States: "These resources include an estimated 35 per cent of the oil and gas, 50 per cent of the coal, and 85 per cent of the oil shale. Substantial amounts of the domestic uranium and geothermal steam resources are also under federal control." Although important energy resources are under private and state-owned lands, the major portion of the nation's energy resources that is most available for early development is "under federal control, particularly offshore oil and gas on the Outer Continental Shelf, and low-sulfur coal reserves in the West."

Such resources plus the sharp rise in oil company profits in 1973 and 1974 has led to proposals that would create a national energy company, patterned after TVA, to explore, develop, and produce new oil and natural gas reserves. TVA has the reputation of being an extremely efficient operation. A *Fortune* article has concluded that "Federal power projects, such as the TVA, have had the healthy effect of lowering the prices, improving the efficiency and even raising the earnings of neighboring private utilities." Whether a national energy company would be as successful at accomplishing similar objectives is uncertain. If it developed new technology and distributed new information about remaining oil and gas reserves to all private producers, it could reduce some risks faced by new energy companies, which would perhaps help to improve the overall competitiveness of the oil and gas industry.

Although direct federal involvement in the discovery and production of new reserves of oil and gas is not yet a reality, a great deal of government intervention will be required if large amounts of liquid hydrocarbons are to be quickly obtained from coal and shale. Because the petroleum-exporting nations can be expected to keep the price of imported oil below the cost of synthetic oil to protect their own markets in the next few decades, American oil companies probably will not undertake a crash program to develop efficient processes for extracting oil from coal and shale without federal subsidies.

Better information about the long-run cost of synthetic oil seems vital in the short run, however, if only to help keep the price of imported oil at levels that the United States and other industrialized nations can afford to pay. Two main approaches are now being debated. In the first, the federal government becomes directly involved in developing new technology and in producing sizable quantities of synthetic oil in government-owned plants that have been scaled up beyond the pilot plant stage.

In the second approach, the government subsidizes the production of synthetic oil from plants owned by private oil companies. Safeguards in the subsidy agreements should require that all new technology and cost information developed at government expense be made freely available to other firms which might want to enter the "syncrude" business when the cost of such oil becomes reasonably competitive with imported oil.

Studies by scientists and engineers at the Massachusetts Institute of Technology suggest that a sizable synthetic oil and gas industry will require an enormous capital investment. Whether oil and gas companies will be able and willing to raise as much capital for this purpose as seems socially and politically desirable is uncertain.

Because a sizable synthetic fuels industry is not likely to be directly profitable at first, the federal government may have to raise most of the capital. On the other hand, if the development of a sizable industry is delayed until most of the low-cost reserves of natural oil and gas in the United States and the rest of the world have been exhausted, federal financing is even more likely because most of the profits from low-cost energy will probably have been paid out as dividends. Lowered net income and assets leave little for private financing of a synthetic fuels industry.

Public Interest Corporations

To maximize net income per worker in a world of low-grade energy resources, in which improvements in the efficiency of converting energy into heat and useful working effects have been largely exhausted, capital investment should eventually be carried to the point of a zero net marginal return. The incremental return on the additional capital investment at that point will be just sufficient to replace the additional capital when it wears out. There will be no surplus that can be used to pay interest and dividends on the additional capital. Because enterprises must act as though interest, dividends, and profits are unimportant when employing marginal amounts of capital, it is questionable whether private profit-making enterprises are the best vehicle for maximizing long-run income.

In those industries in which capital is a very poor substitute for human and inanimate energy, the conditions for an overall income maximum can probably be satisfied by simply imposing income-maximizing standards on all producers of capital goods to be determined by durability and performance characteristics.

Where very little capital and inanimate energy are involved in producing goods and services relative to the amount of human energy, private enterprise may even be better than public ownership. Private owners often work harder for themselves and take better care of their own property than if the tools of production are owned by the state or even a large corporation.

As the amount of capital employed per worker increases and as the ownership of capital becomes more and more divorced from its care and management, however, using economic efficiency to justify private as opposed to public ownership of the means of production becomes less and less persuasive. This doesn't mean that government enterprise is necessarily more successful at maximizing net national product than private enterprise. Some government enterprises have turned out to be very efficient in the use of resources; others have become quite bureaucratic and wasteful.

Great Britain's nationalized coal and steel industries provide a convincing example that there is no magic in government ownership by itself. Output per manhour in the British steel industry is still only about half as great as in the United States. The American post office, which was finally freed from political shackles and set up as an independent, government-owned, nonprofit corporation, is another good example of how government enterprises can be allowed to run down and remain backward.

If there is to be a long-run income-maximizing argument in favor of government ownership it must be on the basis that the government is better able to achieve needed reorganization of the industry or make capital investments that private enterprises are unable or unwilling to undertake.

The main problem with the American health system is not insufficient capital investment but the fact that most of publicly owned hospitals are being operated for the benefit and profit of doctors, surgeons, and hospital administrators rather than the public. Current efforts to correct some of these abuses include such measures as professional standards review organizations and the promotion of health maintenance organizations that provide a wide range of hospital and physician services for fixed, prepaid insurance fees. Such reforms should encourage doctors and hospitals to engage in preventive health care and discourage overutilization of hospital services.

If these innovations do not reduce the incidence of unnecessary operations, improve the quality and general availability of health care services, and constrain the amount of monopoly profits, it seems likely that most doctors will eventually end up as regular employees of either the federal government or of the hospitals in which they are allowed to practice.

The press, radio, telephone, television, and other communications industries and firms, I feel, should remain as free as possible from government takeover or control. Many firms in these industries, I believe, should eventually be converted into independent, nonprofit companies to be operated competitively and in the public interest. A profitable way to achieve this conversion, in many instances, would be for the companies to issue very long-lived income bonds[6] to their shareholders in exchange for their outstanding common and preferred shares.

American Telephone and Telegraph shareholders, for example, have not fared very well in the last fifteen years, despite space-age technology and above-average gains in labor productivity. If the owners were given income bonds with a maximum yield of up to 12 per cent, payable in part from federal taxes, most stockholders would be better off financially.

Textbooks on corporate finance usually assume that management will strive to maximize stockholder wealth, but this goal has been questioned by a number of economists in recent years. William Baumol of Princeton, Jack Downie of London, Carl Kaysen of the Institute for Advanced Study, and John Kenneth Galbraith of Harvard have noted a separation of ownership from control in mature corporations. They have devised explanations of managerial behavior which they believe may be more consistent with this separation. In the *New Industrial State*, Galbraith has suggested that although a few managers might strive to maximize their own return by maximizing that of the stockholders, a more plausible hypothesis is that corporate management will strive to "maximize its success as an organization."

In a world where large corporations are being urged to do their part to clean up the environment, hire the disadvantaged, remain in congested downtown areas, hold prices down to prevent inflation from getting out of hand, and to pursue many other goals besides profit maximization, it makes sense for management and stockholders seriously to consider the possibility of "profitably" converting their organizations into a new breed of nonprofit institutions that would remain competitive yet be able to better project an unselfish image of functioning in the public interest.

In 1975 profit-gouging and many other unscrupulous business practices were found in the private nursing home industry. The resulting scandal led Manhattan Assemblyman Andrew Stein to sponsor a bill in the New York Legislature encouraging an expansion of nonprofit nursing homes, which generally provide better care than private nursing homes.

If all the conditions for a competitive equilibrium were satisfied there might be considerable merit in retaining Adam Smith's faith in an "invisible hand" that will lead private self-interest to serve the common goal unwittingly. In a world where pollution control and some other socially desirable costs are not always born by producers, however, one can as easily accept Herman Daly's hypothesis of an "invisible foot" which leads private self-interest to kick the common good to pieces.

In an economic system rooted to a philosophy of greed and selfishness, corporate executives will remain on the defensive, caught between stockholders desiring higher profits and an outraged or highly suspicious public unhappy about higher prices or behavior that does not seem to be in their own best interest. This basically no-win situation can only exact a heavy psychological toll on those responsible for making economic decisions.

The stock market went practically nowhere except up and down in the 1965 - 1974 decade. One interpretation might be that the market, in its own inscrutable fashion, anticipated that the United States economy will soon approach a steady state equilibrium. Because an end to economic progress could mean financial losses to persons and institutions that have acquired common stock at very high price-dividend ratios in anticipation of continued growth in dividends, prudent investors should seriously consider new institutional arrangements that might better protect their financial investment.

A "profitable" conversion of investor-owned companies into nonprofit organizations would seem particularly desirable for large, multinational corporations to improve their image and perhaps reduce the risk of nationalization without adequate compensation.

Assuming that most private corporations were converted to public interest corporations, the stage might then be set for a rapid elimination of the corporate profits tax, which some economists believe seriously distorts the allocation of capital resources between industries.[7] With the corporate profits tax eliminated and with profit maximization no longer an overriding consideration, corporate executives could then push capital investment to the point of a zero net marginal return and pursue other goals that may be more closely related to the maximization of net social welfare.

Notes

1. W. P. Webb, in *The Turner Theses*, ed. G. R. Taylor (Boston: Heath, 1956), p. 94.

2. Milton Friedman, *Capitalism and Freedom* (Chicago: University of Chicago Press, 1962), pp. 2 - 3.

3. Edward F. Renshaw, "Utility Regulation: A Re-examination," *Journal of Business* (October 1958), pp. 335 - 43; and Paul W. MacAvoy, *The Crisis of the Regulatory Commission* (New York: Norton, 1970).

4. George Sternlieb, "Slum Housing: A Functional Analysis," *Law and Contemporary Problems* (1966), p. 352.

5. Edward M. Kennedy, *In Critical Condition: The Crisis in America's Health Care* (New York: Simon and Schuster, 1972), pp. 16 - 17.

6. Income bonds are more like preferred stock than ordinary coupon bonds in that the holders of these bonds cannot force a company into bankruptcy if it is not able to pay interest on its income bonds.

7. Arnold Harberger, *Taxation and Welfare* (Boston: Little, Brown, 1974), Chapter 6, pp. 122 - 133.

chapter 14

THE DISTRIBUTION OF INCOME

Robert Heilbroner has noted that we are now in a period in which rapid population growth, the presence of obliterative weapons, and dwindling resources may bring international tensions to a dangerous level for a long time. A "stationary," non-expanding capitalism, he believes, "has always been considered either as a prelude to its collapse or as a betrayal of its historic purpose." Heilbroner suggests that the outlook for man "is painful, difficult, perhaps desperate, and the hope that can be held out for his future prospect seems to be very slim indeed."[1]

Although the adjustment to a nongrowth economy may be rather painful, I am at least cautiously optimistic about the prospects for humankind. People concerned about the finiteness of the earth and its limited ability to diffuse and absorb waste products, for example, can take some comfort from the fact that the worldwide growth rate has slowed down. This stabilization allows more time to understand the environment, to formulate solutions to unanticipated problems, and reduces the possibilities of major environmental catastrophes resulting from unconstrained rapid economic growth. Vigilance and concern about the environment should not be relaxed, however, even though environmental problems may not be as hopeless as some critics of continued exponential growth have suggested.

Many of the more serious adjustment problems are already upon us. Whether we like it or not they will have to be grappled with in this decade rather than be postponed to a time when the world population will be much larger, when most of the world's fossil fuels and high-grade mineral resources are used up, when global pollution loads are so large as to threaten human survival, and when almost every country, large and small, can manufacture atomic weapons. The necessity of dealing with such difficult problems as natural resource scarcity, overpopulation, and the Palestinian refugee problem now rather than later, I believe, greatly reduces the prospects for doomsday solutions.

One basis for optimism is the ability of the major world powers to avoid direct military confrontation during the numerous wars that have erupted in and between smaller countries since World War II. It suggests that additional ways may be found to limit arms and further reduce the risk of self-defeating wars between the major countries of the world.

Although another war between Israel and her neighbors cannot be ruled out as unlikely, there are some grounds for optimism. The large build-up of petrodollars, for example, has opened up the possibility of rapid economic growth not only for the oil-exporting nations of the Middle East but also for Egypt, Syria, Jordan, and the Palestinian refugees, if new wars can be avoided.

The developing nations that do not produce oil cannot expect large amounts of financial assistance from petroleum-exporting nations for very long, however. Rapid price inflation for industrial commodities, expanded supplies of exportable petroleum from other regions, and reduced crude oil imports in industrialized nations have already helped to erode the supply of excess petrodollars. As the oil-producing nations of the Persian Gulf begin to use more oil revenues for internal development, the surplus funds that can be used to finance investment projects in other developing countries are likely to decline.

Therefore, if a peaceful solution to the Arab-Israeli dispute is not found in the near future, Egypt and Syria might remain undeveloped for several more decades. Although this possibility may not be a deciding factor, it does provide a reason for hoping that mutually advantageous agreements will eventually be worked out between the oil-producing and consuming nations to maintain political stability in the Middle East, preserve a more or less prosperous world economy, and permit Israel to coexist with the new Palestinian homeland which seems destined to be created on the west bank of the Jordan River.

A stagnating world economy, in the final analysis, is not in the best interest of either the petroleum-exporting countries or other developing nations. The history of economic development assistance in the United States, for example, suggests that it is much easier for governments to appropriate large amounts of economic aid for other countries when they are at peace and their own economies are prospering. The share of American income going into foreign aid peaked in the 1948 - 1951 period when real GNP was increasing at an average annual rate of over 6 per cent. Economic development assistance was cut back fairly sharply by the late 1950s as the United States economic growth began to slow. There was a slight recovery in the amount of economic aid in the early 1960s (Table 14.1). In the 1965 - 1975 decade, when the United States was involved in Vietnam and later experienced a significant slowdown in the growth of output per manhour, official American development assistance declined from approximately 0.5 to about 0.2 per cent of GNP. The history of Great Britain also supports the hypothesis that domestic disturbances and slower growth rates will tend to force industrialized nations to cut back on their international commitments and be less generous in their foreign assistance.

One of the more paradoxical reasons for expecting the share of national income devoted to foreign aid to decline as industrialized nations approach a steady state equilibrium is mounting internal pressures for income redistribution at home. Such pressures have been very strong in Great Britain and could become a paramount issue in the United States.

The Prospects for Income Redistribution

A stationary capitalism, according to Robert Heilbroner, will "be forced to confront the explosive issue of income distribution in a way that an expanding capitalism is spared." In Chapter 8 I noted that money income is distributed in an unequal manner in the United States and that there has been little change in the relative distribution of income and wealth since 1950. In 1970 the lowest fifth of all families received only 5.5 per cent of all family income, whereas the top 5 per cent received 14.4 per cent. Property is distributed less equally. In 1969, 1 per cent of all adults were estimated to have owned over 50 per cent of all common stock and more than 28 per cent of all the wealth in the United States. Herman

TABLE 14.1

Flow of Official Development Assistance Measured as a Percent of Gross National Product[a]

	1960	1965	1970	1971
Australia	.38	.53	.59	.53
Austria	—	.11	.07	.07
Belgium	.88	.60	.46	.50
Canada	.19	.19	.42	.42
Denmark	.09	.13	.38	.43
France	1.38	.76	.66	.66
Germany	.31	.40	.32	.34
Italy	.22	.10	.16	.18
Japan	.24	.27	.23	.23
Netherlands	.31	.36	.61	.58
New Zealand[b]	—	—	—	—
Norway	.11	.16	.32	.33
Portugal	1.45	.59	.67	1.42
Sweden	.05	.19	.38	.44
Switzerland	.04	.09	.15	.11
United Kingdom	.56	.47	.37	.41
United States[c]	.53	.49	.31	.32
Grand Total				
ODA (current prices) $ millions	4,665	5,895	6,832	7,762
ODA 1973 prices	7,660	9,069	9,346	9,976
GNP (current prices) $ billions	898	1,340	2,010	2,218
ODA as % GNP	.52	.44	.34	.35
ODA Deflator	60.9	65.0	73.1	77.8

Source: World Bank.

[a]Countries included are members of OECD Development Assistance Committee, accounting for more than 95% of total Official Development Assistance. Figures for 1973 and earlier years are actual data. The projections for 1974 and 1975 are based on World Bank estimates of growth of GNP, on information on budget appropriations for aid, and on aid policy statements made by governments. Because of the relatively long period of time required to translate legislative authorizations first into commitments and later into disbursements, it is possible to project today, with reasonable accuracy, ODA flows (which by definition represent disbursements) through 1975.

[b]New Zealand became a member of the DAC only in 1973. ODA figures for New Zealand are not available for 1960–71.

[c]In 1949, at the beginning of the Marshall Plan, U.S. Official Development Assistance amounted to 2.79% of GNP.

[d]Case I leading to a −0.4% change in GNP per capita per annum in countries with incomes under $200 per capita would require ODA at $16.7 billion (.20% of DAC GNP) in 1980; Case II with 2.1% growth in GNP per capita would require $24.4 billion (.30% of DAC GNP in that year).

| 1972 | 1973 | 1974 | 1975 | 1980[d] Required for | |
				Case I	Case II
.59	.44	.53	.54		
.08	.13	.13	.13		
.55	.51	.56	.62		
.47	.43	.51	.51		
.45	.47	.49	.50		
.67	.58	.55	.51		
.31	.32	.30	.28		
.09	.14	.10	.08		
.21	.25	.24	.24		
.67	.54	.61	.65		
.23	.27	.36	.47		
.41	.45	.63	.65		
1.79	.71	.47	.42		
.48	.56	.69	.70		
.21	.15	.15	.15		
.39	.35	.34	.32		
.29	.23	.21	.20		
8,671	9,415	10,706	11,948	16,760	24,400
10,059	9,415	9,391	9,452	9,259	13,480
2,550	3,100	3,530	4,100	8,200	8,200
.34	.30	.30	.29	.20	.30
86.2	100.0	114.0	126.4	181.0	181.0

Daly has suggested that distribution is the rock on which most ships of state, including the steady state, are very likely to run aground:

> For several reasons the important issue of the stationary state will be distribution, not production. The problem of relative shares can no longer be avoided by appeals to growth.The argument that everyone should be happy as long as his absolute share of wealth increases, regardless of his relative share, will no longer be available. . . . The stationary state would make fewer demands on our environmental resources, but much greater demands on our moral resources.[2]

Scholars disagree about whether a zero growth economy would lead to a more equal distribution of income. Some are quite pessimistic. Lester Thurow of MIT has suggested that if zero growth were imposed on the current structure of the American economy, "the distribution of family income would gradually grow more unequal, blacks would fall farther behind whites, and the share going to female earnings would fall below what it would otherwise be." Other analysts, like Harvey Brooks of Harvard, are inclined to believe that zero economic growth could only be achieved within the framework of a democratic political system if income were distributed more equally than at present.

To improve their position in a nongrowth economy the poor would have to gain at the expense of the more affluent, which could lead to social and political conflict, more time devoted to bargaining at the expense of greater production, and, as Roland McKean has noted, perhaps "more resources of the spirit squandered in anger, bitterness, and violence."[3]

Though the overall distribution of income and wealth has not changed appreciably in the last few decades, poor families can be considered relatively better off today than in the 1950s. In the first place the number of children and dependent adults per household has dramatically declined, especially in poor households.

At the end of World War II there were more than four adults per family. There are now less than two. The average low-income worker, thanks to improved social security benefits, no longer has to share a meager income with parents and aged relatives. Fewer children per family also means relatively more income per person.

The United States has also become decidedly more egalitarian in specific ways. Education, health, and basic foods are now distributed far more equally than before World War II. Nearly all families have refrigerators, radios, and television sets; more than 90 per cent either own washing machines or live in an apartment house with such machines; 80 per cent have at least one car; and more than 60 per cent of all families own their own homes. Ninety-five per cent of the country's 63.5 million households also have full plumbing facilities.

In 1960, only 38 per cent of black males and 43 per cent of black females between 20 and 29 had completed high school; by 1972 these proportions had risen to 64 per cent for males and 66 per cent for females. The proportion of blacks between 18 and 24 attending college rose to 18 per cent. In the past decade the number of blacks in professional and technical positions has increased by 128 per cent. During the same time the number of black managers, officials, and proprietors has nearly doubled.

The distribution of income and wealth will probably become more equal as a steady state economy is approached for several reasons. Very high incomes are usually the result of fortunes made in real estate development, the exploitation of new technology, and the discovery of new deposits of high-grade mineral wealth.

None of these foundations for accumulating and preserving large personal fortunes is likely to be very important in a steady state economy, when the emphasis will shift from new real estate developments to urban renewal and building replacement, which are often unprofitable. New technology will be directed toward quality improvements and preserving existing wealth stocks rather than new inventions that add to the stock of wealth. As high-grade mineral resources are used up, the thrust of economic activity will switch to recycling and mining of low-grade resources that do not provide as many opportunities for windfall profits.

In the steady state world of the future it will not only be more difficult to acquire large personal fortunes but it will also be more difficult to preserve those fortunes acquired during the era of rapid economic growth. Many wealthy people have been able to escape graduated income taxes by investing in oil wells, undeveloped land, and no-dividend growth stocks. Because oil wells will be anachronisms and because land values and the prices of most capital assets will have stabilized, except for inflationary increases in the general price level, it will be far more difficult for wealthy families and individuals to find profitable investments that do not produce taxable income. With interest and dividend yields about the same as the general rate of inflation and with marriages to impecunious persons, divorces, and inheritance taxes taking a bite out of family fortunes every generation or two, the great capitalistic fortunes are likely to gradually wither away.

The distribution of affluence is less certain for those who have acquired above-average incomes as a result of professional competence or advanced education or both. As I noted in Chapter 9 an oversupply of college graduates seems to be depressing the relative incomes of younger workers with bachelors' degrees. As enrollments at colleges and universities decline it seems likely that the average professor will not fare as well in the future as in the past decade.

Some of the highest incomes are now earned by medical doctors and hospital administrators. An increased supply of doctors coupled with better government controls on health costs will likely reduce the relative income status of this group.

As ZPG is approached, there will be relatively fewer cavity-prone children. It follows that the steady state society of the future will need relatively fewer dentists. Because there will also be relatively less need for scientists, architects, and construction engineers, other professional incomes will probably be significantly narrowed.

Another factor that should help to improve the distribution of effective purchasing power is better social security. In 1950, only about 15 per cent of the federal budget was devoted to cash-income assistance. By the mid-70s that percentage increased to more than 30 per cent. Most workers can now look forward to a dignified retirement.

However, increased social security benefits have not helped to improve the distribution of income in the United States. In 1950 less than 10 per cent of all federal budget receipts were from payroll taxes. These receipts have since increased to about 30 per cent in 1975. The method of financing social security will probably change substantially in the future.

A congressional economic survey has found that higher tax payments outstripped all other price increases in consumer budgets in 1974. Low- and middle-income taxpayers were more affected by this rise than the wealthy. Greater awareness of the regressive impact of payroll taxes has led the Social Security Advisory Council to recommend that the social security tax rate be kept more or less constant in the future and that additional revenues be obtained by either increasing the taxable wage base or by using federal income tax revenues to supplement payroll taxes.

Indexing, or automatic upward adjustment, of retirement benefits for increases in the consumer price index will require substantial amounts of new revenues in the years ahead to keep the social security system financially solvent. If Congress enacts a national health insurance program there is likely to be a further need for new revenue sources to fund the social security system. These factors, combined with greater lobbying efforts by public interest groups, are almost certain to bring about substantial reforms in financing social security benefits.

Other tax reforms may also help to improve the overall distribution of income in the United States. In early 1975 President

Ford proposed a 12 per cent income tax rebate on 1974 taxes to help stimulate an economic recovery. Nearly half the antirecession benefits in Ford's plan would have gone to the wealthiest 17 per cent of the United States population; the 16 million families that filed income tax returns but were not required to pay any taxes would have received nothing.

The final tax bill that was passed by Congress, however, provided tax reduction at the rate of 238 per cent for the poorest taxpayers, a 15 to 28 per cent reduction for middle income groups, and a reduction of less than 6 per cent for wealthy taxpayers. The tax bill also contained a provision to repeal the depletion allowance for large oil companies. This allowance had cost the U.S. Treasury $2 - $3 billion in "tax expenditures" annually and was generally considered to be one of the most glaring tax loopholes. Percentage depletion deductions not only allowed oil companies and owners of oil wells to recoup their original investment costs once, as do depreciation allowances for most other investments, but to obtain additional tax-free income equal to about fifteen times the original investment costs.

Most economists consider the percentage depletion allowance to be a very inefficient way to encourage new exploration and to provide economic protection to the domestic oil industry. The depletion allowance can also be considered a positive hindrance to the production of synthetic oil from coal, shale, and garbage. According to Dr. Gerard M. Brannon, former director of the U.S. Treasury's Office of Tax Analysis:

> The net value of the percentage depletion deduction for $7.00 oil will be $1.25. If processes are developed to turn coal through extensive manufacture into a perfect substitute for $7 oil, the incentive deduction for this valuable process will be about $0.10, since coal depletion is much less than oil depletion. Equally valuable to the U.S. would be machinery that needed less energy input. Percentage depletion offers no tax incentive for this.[4]

Pressure also seems to be mounting for other kinds of tax reforms.[5] These pressures are not limited to the federal government. Property tax relief programs for low- and middle-income householders have increased tremendously. In 1965 only six states had some form of property tax concessions for the aged. By 1970, 28 states had enacted such programs; by 1975, all 50 states and the District of Columbia had some sort of property tax relief for the elderly. Several states also provide relief to all low- and moderate-income families.

The most rapidly growing form of property tax relief is the so-called circuit-breaker, designed to protect family income from property tax "overload" in much the same way that an electrical circuit-breaker protects the family home from current overload. When the property tax bill (or the tax equivalent for renters) exceeds a fixed percentage of household income, the circuit-breaker goes into effect and relief is granted from the "excess" taxes. Wisconsin pioneered this type of property tax reform in 1964. In 1975 there were twenty-five circuit-breaker programs, most of which extended coverage to renters as well as owners.

Families with low and moderate incomes are also beginning to benefit from regulatory reforms in the pricing of electricity. The inner-city poor have not only been required to pay higher prices for electrical power but have also helped to subsidize the extravagant use of electric power by relatively more affluent families.[6] The subsidy is related in part to quantity discounts that have been used to increase electric power consumption in industry and in affluent suburbs, where consumption per family is now more than twice as great as in the inner city.

After extended testimony by reform-minded public interest groups in 1974, the Michigan Public Service Commission ordered the Detroit Edison Company to abandon its promotional rate structure and adopt a uniform price for electricity sold to residential consumers. Later in 1974, the Wisconsin Public Service Commission ordered a nearly uniform residential electric rate structure during summer months for Madison customers.

The next big step in the pricing of electricity is to have public utilities adopt a schedule of increasing prices for larger amounts of electricity during periods of peak demand. Such repricing can be justified on the basis of economic efficiency to offset the higher incremental cost of maintaining standby capacity for peak usage. A progressive rate schedule would also help to redistribute purchasing power to many poor and elderly families whose incomes have been seriously eroded since 1970 by higher electric rates caused by higher fuel prices.

The economic burden of higher fuel prices could be further reduced by moving toward progressive consumption taxes for other types of energy consumption. The proceeds could be used either to finance tax relief for the poor or to provide disproportionate benefits to families with low and moderate incomes.

Some proposals, for example, would impose differentially high excise taxes on automobiles with high gas consumption or excessive horsepower. Others would establish a two-price system for gasoline, either directly or indirectly through tax rebates. Families that consume below-average amounts of gasoline would then pay less per gallon than the generally more affluent families that consume above-average amounts of gasoline.

The public transportation system also appears to be moving in the direction of discounts for no-frill airline tickets and off-peak rate schedules, which can be expected to provide disproportionate benefits to students, retired persons, and other low-income groups.

Young people may also benefit from significant reforms in the present welfare system. Disabled adults are now eligible for basic welfare grants that are fully funded by the federal government and indexed to provide economic protection against inflation. Aid to families with dependent children has been rather spotty, however. In 1972, the average monthly benefit under AFDC for the country as a whole was $53.95 per child, but benefits per recipient ranged from a low of only $14.41 in Mississippi to over $95 in Massachusetts — a sixfold difference in the level of welfare benefits compared to a less than twofold difference in median family incomes for the various states.

The benefits available under AFDC are so low in some states as to imply serious hardship. In other states they are so generous relative to available wages that it is economically advantageous for a man to abandon his wife and children. This is one area where major reforms can be expected.

The existing tax and welfare system also has the disadvantage of encouraging people to have too many children. This problem could be solved in several ways — for example, by providing all poor families with a fairly generous income supplement or negative income tax that is largely independent of the number of children.

The federal government could also become an employer of last resort or subsidize jobs for the disadvantaged in industry or nonprofit institutions. If every able-bodied adult was assured of a job with an income sufficient to lift a family of four out of poverty, aid to dependent children could be limited to those families where one or both parents are incapacitated. The jobs approach would deal directly with the problem of too few employment opportunities for low-income workers. If both parents were able and willing to work, family income could be raised above subsistence levels.

Guaranteeing jobs has another advantage over the negative income tax; it would open up new opportunities for women and would probably be far more effective at keeping the number of births at a replacement level.

Welfare and employment reform planning in the United States might profit from examples of other countries. Many European countries with less per capita income than the United States have been far more successful at eliminating poverty and providing workers with greater job security. China and Cuba have also been surprisingly successful at reducing poverty and narrowing the degree of income inequality under adverse economic conditions. If Congress does not enact tax and welfare reforms along the lines of the Scandinavian countries, revolutionary elements in our own society might push the United States to the brink of abandoning its predominantly free-enterprise system altogether.

Attitudinal surveys conducted in nineteen countries have shown that reported happiness tends to increase with higher incomes. In all societies, more money income typically means more individual happiness. Raising the income of all individuals, however, does not necessarily increase the happiness of all. The average level of happiness in the United States is reported to have increased from the late 1940s until about 1957 but was not much different in 1970 from the earlier level. The citizens of poor countries are sometimes reported to be as happy as if not happier than the citizens of more affluent societies.

These findings have led Richard Easterlin and some other economists to conclude that individuals assess their material well-being not by the absolute amount of goods they have, but by the social norm of what goods they feel that they ought to have in comparison to their neighbors. Rising expectations seem to defeat the positive impact of income growth on human happiness. Those who live in richer times and places tend to perceive their needs in more ambitious terms than those in poorer societies.[7] This suggests that a growth-minded society can get "hooked" on what Philip Brickman and Donald Campbell have termed an "hedonic treadmill."

World Stabilization

Though I believe that Congress will be under enormous political pressure to adopt tax and expenditure measures that will improve the equality of income in the United States as we adjust to a steady state economy, it is by no means clear that comparable pressure will exist to adopt measures which will redistribute income to poorer countries. The data on official development assistance in Table 14.1 show a more or less continual decline in the share of GNP devoted to foreign aid since about 1965.

If the United States and other industrialized nations are to be more active in helping the oil-importing developing nations to achieve economic growth, new sources of financing for development assistance are necessary. One of the more interesting possibilities would be to impose a common tariff on imported oil, with some proceeds being earmarked for economic development assistance not only in the so-called developing nations of the world but also in some of the poorer regions of Western Europe, Japan, and perhaps even the United States. A dollar a barrel tariff on imported oil would provide enough extra tax revenue to almost double the amount of official development assistance that was extended by the United States and other industrial nations in 1975.

Although this proposal may sound outlandish, eighteen major oil-consuming nations met in Paris in 1975 to consider two American proposals for ensuring the development of alternative energy supplies. One proposal called for the consumer nations to establish a common floor price for oil to protect investors in new technology against the risk of falling oil prices. The other proposal would have achieved a similar objective by levying a common tariff on oil imported from outside the group of eighteen nations.

A common tariff might be highly effective at helping to reduce the monopoly profits of the petroleum-exporting nations. If it were not immediately successful at lowering oil prices, it would still encourage energy conservation as well as the development of alternative energy sources. Using the proceeds to finance investment projects in less-developed regions of the world might help to reduce international tensions and create a more healthy, stable, and prosperous environment that would be to the long-run advantage of all nations and peoples of the world.

Notes

1. Robert Heilbroner, *An Inquiry Into the Human Prospect* (New York: Norton, 1974), p. 22.

2. Herman E. Daly, "Toward a Stationary-State Economy," in *The Patient Earth*, ed. John Harte and Robert Socolow (New York: Holt, Rhinehart and Winston, 1971), pp. 236 - 237.

3. Roland N. McKean, "Growth vs. No Growth: An Evaluation," in *The No-Growth Society*, ed. Mancur Olson and Hans H. Landsberg (New York: Norton, 1973), p. 221.

4. Gerard Brannon, "Energy and Tax Reform," *Taxation With Representation Newsletter* (March 1, 1974), p. 2.

5. For a more detailed discussion of opportunities for federal tax reform, see Joseph A. Pechman, *Federal Tax Policy* (New York: Norton, 1971).

6. Ed Meyers and John Musial, "The Electric Scandals of '75," *The Progressive* (March 1975), pp. 24 - 27.

7. Richard Easterlin, "Does Money Buy Happiness?" *The Public Interest* (Winter 1973), pp. 3 - 10.

index